Street Players

Street Players

*Black Pulp Fiction and the Making
of a Literary Underground*

KINOHI NISHIKAWA

The University of Chicago Press   Chicago and London

The University of Chicago Press, Chicago 60637
The University of Chicago Press, Ltd., London
© 2018 by The University of Chicago
All rights reserved. No part of this book may be used or reproduced
in any manner whatsoever without written permission, except
in the case of brief quotations in critical articles and reviews.
For more information, contact the University of Chicago Press,
1427 E. 60th St., Chicago, IL 60637.
Published 2018
Printed in the United States of America

27 26 25 24 23 22 21 20 19 18   1 2 3 4 5

ISBN-13: 978-0-226-58688-5 (cloth)
ISBN-13: 978-0-226-58691-5 (paper)
ISBN-13: 978-0-226-58707-3 (e-book)
DOI: https://doi.org/10.7208/chicago/9780226587073.001.0001

Library of Congress Cataloging-in-Publication Data

Names: Nishikawa, Kinohi, author.
Title: Street players : black pulp fiction and the making of a literary
    underground / Kinohi Nishikawa.
Description: Chicago : The University of Chicago Press, 2018. |
    Includes bibliographical references and index.
Identifiers: LCCN 2018010068 | ISBN 9780226586885 (cloth :
    alk. paper) | ISBN 9780226586915 (pbk. : alk. paper) |
    ISBN 9780226587073 (e-book)
Subjects: LCSH: American fiction—African American authors—
    20th century—History and criticism. | Urban fiction, American—
    20th century—History and criticism. | African Americans in
    literature. | Race in literature. | Holloway House Publishing Co.
Classification: LCC PS153.N5 N57 2018 | DDC 813.009/896073—dc23
LC record available at https://lccn.loc.gov/2018010068

♾ This paper meets the requirements of ANSI/NISO Z39.48–1992
(Permanence of Paper).

Contents

Introduction: From Sleaze to Street

Irvine Welsh's life changed after he found a copy of *Pimp: The Story of My Life* in a "used bookshop in Soho," in London's West End. Besides the title, what caught his attention was the author's name. "How could you not pick up a book called *Pimp* written by a guy named Iceberg Slim?"[1] he mused. The book did not disappoint. Originally published in 1967, *Pimp* was a coming-of-age story unlike any he had read. Abandoned by his father as a baby and left to his own devices by his mother as a kid, Slim recounted a boyhood spent on the streets of Milwaukee and Chicago, where paternal surrogates schooled him in the art of the hustle. He proved a quick study and made his way up the ranks of the underworld. In a time when black men in the North suffered the indignities of police harassment and employment discrimination, Slim became one of the most successful black pimps in the Midwest—a lothario to women and the envy of every other man. Slim had made a way out of no way and, despite the odds, had come out on top.

Hailing from a rough, working-class section of Edinburgh, Scotland, Welsh saw, and heard, aspects of his own life reflected in the pages of *Pimp*. For one, he could relate to "Slim's view of the relationships of the black American ghetto, the hustling, scamming, pimping, drug-dealing, stealing, and rampant aspiration towards wealth"—in short, a world where it was every man for himself, and the trick was how to survive it. But he could also relate to Slim's command of street language, its florid descriptions, acerbic barbs, and vulgar slang—a mode of communication that, though unique to the American ghetto, felt typical of all urban argots. Welsh was so taken with *Pimp* that reading it gave him "the confidence to write in [his] own voice."[2] And so he did, resulting in *Trainspotting* (1993), a best-selling novel about a dope addict who tries to extricate himself from Edinburgh's blight while kicking the habit. The book, written partially in Scots dialect, was made into an internationally acclaimed film in 1996.

Slim had a similarly inspiring effect on a young black man, Tracy Marrow. After his parents died within four years of each other, Marrow moved across the country, from New Jersey to Los Angeles, to live with his aunt. It was there, in the enclave of South Central, that he was introduced to Iceberg Slim. "Ghetto hustlers in my neighborhood would talk this nasty dialect rich with imagery of sex and humor," he recalls. "My buddies and I wanted to know where they picked it up, and they'd told us, 'You better get into some of that Iceberg stuff!'"[3] Slim's reputation as an obscene wordsmith prevailed over the culture of Crenshaw Boulevard. But it was his work as a published writer ("that Iceberg stuff") that provided the key to understanding this culture, a way to connect with older men in the community. Reading Slim was an initiation into their world.

Marrow continues, "We found the books, and we started passing them around to each other." He and his friends devoured Slim throughout their high-school years, inculcating themselves into street culture in the process. Slim's appeal, for them, was self-evident: "Here was a man that a lot of black kids could relate to because he spoke *their* language. The language of the ghetto. He wasn't writing from the perspective of some brother who got outta the hood, but from the perspective of an insider." In time, Marrow decided to adapt that perspective to his chosen art form: rap. He styled his emcee persona "by the same method" Slim had used in his writing—describing street life on its own terms, in its own argot. His career as a performer took off, and he has not looked back since. "I took my rap name in tribute to him," says Marrow, better known as the gangsta icon Ice-T, "and I've never regretted it."[4]

Welsh and Ice-T were born in 1958. Reading Iceberg Slim was a transformative experience for both. But the differences in how these men—a white, working-class Scotsman and a black, working-class American—discovered and made use of Slim's writing point to familiar problems in the study of black popular culture. Welsh came to Slim by accident, drawn in by *Pimp*'s sensationalistic packaging. Though he did not explicitly represent blackness in *Trainspotting*, Welsh did use Slim as a kind of "black mirror," Eric Lott's term for a "blackness imagined to be both other and intimate," capable of helping whites learn more about themselves.[5] On the flipside, Ice-T came to Slim as a matter of course: by word of mouth, and through a community of readers. *Pimp* was already part of the culture into which he entered and to which he would contribute his creative energy. Thus, when Ice-T adapted Slim's writing into rap, it was not so much an act of cultural appropriation as a node in the process of cultural recirculation.

From the cakewalk to the Kardashians, Elvis to Eminem, white appropriation of black cultural forms is a recurring theme in modern social life. It explains the apparent irony that as our popular culture has become more representationally diverse, the structures sustaining racial inequality have remained intact. Greg Tate traces the origins of this dynamic to the slave trade, where the black body was offered up as "capitalism's original commodity fetish." Blacks' "reduction from subjects to abstracted objects," Tate argues, "made them seem larger than life and less than human at the same time"—an image perfectly suited to the project of appropriating blackness with one hand while condemning it with the other.[6] When it comes to Irvine Welsh, bell hooks's formulation of "eating the Other" would seem to be more germane. By consuming different cultures in the marketplace of commodities, white people, she posits, realize "all those 'nasty' unconscious fantasies and longings about contact with the Other [that are] embedded in the secret (not so secret) deep structure of white supremacy." Put differently, whites want a "bit of the Other"—"working-class British slang," hooks reminds us, for having sex with a person of color—but they do not want the basis for their social identity to be challenged by that encounter.[7]

This book is centrally about race and appropriation in late twentieth-century popular culture. Parts of it dovetail with the points made above. But the broader story it has to tell moves beyond the binary oppositions—white versus black, fetishism versus self-possession, appropriation versus authenticity—on which these points rely. Before such distinctions can be drawn, we need to consider how the "Other" of white fascination is produced in the first place. The reason, I suggest, is that this "Other" is not always what it seems. For example, the appropriative processes I have been describing with regard to Irvine Welsh and *Trainspotting* apply equally to Iceberg Slim and *Pimp*. Far from a candid or truthful account of Slim's life, *Pimp* was self-mythologizing fiction—a heady mixture of confession and bombast whose greatest trick was to convince readers that "Iceberg Slim" had been the author's street moniker and not the nom de plume that it was. That trick may have established the author's larger-than-life persona, but its raison d'être was to appeal to the prurient interests of whites. In fact, Slim's literary career was made possible by the fact that his publisher wanted him to be a black mirror.[8] Exactly how all of this happened, and what this story means for continued discussions of race and cultural appropriation, are the subjects of this book.

The story I recount centers on Holloway House, a Los Angeles–based publishing company that became the major force behind diversifying the pulp and genre fiction industries in the late twentieth century. In its early years, Holloway House exploited the liberalization of sexual culture by putting out a rogue's list of classic erotica, tabloid confessionals, and studies of sexual and "deviant" behavior. This 1960s catalog derived largely from materials published in two pinup magazines: *Adam* and *Sir Knight* (later renamed *Knight*). The magazines and publishing operation were intertwined under the ownership of Bentley Morriss and the editorial oversight of Ralph Weinstock. Morriss and Weinstock were former publicists who had parlayed their contacts in the movie industry, local press, and even red-light district into a multi-faceted publishing enterprise. They were white men, and until 1967, so were nearly all their writers. *Pimp* was the first book by a black author that Morriss and Weinstock published. Yet it was not as radical a departure from their usual fare as one might think. *Pimp* combined different elements of what they had specialized in—the confessional frame, voyeuristic depictions of sex and sex work, an exploration of the seedy underbelly of urban America—in a way that would have been immediately appreciated by readers.

Above all, though, *Pimp* put a new spin on the revanchist dictum that had animated all of Morriss and Weinstock's print commodities: in the face of profound social change, men needed to reclaim their "natural" dominion over women's bodies. That Slim was a black man with firsthand knowledge of the black underworld validated this ethos as racially authentic, serving it up as the "real-life" experiences of a native informant. In other words, as the scholarship on cultural appropriation suggests, Slim's blackness amplified his reclamation of masculinity for white readers. It would not have mattered, of course, whether *Pimp* was true or made up. A longtime author at Holloway House, Odie Hawkins, once said: "I knew Iceberg Slim . . . I knew him as a boy. He was *not* a major league pimp—no, no, no. That's a correction that needs to be made."[9] From this we may infer that Slim's life story would have been sensationalized to drive home the image of masculine authority that his black body represented for whites. For them, he was never really a man of flesh and bone but a projection of their darkest fantasies.

But where does that leave someone like Ice-T? Further complicating the story of Holloway House is the fact that Slim's elevation as a culture hero among black men was also conducted through Morriss and Weinstock's enterprise. Over time, the initial act of cultural appropriation gave way to a concerted effort to market Slim and other writers to a completely different readership. That effort, in a phrase, focused on publishing pulp fiction by black authors for black readers. To be sure, Holloway House would not have reoriented its business strategy had it not been profitable to do so. (The shift was not an act of beneficence.) Yet, despite, or perhaps because of, that profit motive, Morriss and Weinstock became deeply receptive to black men's interests and tastes. By 1973, they had effectively turned Holloway House into a publisher of black-oriented fare, phasing out most of its white-authored pulp while releasing scores of books by authors who, rather than appeal to the white gaze, wrote crime, action, and adventure novels for men like themselves. *Adam* and *Knight* survived the cuts, but they were segregated from this side of the business. In their place emerged *Players*, the first pornographic magazine to feature only black models and a black editorial board. These changes cultivated a loyal black readership for Holloway House, and it was within that context that Slim could be rebranded as speaking directly to young men like Ice-T.

Strange, then, that someone like Irvine Welsh would have been the presumed reader of *Pimp* on its debut in 1967, while someone like Ice-T would have been the presumed reader after that, once the book secured its reputation as a cultural touchstone. Stranger still that a white-owned and -operated company made both of these reading positions possible. Beyond the binaries set up by anti-appropriation discourse, how do we begin to understand a conjuncture where white interests aligned with the appropriation and later reappropriation of black culture? The question here is not whether Morriss and Weinstock succeeded in turning white fetishization into black appreciation. As far as reception history is concerned, they did. The more salient question is, How did they do it?[10]

Street Players: Black Pulp Fiction and the Making of a Literary Underground is an extended response to that question. It is the first study to present a complete genealogy of black pulp fiction, one that connects where it came from to where it ended up going. While existing studies of black pulp fiction gloss over its origins, as if they were incidental to its development or too embarrassing to acknowledge, this book makes that background central to its argument.[11] It begins by highlighting the significance of Morriss and Weinstock's starting out in the business of *sleaze*, which I define as mid-twentieth-century print commodities (pulps and pinup magazines) whose aim was to circulate fantasies of putting women in their place. Readers of sleaze felt that they were victims in a world given over to feminization, or the idea that masculine self-possession was being squelched by the demands of social conformity and domestic life. Sleaze rebuffed that trend, assuring readers that men were still on top, and that, despite many challenges to it, the male ego remained intact.[12] *Pimp* and other early black-authored books at Holloway House appealed to readers on precisely these terms. Given their orientation toward a white readership, these pulps may be thought of as what I term *black sleaze*.

The genealogy continues with Holloway House's transformation into something more than an outlet for sleaze. In shifting their attention from white to black readers, Morriss and Weinstock adapted their publishing infrastructure to manage new content. In a relatively short period of time, they flooded the literary marketplace with pulps that, when not set in the ghettos of black America, at least featured streetwise protagonists who came from those spaces. The books lacked originality, but they sold well. Morriss and Weinstock thus revamped Holloway House by commodifying formulas that proved popular among black readers and by hiring hacks to churn out variations on those formulas. In this sense, the emergence of *black pulp fiction*, as distinct from black sleaze, was a function of Holloway House creating a surplus of like-minded literary fare in a well-defined market niche. Over time, that niche became self-referential, cutting off ties to white readers and staging an explicit back and forth between black pulps and the aforementioned *Players* magazine. Readers like Ice-T eventually embraced Holloway House paperbacks as culturally authentic because they circulated within a field of auto-validating print commodities. I refer to this field as the *black literary underground*.

The genealogy of black pulp fiction that takes us from sleaze to street is a story of cross-cultural entanglement, of how the nexus of financial profits and racial fantasies proved remarkably adaptable to different market niches. Stuart Hall's essay "What Is This 'Black' in Black Popular Culture?" offers a theoretical framework beyond cultural appropriation that accounts for the complexities of this story. On one hand, Hall acknowledges the problematic laid out by bell hooks—namely, that "there's nothing that global postmodernism [i.e., consumer capitalism] loves better than a certain kind of difference: a touch of ethnicity, a taste of the exotic, as we say in England, 'a bit of the other.'" He concedes that the culture industry constitutes a "space of homogenization where stereotyping and the formulaic mercilessly process the material and experiences it draws into its web." Yet Hall believes these trends tell only part of the story. The more comprehensive view he advances, based on Antonio Gramsci's theory of hegemony, posits, "There are always positions to be won in popular culture, but no struggle can capture popular culture itself for our side or theirs." In other words, even and especially when appropriation occurs, popular cultural forms leave themselves open to repositioning and reappropriation. That is because, Hall writes, "these forms are the product of partial synchronization, of engagement across cultural boundaries, of the confluence of more than one cultural tradition, of the negotiations of dominant and subordinate positions, of the subterranean strategies of recoding and transcoding, of critical signification, of signifying."[13] Conceived in this way, popular cultural forms become dynamic strategies of representation rather than essentialist markers of identity.

For Hall, race is a variable position in the culture industry, one whose meaning can change over time. The "mark of difference *inside* forms of popular culture," he concludes, "is carried by the signifier 'black' in the term 'black popular culture.'"[14] Following from that point, I use the word "black" to mean different things in black sleaze and black pulp fiction. Elements of fetishization and self-possession, appropriation and authenticity, can be found in both formats. It is not as though one was more "black" than the other, or that we move from white exploitation to black agency between them. Instead, Hall's theorization allows us to recognize how blackness was put to different uses by different actors at different points in Holloway House's history. Race, in other words, became that which was contested, struggled over, and repositioned following Morriss and Weinstock's decision to shift their attention to a different readership. In this way, the "black" in black sleaze and black pulp fiction may be read as a sliding signifier, a term that registers the continuities and discontinuities in the way race was deployed at Holloway House.

The black literary underground requires elaboration beyond Hall's essay because though it involved Holloway House's uses for black pulp fiction, it also exceeded them. In theoretical terms, the black literary underground was not the epiphenomenal expression of a preexisting cultural formation. It was, instead, a *field* constituted by competing and complementary interests within and across cultural formations. My citation of field derives from Pierre Bourdieu's sociology of culture:

Given that works of art exist as symbolic objects only if they are known and recognized, that is, socially instituted as works of art and received by spectators capable of knowing and recognizing them as such, the sociology of art and literature has to take as its object not only the material production but also the symbolic production of the work, i.e. the production of the value of the work or, which amounts to the same thing, of belief in the value of the work. . . . It is a question of understanding works of art as a *manifestation* of the field as a whole, in which all the powers of the field, and all the determinisms inherent in its structure and functioning, are concentrated.[15]

As a structuralist account of cultural production, Bourdieu's field attends not only to the individual work in its material specificity but to everything external to the work that determines its symbolic value. Bourdieu spent much of his career exploring the value distinctions that cultural fields draw between the "high" and "middlebrow" arts, but I find his theory elastic enough to apply to works of racial and gender differentiation as well. Here I draw on him to account for the material and symbolic production of black pulp fiction's value beyond what Holloway House could control.

A Bourdieuian approach to the black literary underground adds an important spatial dimension to Hall's antiessentialist theorization of race. It would not have been sufficient for Morriss and Weinstock simply to identify uses for black pulp fiction that were distinct from those they had set out for black sleaze. Just as the wider market for pulps and pinup magazines made black sleaze desirable as a print commodity, so did black pulp fiction require a context, or field, to legitimate it as worthy of black readers' attention. As we will see, beyond Holloway House, a wide array of actors, from literary critics and book reviewers to urban ethnographers and cultural nationalists, helped determine the symbolic value of black pulp fiction. Their collective discourse, whether "positive" or "negative" toward the literature, independently confirmed that Holloway House was publishing books of considerable interest to black readers. As I refer to it throughout this book, then, the black literary underground was that field of receptivity in which black pulp fiction "made sense" as being by black authors for black readers— even in cases where one or the other was perhaps not technically true.

Finally, we need a theoretical framework to help us understand how

Holloway House itself changed over time as it became a constitutive part of the field of the black literary underground. For this, I draw on cultural historian Robert Darnton's notion of the *communications circuit*. A model for "analyzing the way books come into being and spread through society," the communications circuit "runs from the author to the publisher (if the bookseller does not assume that role), the printer, the shipper, the bookseller, and the reader." But what makes this model a circuit and not something else is the feedback loop connecting reader to author. Darnton continues:

The reader completes the circuit, because he influences the author both before and after the act of composition. Authors are readers themselves. By reading and associating with other readers and writers, they form notions of genre and style and a general sense of the literary enterprise, which affects their texts. . . . A writer may respond in his writing to criticisms of his previous work or anticipate reactions that his text will elicit. He addresses implicit readers and hears from explicit reviewers. So the circuit runs full cycle. It transmits messages, transforming them en route, as they pass from thought to writing to printed characters and back to thought again.[16]

Like Bourdieu, Darnton is interested in the processes by which actors and institutions come together to create different modes of literary production. But Darnton's model contains a temporal dimension that, in supplementing Bourdieu's structuralism, helps us understand changes in and modifications to the field over time. Darnton dwells on the role of the reader because that is the point in the circuit where shifts in reception and production converge. The implication is that a shift in reception could very well alter not only which books get written but also how those books are published and distributed. In theory, the infrastructure of the circuit could remain the same while the qualities that define it could change dramatically.

The communications circuit is thus the primary framework through which I explain the relationship between Holloway House's producers, Morriss and Weinstock, and its legions of fans, black readers. Morriss and Weinstock learned how to become responsive to black readers' interests and tastes, which in turn informed which authors and books they published and, eventually, what kind of business they wanted to run. This degree of responsiveness is actually what distinguished black pulp fiction from its closest analogue and contemporary, so-called blaxploitation films of the early 1970s. Black pulp fiction and blaxploitation had a great deal in common, including their reliance on white

capital, their use of black "fronts," or creative talent, and their preference for masculinist crime, action, and adventure formulas. But, as Ed
Guerrero has argued, whereas blaxploitation's producers were largely
indifferent to moviegoers' feedback, seeing these films as a financial
stopgap during lean years in Hollywood,[17] Morriss and Weinstock did
make an effort to give black readers what they wanted. That difference,
I suggest in this book, can account for blaxploitation's flaming out as a
fad by the mid-1970s and for black pulp fiction's longevity as a literary
phenomenon for over forty years. Acknowledging this is no defense,
of course, for the kind of business Morriss and Weinstock ran. There is
enough exploitation of labor, talent, and culture in the following pages
to make anyone balk. But for a project that aims to figure out how the
black literary underground was made, these disparities would have to
be considered alongside the bonds between black readers and black authors Morriss and Weinstock helped forge. Exploitation and intercon-
nection are inextricable in this story.

By analyzing black pulp fiction through the framework outlined
above, this book makes important contributions to the study of race
and appropriation in late twentieth-century popular culture. Method-
ologically, it links up with interdisciplinary scholarship on the commodification of race, or the idea of racial authenticity, in the American
cultural marketplace. More specifically, it dialogues with longitudinal
studies that have tracked actors and institutions over time, showing
appropriation to be a variable function of market response and adjust-
ment, not simply a single act of white exploitation.[18] As for its object of
study, this book does not limit itself to correcting long-held assumptions about black pulp fiction that pervade American studies and African American studies scholarship (cited throughout and thus not
noted here). Its more expansive concern is to identify new ways of
thinking about the conjunction of race and popular print media in the
age of sexual liberalization. For if there is one thing the genealogy of
black pulp fiction underscores, it is that the commodities published by
Morriss and Weinstock gratified men with extraordinary consistency.
As radical as their shift from white to black readerships may have appeared from the outside, they already had the infrastructure to appeal
directly to black men's interests and tastes. In illuminating how the
sexual politics of that appeal was embedded in the popular print culture of the day, this book aligns itself with feminist, queer, and critical
race studies of pulps, pornography, and cross-racial desire.[19]

*Street Players: Black Pulp Fiction and the Making of a Literary Under-
ground* is organized into eight chapters, divided into three parts. Part 1,

"Origins," introduces the white-oriented sleaze trade as the necessary backdrop to black pulp fiction's emergence. Part 2, "Transitions," examines the period 1971 to 1973, when Morriss and Weinstock, presumably responding to readers' wishes, redirected their communications circuit toward black men. Part 3, "Trajectories," follows the development of the black literary underground from an undefined market niche into a vibrant corner of the black public sphere.

The book begins with a chapter on the pinup prehistory to black pulp fiction. In "Up from Domesticity," I explore the midcentury sleaze market in which Morriss and Weinstock staked their publishing enterprise. By taking a closer look at *Adam*, *Sir Knight*, and a selection of early Holloway House paperbacks, I lay the groundwork for the argument that the literary fare Morriss and Weinstock produced for white men served as an incubator for the black-authored books that followed. In particular, I show how these interrelated print ventures leaned heavily on a confessional mode of writing that assumed to expose the "truth" of men's experiences in American society. Befitting the designation sleaze, this confessional mode reveled in exploring the seedy underbelly of the postwar ideal of suburban domesticity.

Chapter 2, "Street Legends," homes in on the breakout year for black pulp fiction: 1967. I retrace the conditions under which Iceberg Slim and another black author, Robert H. deCoy, made their debuts at Holloway House. Whereas previous critics have largely echoed Morriss's claim that he wanted to give black writers a chance at the company, I outline my reasons for being skeptical. The available evidence suggests that Holloway House picked up Slim and deCoy because their work fit nicely into its catalog of sleaze. At its inception, then, black pulp fiction was directed not to a black audience but to white readers looking in.

It did not take long for Holloway House to realize that their books were being bought and read by many beyond its traditional white base. Between 1968 and 1970, the company struggled to figure out what it would mean to market race-oriented fare to a diversifying readership. Chapter 3, "Black Sleaze," shows how Morriss and Weinstock navigated this new reality. Though they began to appeal to the political consciousness of black readers caught up in the social unrest of the times, they also kept coming back to the sleaze fetish for interracial sex that they knew white men enjoyed, and that continued to be popular in the late 1960s. I contend that this transitional moment in the company's history highlights the overlap between the older market for black sleaze and the new market for black pulp fiction that Holloway House was about to define.

The next two chapters, "Missing the Revolution" and "Return of the Mack," make up part 2 of the book. They consider the years 1971 to 1973 simultaneously. These years merit extended analysis because they bracket the period when black pulp fiction emerged out from under the shadow of black sleaze, backed by Morriss and Weinstock's (still inconsistent) efforts to appeal directly to black readers. Chapter 4 examines how Slim, by now a best-selling author, came to view his pimp persona as counterproductive to black liberation. He spent much of the early 1970s trying to distance himself from that persona, duly performing the role of the self-flagellating reprobate. Yet, as much as he tried to escape his romanticized past, Slim could not help but be propped up by Morriss and Weinstock as the new face of the company. By contrast, Donald Goines, who had read Slim while finishing up a jail sentence, came on to the scene fresh and ready to write his way into notoriety. Chapter 5 contends that Holloway House's marketing of Goines in the same years helped distinguish black pulp fiction not only from its sleaze origins but also from its star author. Goines's five novels published between 1971 and 1973 effectively rewrote Slim's output, making no apologies for its crude sensationalism.

It was through Goines, then, that Holloway House set up the parameters for the market niche that harbored a black literary underground. Part 3 examines how this underground developed from 1974 and into the 1980s. Chapter 6, "Difference and Repetition," takes up the first year in that periodization: 1974. Steering Holloway House away from the old sleaze catalog required that Morriss and Weinstock produce black-authored books in droves—and fast. To do this, they relied on hacks whose serial fiction copied action-adventure formulas from the mainstream pulp house Pinnacle. Intertwined with that effort was the founding of *Players*. This pornographic magazine would be to black pulp fiction what *Adam* and *Sir Knight* had been to Holloway House's early paperbacks. At once a staging ground for new writing and an advertising medium for already published paperbacks, *Players* anchored Morriss and Weinstock's place in the black literary underground. I trace the relationship between black pornography and black pulp in chapters 5 and 6.

Chapter 7, "Reading the Street," identifies 1975 to 1977 as the period when Morriss and Weinstock's operation cornered the market niche for black men's leisure reading. With black pulp fiction and *Players* magazine becoming intertwined, readers were guided on how to read one from the other and vice versa. The effect was self-reinforcing. When it came to books, that effect placed a premium on lived experience—

specifically, the idea that an author would have intimate knowledge of that which he wrote. When it came to pornography, however, the effect was more elastic. *Players* afforded a range of opinion and entertainment so long as black men's ability to consume erotic black womanhood was guaranteed.

The book concludes with a chapter on the history of black pulp fiction since the late 1970s. In "The Difference Within," I recount how Holloway House tried to diversify its market niche by publishing women-in-peril novels and modern-day romances. The arrival of these genres signaled Morriss and Weinstock's effort to appeal to black women readers. But after several failed attempts, black women themselves took up the pen and published their own urban-themed romances, which then came to dominate the black literary underground in the 1990s. Variously labeled "urban fiction," "street lit," and "hip-hop lit," their books dovetailed with young black men's recirculating black pulp fiction through rap. Of course, the more Slim and Goines became associated with rap's cultural networks, the less need there was to turn to the communications circuit to indulge in pulp storytelling. In the end, I argue, Morriss and Weinstock's hold on the black literary underground was undone by these readers' reappropriating black pulp fiction for their own purposes.

In tracking Holloway House's move from sleaze to street, I aim to tell a particular story that nonetheless has broader implications for how we think and write about race and appropriation in American culture. That I end the book with urban fiction and hip-hop underscores the strange and unpredictable turns this story takes. But it is precisely in those turns, I think, that we can see where cultural appropriation makes reappropriation possible, and where the racial "Other" slides into something like racial community. Thus, at these turns, we can begin to appreciate Stuart Hall's point that, "however deformed, incorporated, and inauthentic are the forms in which black people and black communities and traditions appear and are represented in popular culture, we continue to see, in the figures and the repertoires on which popular culture draws, the experiences that stand behind them."[20] This book is centrally about how black readers contested with white readers to bring those experiences—their experiences—to light.

PART ONE

Origins

ONE

Up from Domesticity

A beaming Marilyn Monroe, left hand held high in the air, as if caught in mid-wave, graced the cover of a new men's magazine in December 1953. On its debut, *Playboy* was showcasing a photograph for which the starlet had posed in 1949, before she became famous. Monroe was both cover girl and centerfold of the new magazine. But she was not the first female figure to catch the reader's eye once he started flipping through it. That distinction went to the disembodied head of a heavily made-up, middle-aged woman. Taking up half the page, the head gazed down upon on the figure of a much smaller man, a sad sack whose pockets were turned out to show he had no money left. The tableau illustrated the first piece of featured writing to appear in the magazine. It was titled "Miss Gold-Digger of 1953."

The article by Bob Norman bemoaned the passing of those days when "a man knew where he stood," and specifically when "alimony was reserved for the little floosies [*sic*] who periodically married and divorced millionaire playboys as carless [*sic*] with their lucre as their love." The problem today, according to Norman, was that alimony had become "democratic"—any woman, "even the simplest wench," could ask for it. He ran down the list of recent divorce cases in which working stiffs had been taken for a ride by their exes. Truck driver, salesman, television director: all had been victimized by a system that favored a woman's claim to as much as half of a man's earnings. In this system, men's "economic survival" came at the expense of supporting women from whom they could no longer expect any domestic or sexual benefits. Norman concluded the piece on an ominous note: the gold digger of 1953 was still after "wealthy playboys," but she could "also be after you."[1]

Far more complementary to Monroe's turn as a star pinup was the anonymous piece "An Open Letter from California." The story it told was the stuff of fantasy. An "eastern boy" had moved to Southern California to "soothe an ugly ulcer and some jangled, city-type nerves." There, in his "six room house" with "palm trees and a private swimming pool," he found that the warm weather and laid-back atmosphere suited him just fine. As did his new female friend, a buxom brunette whose poolside pictures he made sure to include in the letter. Apparently uninhibited, the woman can be seen frolicking in and out of the water with nothing on except something to cover her head. The pictures build up to a simple question: Jealous yet? "Yeah, California is a helluva fine state," the author deadpanned.[2]

This book begins at the conjuncture of misogyny and libertinism—the point where gold diggers and pinups meet. What might look like opposing positions to us today were, in fact, two sides of the same coin in midcentury America. Before *Playboy* cleaned up its act and became a mouthpiece for sexual liberalism in the 1960s, it was like any of the other stridently masculinist pinup magazines from the 1950s. Sporting names like *Stag*, *Rugged*, and *Monsieur*, these periodicals were products of their time. They decried women's increasing ability to assert their socioeconomic independence from the private sphere, but they also celebrated women's increasing availability as sexual objects in public. The fact that the latter was, to a large extent, made possible by the former did not trouble readers of these magazines. They were more than capable of reconciling the belief that wives belonged in the home with the fantasy that singles belonged in their beds.

Bentley Morriss and Ralph Weinstock were wholly committed to the idea that men could have it both ways. They liked the *Playboy* model, and, from their perch in Los Angeles, they correctly predicted that there was enough room in the market for their own magazines. *Adam* debuted in 1956 with an editorial that explained its choice of title: "To what more delightful thing can a man dedicate himself than the *ladies!* Not since Adam gave up a rib to create Eve has there been anything better than the *ladies!*"[3] The statement may have lacked the bite of *Playboy*'s gold-digger commentary, but it still connected women's sexual availability ("*ladies!*") to their dependence on men (Adam's rib). *Sir Knight* honed the misogyny-libertinism line when it debuted in 1958. It was, in the words of its editorial, "dedicated solely to fostering the proposition that every male with corpuscles pink and surging in his veins has the right to pursue all the happiness he can grasp for himself." The magazine welcomed "womankind" into the fold, but only if she was "willing to ride on the saddle behind him."[4]

I begin with *Playboy*, *Adam*, and *Sir Knight* because the print culture of which they were leading examples constituted the foundations of black pulp fiction. That culture was rakish yet leering, defensive yet outspoken; it embraced the fact that it circulated on the margins of wholesome popular culture. The books and magazines produced within the culture could only be purchased in specialty adult bookstores, which tended to be located in the seedier parts of town, or, as Gay Talese immortalized at the beginning of his book *Thy Neighbor's Wife* (1981), out from under the counter at your local suburban newsstand. (Eventually they would become available by mail order.) In their flouting of social niceties and their unapologetic treatment of women as sex objects, these print commodities made up the literary underground of their day. In retrospect, we call that underground by a name that signifies a whole ethos of crude masculinism: *sleaze*.[5]

In this chapter, I examine the core ideology around which Morriss and Weinstock built their empire of sleaze: that domesticity was a trap. The threat of feminization posed by the domestic sphere was, of course, hardly new. As Ann Douglas and others have shown, that threat had been a constitutive part of American life since the nineteenth century, when stereotypes of gender difference were mapped onto the separate spheres (public, private) of daily existence.[6] What was new, then, was the seemingly infinite variety of ways this ideology could be expressed. Never before had the collective id of American masculinity enjoyed so many outlets for expression. Within print culture alone, the combination of text, graphics, and photography in mass-produced packages allowed for the dissemination of antidomestic sentiment on an unprecedented scale. And with scale came the desire for more. Soon sleaze was in a race to outdo itself—to see how much it could get away with, both visually and textually. *Playboy* dropped out of the race in the 1960s, rebranding itself as a vehicle for upmarket taste. Morriss and Weinstock, however, very much stayed in it—long enough to hit the craze for black sleaze.

But before I get to that, I spend this chapter taking a closer look at how sleaze operated in *Adam*, *Sir Knight*, and the early titles of Holloway House. Though these print commodities had antidomestic themes in common, they were also materially conjoined by Morriss and Weinstock's overarching business structure. Because sleaze often found itself on the wrong side of decency ordinances and censorship laws—to say nothing of the social opprobrium foisted on its articles, cartoons, and pictorials—it required a high degree of self-contained organization. Morriss and Weinstock could not rely on the mainstream publishing industry, or local authorities, to give them any breaks. What they did, then, was distribute their own media, populate it with hackwork, and create the illusion that the hackwork was the real thing (that is, not hackwork). Beyond the fact that alternately demeaning and objectifying women was simply in bad taste, these were the business strategies that made sleaze the literary underground of its day.

American Venus

Like many Angelenos then and today, Bentley Morriss and Ralph Weinstock were transplants to the city. They had moved from Chicago and Detroit, respectively, to attend college at UCLA. After graduation, they set out to find work in the local media industry. Morriss and Weinstock did a little bit of everything at first: promotion, advertising, scouting for talent—whatever the bigger fish needed. Though little about Weinstock is known during this period, Morriss seemed to thrive in his role as a media insider. In 1947 he emceed an American Jewish Congress fund-raiser headlined by Jimmy Durante and Burl Ives; later he became president of the local B'nai B'rith lodge.[7] Morriss's ambition was further reflected in his choice of a pseudonym.[8] He derived it by combining the names of two posh-sounding British automobile manufacturers: Bentley Motors Limited and Morris Motors Limited. "Bentley Morriss" indeed had "hilarious class connotations," but it also revealed the power of self-invention in the industry.[9] Not for nothing did pseudonymous authorship become the foundation for Morriss's publishing enterprise.

By the 1950s, Morriss and Weinstock had secured enough contacts and capital to start their magazines. They set up operations in an area that was perfectly suited for this sort of business. According to urban historian Robert O. Self, the zone demarcated by North Hollywood, Silver Lake (to the east), and West Hollywood began to lose residents to Beverly Hills and Bel Air around the middle of the century. Flight from the area meant that "the class character of both the principal thoroughfares and surrounding residential neighbourhoods" shifted downward. It was not long before "porn theatres and other sex businesses" were replacing more conventional retailers. West Hollywood was a special case even within this zone, as it was "an unincorporated urban island entirely surrounded by Los Angeles but under the administration of the county." The somewhat lax oversight of this zone-within-a-zone made it particularly attractive to "gay residents and straight commercial sex."[10]

It thus was no coincidence that Morriss and Weinstock based *Adam* and *Sir Knight* in West Hollywood. The former was issued by Knight Publishing, with offices in the Prismatic Building.[11] The latter was a product of Sirkay ("Sir K") Publishing, located at 8835 Sunset Boulevard. *Adam*'s building and *Sir Knight*'s address were probably one in the same, given Morriss's reputation as a hands-on publisher who liked to oversee the daily operations of his companies. At any rate, what mattered was that the neighborhood was good for business. This stretch of Sunset Boulevard— Tinseltown's backyard, so to speak—welcomed more than enough talent to prop up a pinup enterprise. Cheap rents and a boozy nightlife provided a steady stream of models, dancers, and wannabe starlets who could be persuaded to push the bounds of decency. The milieu also attracted writers, usually men, either trying to catch a break in show business or slouching toward the midlife of their careers. In short, this was a neighborhood for the struggling artist, and men and women offered up different talents for Morriss and Weinstock to exploit.

Women filled exactly one role in their operation. *Adam* and *Sir Knight* were produced with the express purpose of gratifying the male gaze. The magazines' visuals captured what Laura Mulvey has called women's "to-be-looked-at-ness"—that is, a state of objectification in which the depicted female figure "holds the look, and plays to and signifies male desire." Mulvey contends that the female figure in classical Hollywood cinema, and in related culture industries ("from pin-ups to strip-tease"), at once fascinates the male gaze (in a scopophilic extraction of pleasure) and reinforces its activity (by feeding back into its narcissism).[12] This is the visual language also taken up by *Adam* and *Sir Knight*. Compare the following images from both magazines: a model in the great outdoors (figure 1.1); a cover girl with fabric (figure 1.2); another model in a sheer negligee (figure 1.3); and another cover girl alongside a table of fruit (figure 1.4). Figures 1.1 and 1.4 show women whose eyes are obscured or directed away from the reader. By contrast, figures 1.2 and 1.3 show women who stare directly at the reader. Yet the variability in these acts of looking does not count for much here. That is because all four figures invite the male gaze by virtue of how they are framed. Whether awaiting capture by a voyeuristic glance (unknowing innocence) or legitimating the reader's desire with a "come

FIGURE 1.1 Pictorial image from "Meet Sweet Sue," in *Adam* 1, no. 4 (1957). Courtesy of Knight Publishing.

hither" look (knowing seduction), these women reinforce masculine self-possession by evoking an essentially feminine passivity.

We can push this analysis even further and identify the key element to which the reader's gaze is drawn. Whatever the state of undress, the women in these images are positioned to accentuate a specific part of

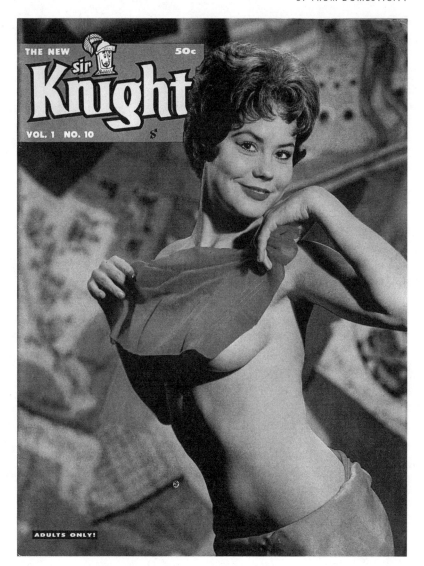

FIGURE 1.2 Front cover of *Sir Knight* 1, no. 10 (1959).

the body. That obviously goes for figure 1.1, but it applies to the other three as well: the tease of concealment and anticipatory revelation swirl around their breasts. The obsession with breasts was standard during this time, as the buxom models of wartime pinup calendars continued to influence popular standards of sex appeal. French film critic André Bazin once described this idealized figure as an "American Venus."

FIGURE 1.3 Pictorial image from "Trick for the Taking," in *Adam* 1, no. 8 (1957). Courtesy of Knight Publishing.

"With her narrow hips, the pin-up girl does not evoke motherhood," he wrote. "Instead, let us note particularly the firm opulence of her bosom. American eroticism . . . seems to have moved in recent years from the leg to the breast."[13] True to that ideal, *Adam* and *Sir Knight* decoupled breasts from their reproductive function and turned them into

FIGURE 1.4 Front cover of *Sir Knight* 2, no. 1 (1960).

points of masculine sexualization. An editorial statement joked, "As long as watchers of women are liable to public scorn, while watchers of small birds win public acclaim, ADAM and his readers have a cause to promote. For what red-blooded, adult male, wants to watch small birds while women remain available?"[14] Sex appeal, rather than reproductive ability, was attached to size: the bigger, the better.

To be sure, sexualizing women's breasts was of a piece with the anti-domestic ideology of sleaze. Women could be the playthings of men's imaginations precisely insofar as they disclaimed or negated familial and matrimonial ties. The woman who tied a man down was assailed in predictable ways. Above a drawing of a couple getting their marriage license was a joke about the "three stages of man": "First—tri-weekly," "Second—try-weekly," "Third—Try-weakly."[15] But living in a sexless marriage was the least of man's worries. Sleaze saw all women as potential gold diggers—con artists who, after springing the trap of domesticity, could drain husbands of their money. The best a man could hope for was a wife who was a spendthrift. Divorce was a more serious threat, given that a man would have to part with his money and his domestic favors. A cartoon of a nicely dressed woman driving alone in a car shows a sign plastered on her rear window: "Made in Texas, New York, California, Mass., Ark., & Wash, D.C."[16] But even appearing on a divorcee's long list of victims seemed preferable to dying at a woman's hands. A historical article on women who killed men close to them by poison ended with the then recent case of Marie Besnard, an elderly Frenchwoman who allegedly poisoned thirteen people, including her husband, because of "her love of money, and her total disregard for the manner in which she obtain[ed] it."[17] Harboring such a low view of married women, is it any wonder that *Adam* joked in 1960 that the bachelor's "dream wife" was "a beautiful, nymphomaniacal deaf mute with a large inherited income"?[18]

The nastiness of sleaze's antidomestic ideology expressed a broadly held, if impolite, view that the de-individualizing aspects of modern American life could be blamed on women, and specifically on a figure known as "mom"—the quintessential domestic female. From communism to corporate bureaucracy to mass culture, mom was blamed for forcing the American male to suppress his desires and conform to groupthink. Fittingly for sleaze, the most outspoken proponent of this ideology, "momism," was a Princeton-trained pulp author named Philip Wylie. Wylie's 1942 diatribe *Generation of Vipers* crystallized the male backlash against feminization. In it he contrasted mom to the "Cinderella" most men think they are marrying:

The devil whispered. The pretty girl then blindfolded her man so he would not see that she was turning from a butterfly into a caterpillar. She told him, too, that although caterpillars ate every damned leaf in sight, they were moms, hence sacred. Man was a party to the deception because he wanted to be fooled about Cinderella, because he was glad to have a convenient explanation of mom, and also because there burned within him a dim ideal which had to do with proper behavior, getting along, and, especially, making his mark. Mom had already shaken him out of that notion of being a surveyor in the Andes which had bloomed in him when he was nine years old, so there was nothing left to do, anyway, but to take a stockroom job in the hairpin factory and try to work up to the vice-presidency. Thus the women of America raped the men, not sexually, unfortunately, but morally, since neuters come hard by morals.[19]

Wylie blamed mom for every lost opportunity and every dashed hope in a working man's life. In collapsing wife and mother onto the single figure of mom (mainly through the metaphor of the butterfly turning back into a caterpillar), he instilled in readers the fear that there was a vast conspiracy against manhood. The whole thing, from boyhood to marriage, was a "deception," a process of emasculating the American male by chaining him to the home.

By the late 1950s, Hugh M. Hefner, the owner of *Playboy*, was steering his magazine away from the outright misogyny of momism. The move was necessary given that *Playboy*'s bachelor ideal was a man of urbane refinement, not crass objectification. Attuned to the class aspirations of his readership, Hefner sought to cultivate an aesthetic of taste around wine, women, and cars. Happily for him, the less *Playboy* railed against women, the more it attracted new consumers and upmarket advertisers. But Hefner's editorial shift was not the industry norm. As pinup historian Dian Hanson explains, the late 1950s "saw a battle waged between the new and the old for dominance of America's newsstands." At stake was control over the direction of the men's magazine market: "Hugh Hefner . . . led one army and George E. von Rosen, publisher of *Modern Man* led the other. On Hefner's side, the Girl Next Door, cocktails, jazz and journalism; on von Rosen's, strippers, cars, guns and fishing features. It was youth against age, white collar against blue collar, Madonna against whore, Cro-Magnon against Neandertal [sic]."[20] In this "battle" for market control, *Adam* and *Sir Knight* stood squarely on *Modern Man*'s side. And that meant both magazines were confined to the margins of good taste while *Playboy* adapted its message to the dawn of the 1960s.

If mom was too overbearing and the girl next door was too saccharine, what kind of woman was left for Morriss and Weinstock's readers to fantasize about? The answer was simple: she who sold sex for money. In pictorials, short stories, feature articles, and jokes and cartoons, *Adam* and *Sir Knight* consistently extolled women who put a price tag on sex appeal. The logic went like this: if women are out to get men anyway, then the least deceptive ones are those who sell their bodies and services in the free market. In this scenario, men at least had the opportunity to exercise choice in the matter, and long-term commitment was, of course, not an issue. This is why nude models, burlesque dancers, and even madams garnered praise, if not grudging respect, in these magazines. In 1962, for example, *Sir Knight* quipped, "The difference between an amateur play-girl and a professional is easily defined—a professional is a girl who checks a man's advances until he advances her a few checks."[21] The same issue featured a short story about a call girl, a profile of four topless dancers, and a photo spread of a former jazz bar turned strip club in Hollywood. The previous year, *Adam* ran a story on how the married man could spice up his sex life. One tip stood out: pay your own wife before doing it. "All sex is bought and paid for," the author reasoned, so "when a cash payment-in-the-hand is made, one feels that he's getting something special and labors to get his money's worth." "Deposit a coin and see," he urged.[22] That issue featured an article on prostitution in France, a pictorial of a nude model emporium in London, and a defiant manifesto titled "Burlesque Will Never Die."

In the world of sleaze, the American Venus was a whore—and she both knew it and marshaled it to her advantage. Needless to say, this illiberal view of womanhood affected who was willing to associate themselves with *Adam* and *Sir Knight*. Whereas Hefner attracted nationally recognized brands to advertise in *Playboy*, Morriss and Weinstock had to be content with advertising other small businesses specializing in sleaze. In sidebars and on entire pages of *Adam* and *Sir Knight* there appeared scores of mail-order advertisements for sex-related products: amateur photographs, dirty-joke records, adult comics, and sex toys. Post office boxes on both coasts promised to send catalogs of so-called stag books and film reels. Nude models made the reader want to buy a camera so he could set up amateur photo shoots. It was all a bit tawdry. But that was the point. For sleaze, a man's desire was a blunt object: there was little mystery as to what would get him aroused. Thus, rather than encourage the consumption of things that would attract women, as *Playboy* did, *Adam* and *Sir Knight* cut to the chase and crudely offered the thing itself on a plate.

The explicitness of the magazines' appeal to male readers was not lost on the authorities. In October 1957 Philadelphia police issued warrants for the arrest of *Adam*'s editor-in-chief Lothar Ashley and four other officers of the magazine. They were charged with "distributing obscene and lewd publications."[23] If there was any relief that the long arm of the law could not reach from Pennsylvania to California on an obscenity case, that all changed in April 1959, when Los Angeles authorities seized materials from the offices of Knight and Sirkay following an indictment by a Tulare County grand jury. Morriss, business associate Kurt Reichert, and model Virginia "Ding Dong" Bell were charged with "conspiracy to violate Section 311 of the Penal Code, which prohibits magazines containing obscene and indecent materials such as pictures of women in various nude poses."[24] Rural Tulare County, home of Sequoia National Park, was still a far cry from Los Angeles, but its case hit home. Bell was a stag movie icon, and her pictorial in *Adam* precipitated the legal proceedings. The case eventually "settled for a misdemeanor plea deal," but the experience served as a reminder that publishing sleaze was a risky business.[25]

The upside for Morriss and Weinstock was that federal law was inching over to their side. The landmark US Supreme Court decision *Roth v. United States* (1957) did not grant First Amendment protections to those materials deemed obscene, but it did grant localities tremendous leeway in establishing for themselves what obscenity meant. "The standard for judging obscenity," the 6–3 opinion of the Court noted, "is whether, to the average person, applying contemporary community standards, the dominant theme of the material, taken as a whole, appeals to prurient interest."[26] According to Robert O. Self, with no national standard affirmed by the Court, "many state courts and legislatures liberalised . . . obscenity and pornography restrictions" over the next decade. Consequently, in the zone marked off by North and West Hollywood and Silver Lake, "commercial pornographers . . . develop[ed] an array of aggressive forms, seeking access to an ever-increasing consumer market for what many called 'smut.'"[27] The *Roth* decision meant that sleaze would not only live to see another day—it could expand so long as it played up its nonprurient credentials. And expand is exactly what Morriss and Weinstock did in 1961 when they started Holloway House.

Reprint, Recycle, Repeat

By the early 1960s, Los Angeles had become home to "much of the nation's mail-order erotica, pulp paperback trade and pornography."[28] Morriss and Weinstock were at the center of a growth market, and they came to accept their legal predicaments as a cost of doing business in the field. They relocated to 8762 Holloway Drive, just down the street from Sunset Boulevard, and named their new venture after the building. In September 1961 executive editor Masamori Kojima announced that Holloway House would publish affordable paperbacks "keyed to contemporary events and personalities of universal interest."[29] Its debut titles hewed closely to that description. *Hemingway: Life and Death of a Giant* was a biography of the hard-living author by former spy Kurt Singer, while *The Trial of Adolf Eichmann* was an account of the ex-Nazi officer's trial in Israel by *Los Angeles Times* staff writer Dewey W. Linze. Hemingway had committed suicide on July 2, 1961, and Eichmann's trial had adjourned on August 14, 1961. That meant these books had an extremely fast turnaround. It was an early sign of Holloway House's publishing strategy: to treat books like they were magazines, highlighting their topicality and quick and easy consumption.

One important aspect of this strategy involved distribution. At sixty cents per copy, Holloway House paperbacks cost only a dime more than issues of *Adam* and *Sir Knight*; they could also be bought from the same newsstands where men's magazines were sold. This material interchangeability was facilitated, in part, by a shared means of delivery: All America Distributors Corporation (AADC). Morriss's wholesale company treated all print commodities equally—as so much product to be moved.[30] AADC allowed Morriss to bypass conventional distribution networks, effectively cutting out the third party in negotiations between publisher and retailer. The ability to gain entry into the market through direct means evidently outweighed the risk of distributing risqué material on his own. Over time, the success of AADC probably convinced Morriss that he could expand the range of print commodities on offer. Paperbacks, too, could be sold at the newsstand and through mail order. Thus, whenever the AADC logo appeared on the cover of a book or magazine, it signified, above all, an interconnected distribution network involving Knight Publishing, Sirkay Publishing, and Holloway House.

But before these print commodities even entered the market, they were already interconnected at the level of production. That is because Holloway House reprinted a great deal of material from the magazines in book form. After the Hemingway and Eichmann books, for example, there arrived a two-volume edition of Giacomo Casanova's memoirs (1961), which *Adam* had published in installments beginning in 1957; a compilation of Leo Guild's columns for *Sir Knight* titled *Hollywood Screwballs* (1962); and an anthology of short stories, *The Best of Adam* (1962). The company's output over the next seven years derived almost exclusively from *Adam* and *Knight*, the latter of which dropped "Sir" between 1962 and 1963. Take the 1965 catalog of titles:

Ladies on Call by Lee Francis
The Tortured Sex by John S. Yankowski and Hermann K. Wolff
The Yankowski Report on Premarital Sex by John S. Yankowski
Only When I Laugh by Henny and Jim Backus
Satyricon: Memoirs of a Lusty Roman by Petronius, translated by Paul J. Gillette
Prostitution, U.S.A. by Mike Bruno and David B. Weiss
An Uncensored History of Pornography by Paul J. Gillette
My Name Is Leona Gage, Will Somebody Please Help Me? by Leona Gage

With the exception of the Backuses' memoir of Old Hollywood, these titles reflected the magazines' preoccupation with sex. From the *Satyricon* of ancient Rome to contemporary "fallen woman" confessionals (Francis was a Hollywood madam, Gage a former Miss USA) to "case studies" in sexology and sexual behavior: Holloway House specialized in turning serial concerns into stand-alone books.

Ironically, the variety of Holloway House's catalog made the company appear more respectable than your average pinup magazine. In post-*Roth* America, it was common to assess prurience based on whether something could be called erotica or sleaze. Erotica, according research librarian Robert S. Bravard, served a specific, almost anthropological, purpose: namely, "to uncover what the sexual act 'means' to the variety of mankind." Sourced and reprinted "from the Italian Renaissance to Paris publications of the 1930's," erotic literature made historically grounded sexual knowledge available to the masses. Its uses thus could not be prurient. Sleaze, on the other hand, consisted of "items written by contemporary hack writers" that "reflect attitudes and obsessions of our current era," and that provide little more than "a simpleminded recitation of sexual behavior." Bravard was especially dismissive of literature that "purports to be either case histories of all manner of deviations or historical surveys of the same." "Much of this is obviously quite fictional," he warned, "and there seems to be no way of separating the dross from the valuable." Fortunately for Holloway House, Bravard judged its catalog consistent with that of an "erotic publisher." In fact, he complimented the company's "reprint program," saying its books were "basic to any erotic fiction collection."[31]

What Bravard failed to notice was how Holloway House's production model actually blurred the line between erotica and sleaze. The company published both kinds of works and made every effort to highlight their common interest. In so doing, it showed how historical value was bound up with contemporary lust, sexual knowledge with lurid description. Take, for instance, the previously mentioned memoirs of Casanova. The first volume's foreword situated this work within the history of an idea: "For more than a hundred years, the name of Casanova has been synonymous with the act of physical love—of male sexuality. It has, in fact, long ceased to be a name. It is a description, an epithet, a term of admiration, depending on the mood of the user."[32] But the front cover of the book was more direct about its intentions (figure 1.5). Above the picture of a man seducing two buxom, scantily clad women, the cover crowed, "A truly fabulous lover tells all! The incredible number of women he loved in wildly different ways staggers the imagination. Adult reading!" Where did knowledge end and puerility begin? Holloway House thrived in that gray zone.

Further eroding the erotica versus sleaze distinction was the fact that Holloway House's catalog was produced by just a handful of authors. Here the books' origin in magazine work was key. To secure content for their monthly issues, *Adam* and *(Sir) Knight* called on professional hacks who could script antidomestic tropes into any number of generic storylines. These writers turned literary pornography into a science, perfecting formulas designed to recycle a coherent sexual ideology—that of the rake, the seducer, the cad—in as many different forms as possible. The diversity of content in the magazines then led to the publication of different kinds of paperbacks. Yet this recycling process was not facilitated by a sprawling infrastructure. Instead, a single freelance writer was responsible for producing the bulk of Morriss and Weinstock's literary content. That writer turned out to be one of the greatest American hacks of the twentieth century. He wrote for scores of magazines between the 1950s and his death in 1996 and assumed hundreds of aliases and pen names in the process. In the 1960s, he commanded a small army of pseudonyms to make a career out of sleaze. His real name was Paul J. Gillette.

Gillette's papers, which take up seventy-nine boxes at Penn State's Eberly Family Special Collections Library, offer an unparalleled view of how the midcentury pulp and pinup trades worked. His name appears in the list of books Holloway House published in 1965. He is identified as the author of *An Uncensored History of Pornography* and translator of Petronius's *Satyricon*. But Gillette was also the man behind the sexologist personas John S. Yankowski and Hermann K. Wolff, as well as the journalists Mike Bruno and David B. Weiss. Combining all of this work means he was responsible for five out of the eight books the company brought out that year. This was the low-cost business model Morriss and Weinstock had been looking for. They had published one book—a collection of cartoons poking fun at President Lyndon B. Johnson—the

A truly fabulous lover tells all! The incredible number of women he loved in wildly different ways staggers the imagination. Adult reading!

75¢

HH-103

The Many Loves of Casanova

Uncensored personal memoirs of Jacques Casanova

VOL. 1

Bill Edwards

A HOLLOWAY HOUSE ILLUSTRATED PAPERBACK

FIGURE 1.5 Front cover of *The Many Loves of Casanova*, vol. 1 (1961).

year before, and only ten books in three years before that. Their new model, however, allowed them to publish at least ten books per year, each apparently different from the next but each in fact derived from the same freelancer's hand. Thanks to Gillette, Holloway House built a sleaze empire out of a fast and affordable way of recycling antidomestic ideology in print.

Gillette stepped into sleaze through *Playboy*. His specialty was adapting the naughty bits from classical and European literature into modern erotic tales. Between August 1961 and May 1963, he sold nine such pieces—mainly by Petronius and Marguerite de Navarre—to Hefner's magazine under the series title "Ribald Classic." Toward the end of that run, however, Gillette saw more and more of his pieces returned. As *Playboy* swung upmarket, it left old-timey erotica behind. But that was hardly the case for Morriss and Weinstock. In 1963 *Adam* and *Knight* started to buy Gillette's work to fill in their own "Ribald Classic" series. For a time, whenever he got a rejection from *Playboy*, Gillette would simply turn around and submit the piece to *Adam* or *Knight*; it usually sold. In February 1963, for example, Morriss's umbrella company—Consolidated Advertising Directors, Inc. (CAD), whose office was also located at 8762 Holloway Drive—paid Gillette sixty-five dollars for delivery of "The Advance of Medicine," an excerpt from Marguerite's *Heptaméron*, to *Knight*. In August of that year, CAD paid him fifty dollars for delivery of "Innkeeper's Daughter," a story by Giuseppe Gigliotti, to *Adam Reader* (a spinoff of the original).[33] Both excerpts had been rejected by *Playboy*, and both found a buyer in CAD. It was not long before Gillette started submitting his writing directly to Morriss and Weinstock.

Sleaze historian Stephen J. Gertz has complained that Gillette's compositions are not so much adapted translations as outright fabrications. To put one together, he first "condensed, abridged, and paraphrased" a previously published translation in English. Gillette then inserted his own flights of fancy where he thought the narrative needed more sex, more coherence, or some combination of the two.[34] Gillette's work on the Marquis de Sade is representative here. As Loren Glass has shown, Sade mania hit the United States when Grove Press began publishing a multivolume edition of his collected writings in 1965. To achieve this feat, Grove collaborated with Richard Seaver and Austryn Wainhouse, who had originally translated the writings for Maurice Girodias and his Paris-based Olympia Press.[35] Holloway House wanted in on the action, so it allowed Gillette to create Frankenstein versions of Sade based on the Olympia editions. After bringing out a selection of his works, which included *Justine*, *Juliette*, and *Philosophy in the Bedroom*, in 1966,

Gillette turned his attention to *120 Days of Sodom*. He sent Weinstock photocopies of the Olympia edition and proposed a radical reworking of the text, focusing not on a Sadean libertine but on Madame Duclos, a prostitute. He detailed: "What I would do in the editing arrangement of which I spoke is put the 'dye see,' etc., types of dialogue in modern idiom, change the paragraphing, set it up in chapters, smooth out sentences which are inordinately complex, delete references to the individual listeners (Blangis, Curval, etc., of the SODOM cast) and improve terms when one-word changes are possible." All this, Gillette wrote, could be done "in about 15 days."[36] Weinstock took him up on the offer, and the result was *Marquis de Sade's Francon Duclos: The Memoirs of a Paris Madame* (1967), Holloway House's unique version of *120 Days*.

Gertz's criticism of Gillette is withering. There was nary a translation to speak of—only bastardized treatments of other people's work. Characters and storylines bore only a faint resemblance to their source material. Nothing of the original author's style survived. To top it off, the anachronisms Gillette inserted into the text were so ludicrous as to almost willfully invite derision. In *Francon Duclos*, for example, a taxicab makes an appearance in eighteenth-century France. In *Juliette*, the title character leans against a telephone pole. And in *Satyricon*, Trimalchio plays tennis and admires his dining-room clock. "Clocks and tennis," Gertz harrumphs. "Rare sights in ancient Rome."[37]

Yet it may be a mistake to presume that these anachronisms, as well as other textual infelicities, were unintended. Indeed, the point of chopping up and rewriting the classics would have been to make them relatable to modern readers, and specifically readers of sleaze. From that angle, Gillette did exactly what he had set out to do. Unlike Seaver and Wainhouse, he was not interested in the scholarly, intellectual, or cultural value of Sade—or any other figure of standing, for that matter. Gillette's mission was straightforward: ratchet up the hedonism and depravity, turn male characters into alter egos for the reader, and create pinups out of female characters who exchange sex in the free market. And who could forget mom? Gillette reserved a special degree of scorn for her. In *Satyricon*, for example, Trimalchio's wife Fortunata appears as the consummate gold digger: "Notice the way she scurries around the room, her nose held proudly in the air." Already we suspect Fortunata of pretending to be more than what she is, or deserves. Sure enough, the narrator reveals that she used to work "in the bawdy houses," where she made a pittance owing to a lack of customers. "But, look at her now: She's in heaven," Gillette observes. "And Trimalchio worships her. If, at noon, she says it's midnight, he'll believe her."[38] No longer having to work for her appeal, Fortunata has succeeded in bending Trimalchio to her will, turning him into a docile husband. She was a prostitute, but, lamentably, she has become a mom.

Toward the end of 1963, Gillette started supplementing his erotica treatments with articles on contemporary sexual mores. This was exactly the kind of writing that Bravard bemoaned: studies and surveys that, in essence, functioned as delivery mechanisms for titillating sex scenes. One of the first pieces he wrote in this vein, "Interview with a Call Girl," sold to *Adam* in December 1963. The twenty-five-hundred-word article, which he published under the pseudonym Jim Dottle, netted Gillette one hundred and thirty-five dollars.[39] The interviewee in Gillette's piece was no more real than his translations of Latin into English; she was made to say what Gillette wanted her to say. This was characteristic of all his nonfiction. Indeed, there is no evidence from his papers to suggest that Gillette relied on anything but the odd periodical clipping and his own wild imagination to populate his studies and surveys with thousands of people. In this way, his contemporary writing was manufactured by throwing his voice to anyone who had something to say about sex.

The self-contained nature of Gillette's work led to many situations where he would cite himself or one of his many pseudonyms. The primary source of data in *Psychodynamics of Unconventional Sex Behavior and Unusual Practices* (1966), for example, was the aforementioned *Yankowski Report on Premarital Sex*, a trimmed-down, sexed-up Kinsey Report for the sleaze set. Gillette was Yankowski, of course, so passages like this one were entirely self-referential: "Yankowski . . . found that a full 90 percent of all women who reported participation in fellatio said that they either removed their mouth from the penis before ejaculation took place or spit out the substance immediately afterward." Gillette dismisses a couple of reasons for why this might be so—the need to keep clean or the "unpleasant taste"—before settling on the reason Yankowski gives: "the reluctance is motivated largely by psychological factors," as indicated by the fact that "a full 100 percent of all females who reported fellatio said that they experienced guilt and shame after their initial indulgence in the act," and that "a full 35 percent of all who reported continuing participation said that they still experienced guilt and/or shame."[40] The recycling of completely made-up sexual data confirmed what readers wanted to believe at the same time that it validated Gillette's and Yankowski's "research."

The recycling process spilled over into other jobs. Gillette's papers reveal that, beginning in 1964, Gillette sold hundreds of pieces to tabloid magazines such as *Hush Hush, Cloak 'n' Dagger, Vice Squad, Naked Truth, National Examiner,* and *Confidential.* For him, tabloids' stock in trade—scandal, gossip, exposé—was coextensive with sleaze's cynical, de-idealizing worldview. It only made sense, then, that Gillette would adapt his tabloid magazine work into more books for Holloway House. *Prostitution, U.S.A.,* for example, was basically a compilation of stories Gillette had written for the scandal rags under different pseudonyms. The Washington, DC, chapter, for example, cited a December 1964 story from *Vice Squad* (authored by the hard-nosed white-ethnic duo of Bruno and Weiss) about a prostitution ring whose madam, Jeannette Park, had murdered her boyfriend. But Gillette was not one to pass up the opportunity for self-aggrandizement, even when he was using a pseudonym. He appears in the book as a "New York author" who presses the US senator in charge of investigating the DC ring for answers: "Why . . . had the list of [clients'] names remained secret and had the matter failed to be investigated by the Senate Rules Committee?"[41] With Bruno and Weiss at the helm, Gillette could play the reporter asking hard-hitting questions of the Washington elite.

Within and across print commodities, Gillette had effectively created a sleaze echo chamber. Reprints fueled recycling, which led to more reprints and ever more recursive forms of recycling. Though he wrote in an array of registers and put on innumerable masks, Gillette was essentially repurposing material from magazines to books and back to magazines and into more books. This became the model for Holloway House's literary production. It kept the publisher materially intertwined with the pinup trade, and it kept its books ensconced in what amounted to a self-referential universe of misogynist sentiment.[42]

Ghost Confessionals

What were women reading that was remotely comparable to such fare? In magazines such as *True Confessions, Revealing Romances,* and *Secrets,* stories hewed to a formula that valued the very domesticity from which sleaze sought escape. First, the protagonist would err in straying from the bonds of domesticity. That mistake would cause her to fall into ruin or disrepute; for a time, she would have to suffer for having left the security of the home. Eventually, though, either the protagonist would come around or her luck would turn, and she would find a way of bouncing back, affirming the lesson of not straying in the first place. The stories were pitched as "true-life" romances, making them popular with young, working-class, and single women readers.[43] In embracing domestic ideology, these stories, and the confession magazines in which they appeared, flipped the script on *Playboy*, *Adam*, and *Knight*, though they occasionally shared editorial ground with scandal rags like *Vice Squad* and *Confidential*.

By the mid-1960s, the confession story was primed for crossover success in the sleaze market. It had all the ingredients of a sordid literary romp, couched in the language of a cautionary tale. If erotica relied on sexual knowledge to license readers' delight in the lurid and sensational, the first-person confessional rested on the slipperiest, yet potentially most convincing, alibi of them all: frankness. So long as the narrator bared all for readers, there seemed to be no limit to how low she could fall. Morriss and Weinstock sought to capitalize on the confession craze.

The point person in that effort was Leo Guild, another author who went by many names. A former columnist for the *Hollywood Reporter*, Guild came to Holloway House with the inside track on Tinseltown gossip. He turned this advantage into a successful, if not infamous, freelance career. On its own, a book about a star in the news could pull in a $5,000 to $10,000 advance. But if the star signed off on her own book, using Guild as her ghostwriter, then the advance could "break the $50,000 mark," and "subsidiary sales would be enormous." This was the arrangement Guild made with over twenty-five celebrities from the 1950s to 1960s, as he himself detailed in a November 1967 *Los Angeles Times* article appropriately titled "Confessions of a Celebrity Ghost Writer."[44] The article revealed that he had ghosted books by his former boss Bob Hope, burlesque dancer Lili St. Cyr, and Austrian-born American actress Hedy Lamarr.

But these were Guild's high-end deals. Among the rest could be found Holloway House's earliest sleaze confessionals: washed-up actress Barbara Payton's *I Am Not Ashamed* (1963), Hollywood madam Lee Francis's *Ladies on Call* (1965), and *Jayne Mansfield's Wild, Wild World* (1963), coauthored by the hard-living sex symbol and her then husband Mickey Hargitay. Payton, Francis, and Mansfield were fodder for scandal rags and men's magazines. Guild had interviewed the women using a tape recorder, blowing through "50 one-hour tapes" in order to get enough material to "write a good book." Of course, accuracy was not at the forefront of Guild's mind when he wrote up the material. The point in hiring a ghostwriter, he contended, was to add organization and "dramatics" to a life where neither seemed to be present. Unsurprisingly, then, when he tried to reconcile contradictory accounts from Mansfield's "two dozen scrapbooks filled with clippings," she was said to have retorted, "Oh, make it up."[45]

But exactly how did Guild adapt a genre typically associated with women to male-oriented sleaze? *I Am Not Ashamed* provides a case in point. By the time the book was released Payton had been on a steep decline. In 1949 the blonde bombshell came out of nowhere—Cloquet, Minnesota, via Odessa, Texas—to make her way in Hollywood. She picked up bit parts and had a few starring roles through 1953. But then alcohol and drug abuse, as well as several torrid love affairs, derailed Payton's movie career and made her a pariah in the studio system. Guild pens the memoir from the perspective of having caught up with Payton in her current dingy environs. "Today, right now I live in a rat-roach (they're friends) infested apartment with not a bean to my name and I drink too much Rosé wine," he writes. "I don't like what my scale tells me. The little money I do accumulate to pay the rent comes from old residuals, poetry and favors to men. I love the Negro race and I will accept money only from Negroes." Broke, drunk, overweight, and solicitous not just of men but of the racial Other: Guild frames Payton as a figure of utter debasement. All of which is to be expected from the confession genre. But then Guild signals how male-oriented sleaze would handle this story of a fallen starlet. "Does it all sound depressing to you? Queasy?" Guild, as Payton, asks. "Well, I'm not ashamed. I have hope. I don't live in rosy-hazed memory. I look to the future."[46] This is a bold departure from the typical confession storyline. Rather than promise redemption by way of shame and regret, Guild doubles down on Payton's debasement—she fully identifies with what she has become.

Predictably, *I Am Not Ashamed* avoids the usual resolution to the confession narrative—returning to the security of marriage or the family—and revels instead in antidomestic ideology. In particular, exchanging sex for a break in the industry is a recurring theme in the narrative. Men, women, white, black, rakes, introverts: Barbara takes all of them on in her climb to the top. Was the real Payton so promiscuous? It hardly matters, for in Guild's hands each scenario is meant to offer its own pornographic kick. We know what to expect, for example, when Barbara decides to seduce one of Hollywood's "most beautiful actresses, happily married with children," to try to get a part in "a big epic." Unsure whether the actress will take the bait, Barbara follows her into her dressing room, testing whether theirs will be a platonic or romantic encounter. The woman undresses, and Barbara describes what she saw: "Well, she was standing there with the greatest pair of boobies you ever saw sticking straight out. And she just seemed to be riveted to the spot." Barbara "took the cue" and "cupped both her breasts"; the woman then "swooned onto the couch, writhing in some kind of ecstasy."[47] Thus commenced their torrid love affair, which transpired during the shoot since Barbara (of course) got the part.

Though sex appeal is Barbara's greatest resource, it is also her biggest liability. She consistently fails to distinguish image-making from self-exploitation, and it is not long before she is explicitly trading sex for favors and money. As her star begins to dim, a desperate Barbara asks a screenwriter to use his clout to get producers to cast her in his script. Although he fails in doing so, they go to bed anyway: "After all, he *had* tried," Barbara reasons. With no work on the horizon, however, she begins to rely on payments from dates and boyfriends to make ends meet. When one supposedly confused lover does not slip her a little money, she is offended, and must ask herself: "Was I a hustler, a whore, a call girl? Of course not! But the question rankled. I took stock of myself. It was almost true. My prime source of income was from men—just a handful—but men who gave me money when I spent the night with them." The realization leads Barbara to take a hiatus in Mexico, but the break does not change her outlook. Back in Hollywood, she practically self-finances her own feature with money from a Texas oil man, who asks in an ominous tone, "What's in it for me?"[48] A short time later, destitute and wasting away from drink in a Sunset Boulevard apartment, Barbara has sex with her landlord to pay each month's rent.

Barbara's descent into a pit of despair elicits puerility and schadenfreude in the reader; it is a bizarre combination whose ultimate effect (honed by Guild) is to feast on the protagonist's vulnerability. This point is highlighted in a series of photographs that appear in the book's unpaginated insert. Tracing Payton's rise and fall from 1944 to 1963, the images show her as a young bride in Texas, as a beautiful, buxom Hollywood starlet in the early 1950s, and then as an overweight, matronly criminal who passed bad checks and was once arrested for soliciting a police officer. Toward the end of the insert there is a two-page spread comparing Payton in 1952, posing for photographer Andre De Dienes, to Payton in 1963, "fat and wasted-looking" and posing for pictures that would be included in the book. A handful of photographs are featured in the insert, but Payton biographer John O'Dowd describes the latter of the images in the two-page spread as "a true abomination." Payton is shown "lounging on a couch at the motel, with a stripper's fur boa slung over her shoulders," wearing only a "tiny, black bra on a torso that was frighteningly swollen."[49] Payton's eyebrows are raised, her lips puckered, in a sad parody of what her addled mind probably thought was a sensual pose.

Yet, as completely used-up as Barbara is, the way she tells her story (which is the way Guild writes it) conjures the image not of a distraught victim but of a weary yet defiant cynic. Which is not to say the real-life Payton was invulnerable, or that she in any way resembled the protagonist of *I Am Not Ashamed*. It is only to say that Barbara, the specter of Guild's imagination, fully accepts her fallen condition. "If I'm a disreputable harodyn [*sic*], then tough, that's what I am," she says early on. "Where I am today, no matter how bad it looks to you, is where I belong. I can be me."[50] Regardless of the veracity of Guild's version of events, this refrain—I am of and fully identify with this horrible state—constitutes the narrative's ultimate truth. This is confession without guilt, a license to delight in the recognition of someone else's debasement.

Race is a muted, though significant, part of such recognition. As the narrative progresses, Barbara's increasingly self-destructive behavior is mirrored by her increasing identification with blackness. "I love the colored people and they love me," she asserts. "When they have relations with a white girl, it's because they need to be wanted, to belong, to be caressed. The passion is not animal—it's soul-like." Barbara's admiration for black people stems from the belief that, as an oppressed minority, only they can understand what it means to be down and out. Yet her fetish for black male "passion" merely substitutes a racism of stereotype for a racism of antipathy. Barbara's ignorance allows her to romanticize black men in a way that explains why she ends up working for a black pimp. Having operated as a free agent for too long, Barbara finally construes the pimp's offer to handle her business as an expression of care: "He brought me food and put me in his apartment and I started to take on a few Johns a day and he saw to it I wasn't cheated."[51] Even here, at the point where Barbara is completely divested of agency, Guild manages to find a silver lining. At least with the pimp Barbara knows where she stands.

I Am Not Ashamed hinted at how race could be folded into Holloway House's antidomestic project: living at the margins of society, black people's mere existence seemed to constitute a rejection of the square, sissified world. That, at least, is how it seemed to sleaze's white imagination. And Guild took up the challenge of writing a complete narrative around that idea when he and Kipp Washington penned *Some Like It Dark: The Intimate Autobiography of a Negro Call Girl* (1966). But just who was Kipp Washington? According to the book's foreword, the name was a pseudonym for a singer Guild had met at New York City's Cellar Club. Entranced by her light-skinned beauty, he initially had thought "she might be a model, actress, singer but never a call girl." After all, Kipp "had that look of innocence." Guild quickly learned, however, that Kipp's looks concealed a deep-seated cynicism, "a kindred quality" he appreciated. Learning more about her checkered past, he was convinced a book was in the offing. Guild made her an offer, and the deal was done: "Kipp Washington wrote this book."[52]

Or did she? In his "Confessions" piece, Guild said he had been commissioned by Bernard Geis, publisher of Helen Gurley Brown's *Sex and the Single Girl* (1962) and other salacious titles, to ghostwrite the autobiography of African American actress and performance artist Dorothy Dandridge. Unfortunately, their collaboration had been cut short when Dandridge died in 1965.[53] A different source, however, has said that Earl Conrad, a popular author who had "many impressive black-white books" already to his credit (partial or otherwise), replaced Guild on the project and that Guild would not go away until he was paid a "cash sum plus 10 percent of royalties." Meanwhile, Earl Mills, Dandridge's former manager, brokered a book deal of his own with Holloway House.[54] As a consequence, both Conrad's *Everything and Nothing: The Dorothy Dandridge Tragedy* and Mills's *Dorothy Dandridge: A Portrait in Black* appeared in the same year: 1970.[55] Guild may have funneled his notes into helping Mills write his book. But it is also likely that he used them to cobble together *Some Like It Dark*. The material could have been put to use in this text in ways that pseudonymity cloaked as a matter of record. "A pretty colored girl to a white man is just a chocolate bar to devour and enjoy for a few moments," Dandridge allegedly wrote to Guild.[56] Whoever Kipp may (not) have been, the ghostwriter made this statement an implicit motto for his book.

The dirty pun on the title of Billy Wilder's lighthearted comedy *Some Like It Hot* (1959) reveals the lurid core of Kipp's narrative. As a professional black woman escort, she is the exact inverse of Barbara. For if Barbara projects her debasement onto black people, Kipp is exactly that screen onto which white clients project their "perversions." For instance, a Detroit steel baron combines different perfumes and fragrances on Kipp's body during a sexual encounter. She notes fondly, "It was the cleavage of my breasts that sent him into paroxysms of passion. . . . He dabbed a drop of perfume into a rivilet [*sic*] of perspiration on my breasts and that did it. He took long sniffs and then had an orgasm." In another chapter, a movie director evinces the more standard scopophilic desire as he requests to make love in front of a projection screen. But the scenes he displays are unique to his own distorted fantasies, with the background transitioning from the sea to a laughing audience to an old-timey dance hall to a baseball game and to a jungle. "Just a phallic symbol," he explains when a snake slithers up to the camera in the last scene. And then there is the client, an actor, who is drawn to Kipp after learning she has broken an arm in an accident. He remarks casually, "I'm 55 years-old. I've had men and animals and five Japanese broads at a time, and I even screwed a corpse. But it's sick or injured girls that turn me on. Some crazy psychologist worked on it with me once. He said I was so pressured to give perfection in my work, I adore people with imperfections." Despite this unusual sexual history, the actor finds himself struggling with impotency. Can Kipp help him? "Kipp," he tells his psychiatrist (who is brought along to counsel him during the proceedings), "is a prostitute. She is colored. She had a broken arm. Is it true that I can only love a woman who has three strikes against her to start with?"[57] This man has a fetish for handicaps, racial and otherwise.

What to do with this lineup of sad sacks and insecure egos? Might *Some Like It Dark* be a riotous send-up of sleaze after all? It could have been were it not for the fact that nearly all of the men in the narrative share a bond that rationalizes their insecurities and off-kilter desires: marriage. "Ten years ago I was married to a bitch," explains an aging comedian with whom Kipp works at a resort in the Catskills. "One night I got so mad I almost choked her to death. After that I divorced her." But that was also the night his impotency set in. As awful as that sounds, this logic—of blaming men's inadequacies on the castrating "bitch"—serves as the motivation behind many of Kipp's remunerated exchanges. The steel baron, for instance, is "divorced," because of which he "feel[s] like a hundred." Although he is resolute in not wanting to get remarried—"You don't marry for love. You marry to enhance your social prestige or to assist you in business"—when he loses control of himself during a sexual encounter he calls Kipp "a stinking bitch." Befitting his visual fetishes, meanwhile, the director includes in his projector set-up two scenes of his wife: the first, he says, was taken "when she was complaining about my being late to a party she wanted to go to," and the second, Kipp notices, showed "his wife undressing by the pool" and was shot "without her knowing it." The director sneers at his wife's breasts, which "sagged almost to her belly button," and says to her image, "Smile you old bitch while I screw the ass off a girl 100 times better than you." The actor does not harp on an ex-wife like the others, but that is because he is a bigamist, so much as he can remember: "Not only am I married, but I think I am married to two women. There was a mix-up in my divorce." At any rate, he says, "They both have too much lard on them." The trick to curing his impotency, then, is to immerse the actor in a fantasy of getting back at these two women. Kipp slaps the actor "with [her] one good hand," and after slapping him some more, he finally lashes out—"Why you bitch"—and slaps her back. "As pretty as you please his equipment came on like 'Gang Busters,' and he slid into me with every inch of his manhood," boasts Kipp.[58]

Kipp's character thus serves as the racial Other whose (paid-for) sexuality opens up the fantasy space men need to alternately escape from and strike back at emasculating white womanhood. In Guild's hands, black womanhood is synonymous with a streetwise free agency—an attitude toward sexual exchange that is the precise opposite of the stultifying bonds of domesticity. Given all of that, it should come as no surprise that yet another cheating husband compares Kipp to "an Adam Magazine center spread."[59] The self-referentiality of Morriss and Weinstock's fantasy world would have made it perfectly clear that an *Adam* centerfold possessed the sexual know-how of a Kipp Washington. But it did not even take an obscure reference to make that point. The paperback's front cover (figure 1.6) bore the image of an *Adam* pinup model, one Coreen Rodella, from 1958.[60]

It takes a black woman with no hang-ups or strong emotional attachments to others to negotiate the minefield that is male anxiety. And that is what Kipp does with aplomb. Love, she writes toward the end of the book, is "a luxury I couldn't afford." By which she means, "With me there was no love. If a man made love to me he paid for it."[61] The clarity and ease with which Kipp talks about her career—a function of Guild's own imagination, it bears repeating—are qualities of the ideal woman in midcentury pulps and pinup magazines. Kipp keeps her family at a remove, has very few friends, and submits to others' will for a price. She is the antidomestic dream come true.

Sleaze was a paradoxical operation. On one hand, the threat of censorship and the trade in risqué fare made it a relatively small, tight-knit business. Knight, Sirkay, and Holloway House were intertwined entities that answered to Morriss, financially, and to Weinstock, editorially. CAD served as a kind of parent company given that many books would start off as magazine contributions. The lot of them moved into an office building at 8060 Melrose Avenue, which Morriss had constructed

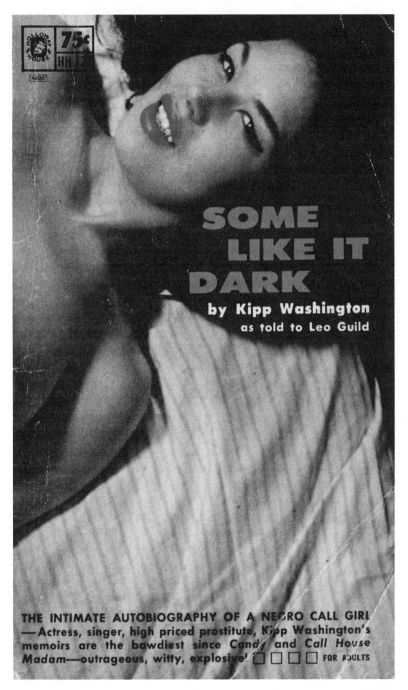

SOME
LIKE IT
DARK

by Kipp Washington
as told to Leo Guild

THE INTIMATE AUTOBIOGRAPHY OF A NEGRO CALL GIRL
—Actress, singer, high priced prostitute, Kipp Washington's
memoirs are the bawdiest since *Candy* and *Call House
Madam*—outrageous, witty, explosive! □ □ □ □ FOR ADULTS

FIGURE 1.6 Front cover of *Some Like It Dark: The Intimate Autobiography of a Negro Call Girl* (1966).

for $530,000 in 1963.[62] The only business that did not move into the building was AADC, which handled distribution for some properties other than Morriss and Weinstock's. Even so, Morriss's drive toward consolidation meant that AADC's offices were situated close by—just a half mile away on Melrose Place.

The small-scale nature of this operation was belied by the fact that, in print, Morriss and Weinstock were creating a veritable universe of male resentment and female sexualization. The echo chamber they set up between *Adam*, *Knight*, and Holloway House created a self-fulfilling fantasy that all wives were "bitches" and all lovers were "whores." Crucially, Morriss and Weinstock could only accomplish this by relying on incredible sleights of hand. Pseudonyms, ghostwriters, fake translations, made-up memoirs: the hacks they hired pulled out all the stops to make it appear as though sleaze was a bigger phenomenon than it actually was. That a handful of men were responsible for the vast majority of their output did not stop Morriss and Weinstock from saturating the market with sleaze. The goal was not to step outside the boundaries of what they knew would sell. The goal, rather, was to sell much, much more of it—to the point where the entire operation became self-referential.

Black pulp fiction came to fruition not despite but because of this operation. In order to clarify that point, we need to examine more deeply the mediating format of which *Some Like It Dark* was an early example. Black pulp fiction did not appear at the exact moment Holloway House started publishing actual, as opposed to ghosted, black authors. First, there had to be black sleaze.

TWO

Street Legends

Watts, Los Angeles, August 1965. A contested traffic stop boiled over into a violent confrontation between black residents and white police officers. That flash point would set off what was then the most destructive urban riot in the nation's history. Stores were looted, buildings vandalized, and cars set ablaze. Clashes between residents and the police (backed by the Army National Guard) left more than thirty dead. Whole city blocks resembled war zones. To whites, the unrest looked like wanton destruction. African Americans saw it differently. Watts, for them, was the outcome of years of hostility and neglect. They understood that, behind its reputation as a postwar paradise, Los Angeles was not so different from the South. Joblessness, police brutality, residential segregation: these facts defined life in the City of Angels as much as they did life under Jim Crow. Bentley Morriss took note. The riots marked an opportunity to publish new voices—ones coming out of Watts.

Legend has it that Holloway House took out an ad in the *Los Angeles Sentinel*, the city's African American newspaper, looking for black writers to join their ranks. Before long, Robert Beck, a self-employed exterminator, walked through the doors with a writing sample. Beck was a former hustler and pimp from Chicago. Having settled in Los Angeles after what proved to be a final stint in the penitentiary, Beck answered the ad eager to see if he could turn the stories of his youth into a literary career. Morriss loved the sample and approved a contract on the spot. The middle-aged author may not have been a voice of Watts, but his work certainly gave voice to the profound disillusionment that had made Watts happen. When the complete manuscript arrived, Milton Van Sickle, Holloway House's veteran sleaze editor, knew he had a winner: "I read [it] and told my bosses it was the best book we ever published."[1] *Pimp: The Story of My Life* arrived in March 1967, and with it was born the larger-than-life persona known as Iceberg Slim.

Behind Beck's decision to submit his manuscript was his then common-law wife, Betty Mae Shew. Legend has it that she urged Beck to approach Holloway House after seeing the ad herself. Mark McCord recounts the episode this way: "'Black writers needed! Publisher will pay you for your stories,' read the ad in the *Los Angeles Sentinel*. Betty was floored. This was the break they were looking for. According to Betty's recollection, Bob doubted that anything would come of it."[2] Justin Gifford relates a similar story: "One day, Betty spotted an ad in the *Sentinel*. . . . The ad read: 'Black Writers Needed. We are looking for black writers that have riveting stories about the black experience.' They decided to submit a short scene of about twenty pages. It was a short story of Beck's life at the height of his pimp success."[3] The 2012 documentary *Iceberg Slim: Portrait of a Pimp* confirms the legend with evidence we can see for ourselves. Shew describes the exact moment she came across the ad in the paper. During her voiceover, the camera zooms in on an inset from the *Sentinel* that features the same language Gifford cites in his work. After Shew's narration, the camera cuts to Bentley Morriss, seated in an office chair. Looking directly at the camera, he states, "At that time, there was no venue for a talented young black author, period."

Morriss is wrong, of course. Nineteen sixty-five saw *The Autobiography of Malcolm X* (as told to Alex Haley) and Claude Brown's bildungsroman *Manchild in the Promised Land* become national best sellers. Experimental writers such as Charles S. Wright, William Melvin Kelley, and Ishmael Reed garnered major book deals around this time. And in 1968, responding to the pitched state of American race relations, presses eagerly promoted black men's writing from prison, with Dial publishing Nathan C. Heard's *Howard Street*, written in Trenton State Penitentiary, and McGraw-Hill bringing out Eldridge Cleaver's *Soul on Ice*, penned at Folsom State Prison. In short, young black men's writing was a literary phenomenon in the mid- and late 1960s. Holloway House never had an exclusive claim to this body of work. Why, then, would Morriss suggest otherwise? What does the legend of Iceberg Slim do for Holloway House?

My own inquiry into these questions has led me to conclude that the legend is misleading at best and an outright fabrication at worst.

There is no record in the *Sentinel* archive of a single Holloway House want ad, much less one seeking black writers. No such ad appears in the newspaper's digital archive, which spans 1934 to 2005 in the ProQuest Historical Newspapers database. That leaves us with the curious artifact featured in the documentary. I tracked down the exact page on which the want ad was supposed to appear based on an analysis of the surrounding material we see as the camera zooms in. The page is 4B, from the Thursday, July 15, 1965, issue of the *Sentinel*, a full month before Watts. Instead of one for Holloway House, there is an advertisement for Johnnie Walker scotch whiskey.[4] There may be an innocent explanation for this: a quirk of reprinting or some contingency of data transfer. I am not convinced. Taking a closer look at the want ad shown in the film, one sees discrepancies that cannot be explained away: cofounder Ralph Weinstock's name is misspelled "Wienstock," and the company's street address, 8060 Melrose Avenue, appears instead as "6080 Melrose Ave." The typos indicate something other than coincidence. This is how legends are maintained.[5]

Nearly all published writing on black pulp fiction has taken Morriss at his word. Because a small fraction of the novels, abstracted from their material conditions of production, distribution, and circulation, tend to be the focus of such writing, little has been done to determine the veracity of the story Morriss has propagated for years.[6] My own sense is that the more that gets written on black pulp fiction—biographies, news stories, theses and dissertations, scholarly articles and book chapters—the less we know of Holloway House. The company's story has become the kind of context most everyone takes for granted: invisible because its function is to prop up what we already know.

In this chapter, I aim to complicate black pulp fiction's narrative of origin. Indeed, for reasons that will become clear, I decline to apply the term black pulp fiction to what Holloway House published during this period. My intention, it should be noted, is not to substitute one narrative of origin for another. Instead, it is to displace the conceptual grounding that an origin story lends to retrospective accounts of black pulp fiction. The grounding we have right now is itself a product of Holloway House's self-promotion. As such, it obscures, rather than illuminates, Morriss and Weinstock's integrated pulp and pinup enterprise. In order to understand what they thought they were publishing with a book like *Pimp*, we need to reconstruct what that enterprise was doing in 1967.

In the following, I explain how Holloway House's appropriation of street culture into mass-commodified pulp fiction was conducted through *racial masquerade*. On one hand, masquerade was the object of readers' fascination: a performance taken up by urban black men in order to make a way out of no way—that is, to make the inhospitable circumstances of ghetto life actually work for them. Yet masquerade was also the vehicle for that fascination: a way for white men to see themselves as black, and for Holloway House to integrate urban black men's outlaw ethos into extant sleaze paperback formulas. It is essential to consider both levels of masquerade in order to move beyond the notion that the street came to Holloway House. It was, if anything, the other way around.

Pseudonym as Strategy

The masquerade begins with a name—or, rather, the slippage between Robert Beck and the many names he went by. According to Gifford's biography, Beck was born Robert Lee Moppins Jr. on August 4, 1918, to Mary Brown and Robert Moppins Sr. It was only in 1932, long after Robert had left the family, that mother and son started to go by the last name Maupins. The altered spelling, according to Gifford, was symbolic—Mary's way of marking a fresh start after an abusive relationship. Maupins became Beck thirty years later, in 1962, when he was released from jail for the last time. He took the name as a way of reconciling with his mother, who had relocated to Los Angeles and married one Ural Beck.[7] So Beck was only Beck for a brief period before he made his way to Holloway House. He had chased a paternal inheritance for most of his life, never quite settling into a given name.

Against this backdrop, Beck exercised a particular kind of authority in writing *Pimp*. Barred from assuming the name of the father, he approached writing his memoir as an opportunity to name himself. Under the label "Biography," the synopsis on the back of the paperback read: "PIMP is the life story of the man known as Iceberg Slim. It is a completely frank story, told without bitterness and with no pretense at moralizing. This is unlike any book ever published. No one before has dared to tell such a story. No one who hasn't lived as a pimp could possibly imagine the smells, the sounds, the fears, the petty triumphs: The world of the pimp."[8] Keeping his real name under wraps, the paperback construed "Iceberg Slim" as a kind of password for entrance into a secret world—a black subculture that readers had no knowledge about. In a way, then, it was the pseudonym that authenticated the author's claim to the street. Slim had written Beck out of his life and replaced him with his own mythos.[9]

That mythos centers on self-nomination as a strategy of survival. In the absence of biological paternal influence, boys become men by gaining a reputation on the street—and earning new names in the process. This is the theme of *Pimp*, a coming-of-age story in which a young black man rejects the confines of domesticity for the open terrain of the urban jungle. Born in Chicago after the Great War, Bobby is the only son of parents who fled the South to chase their dreams in "the promised land up North." But the city has a bad influence on Bobby's father, who, in pursuing his vices, becomes resentful of his familial bonds. One night, after Mama refuses to give Bobby away for adoption, he hurls the baby "against the wall in disgust." Bobby survives, but his parents' relationship is over. Mama and Bobby move to Rockford, Illinois, to live with a hardworking family man, Henry Upshaw, the owner of "the only Negro business" in town. Bobby enjoys staying with Henry—he later refers to him as "the only father I had ever really known"—but this time it is Mama's turn to be ensnared by the fast life. A con man named Steve steals her heart and convinces her to go back to Chicago with him. In leaving Henry a broken man, bereft of "pride and dignity,"[10] Mama seals Bobby's fate as a son of the street.

With this troubled family history restricted to the first chapter of the book, the rest of *Pimp* chronicles the narrator's making a name for himself in the black underworld of the greater Midwest. He comes into his own in Chicago, where he falls under the tutelage of a longtime pimp nicknamed "Sweet Jones." He gives the narrator an empowering narrative within which to locate himself. After slavery, Jones says, black men moved to the city and saw white men "still ramming it into the finest black broads" and black women "still freak[ing] for free with the white man." Sensing an opportunity, the "first Nigger pimps started hipping the dumb bitches to the gold mines between their legs." Soon these men were "the only Nigger big shots in the country," celebrated for putting one over on the white man and admired for their fancy cars and clothes. Who could begrudge their success? "Those pimps was black geniuses," Jones asserts. "They wrote that skull book on pimping."[11] Going by the moniker "Youngblood" (or "Blood"), the narrator is made to feel as if he has entered a guild of the highest order.

Pimp thus presents a rather unsentimental education. It follows Bobby's journey as he embraces the very fast life that destroyed his family. Lacking a biological paternal inheritance, he learns to rely on a network of paternal substitutes to teach him how to become a man. Crucially, every black man he meets outside of Mama's orbit goes by a nickname. Theirs is a subculture that, in direct contrast to the square world, puts black men on top. And if the lore of this underworld is known figuratively as a "skull book," then *Pimp* manifests Bobby's education in that precise form. In other words, Holloway House's paperback literalizes the idea that a skull book should exist.

No wonder, then, that *Pimp*'s climax—the narrator's graduation, as it were—reads as though it were fulfilling a prophecy. By age twenty, Blood has become a fearsome, high-flying pimp with five women under his control. He is in a bar with another mentor, Glass Top, when someone nearby fires a gun. High on cocaine, Blood remains in his seat, oblivious to the commotion, while Glass Top ducks for cover. The bullet ends up going clean through Blood's hat, knocking it off his head, before grazing its intended target. As if it were the most normal thing in the world, Blood picks up his hat and puts it back on his head. Amazed by his protégé's demeanor, Glass Top announces as they walk out, "Kid, you were cold in there, icy; icy, like an iceberg. Kid, I got it. You're getting to be a good young pimp. All good pimps got monickers [sic]. I'm gonna hang one on you."[12] Glass Top bestows upon Youngblood the name that adorns the cover of the book. It is the key moment where the subject of autobiography and the author of *Pimp* become one.

There is something to the idea that, in Robin D. G. Kelley's words, "Iceberg Slim was forged in the fires of Watts."[13] Slim's mythos powerfully speaks to the fate of urban black masculinity in the deindustrializing city. Isolated from its broader urban environs, the postwar ghetto offered little in the way of opportunities for social and economic mobility. Where the jobs did not dry up, white-controlled unions kept black workers out. And where property ownership was in touching distance for some heads of household, restrictive covenants and other discriminatory measures ensured that they stayed right where they were. The ghetto was a trap set by the square world to keep blacks in their place. Which is precisely why pimping could be cast as a reclaiming of urban black masculinity. For Blood, the choice is clear: he can either "be a boot black [sic] or porter for the rest of [his] life in the high walled white world," or he can exploit black women "to get piles of white scratch [money] from that forbidden white world."[14] The narrator opts not to play by the rules of a rigged game. Instead, he scales white America's "walls" without leaving the ghetto. By using black women's bodies to bring white money to him, he is able to line his pockets while keeping his identity of masculine self-possession intact. Pimping, then, is about affirming the American male's place in society even when it does everything it can to stymie blacks from becoming self-made men.

There is also something to the idea that, again to quote Kelley, Slim had deep roots in African American vernacular culture—specifically the "tales, 'toasts' (bawdy oral poetry), and song" that alternately "revered and reviled" the pimp.[15] Part of what Sweet Jones means by "skull book" is a vibrant oral tradition that framed the pimp as a hero of sorts. To be sure, the pimp of lore is no John Henry, the steel-driving man— indeed, he would be the last person to work himself to death. No, the pimp's appeal resides in something less outwardly heroic: his guile. According to Arthur Kempton, Slim propagates the idea that "black men selling white men sexual access to women was a sly, sweet reversal of the power relationship that governed the transaction of interracial sex in the briar patch."[16] In this account, the pimp is a trickster figure (in the tradition of Br'er Rabbit) who reverses the sexual economics of chattel slavery. Through his hierarchy of exchange, white men are taken for suckers, and black women collect all day long. Like any trickster, the pimp is a consummate opportunist. Rather than overthrow the system, he is keen on making "adaptive behavioral advantages" that would help him, and only him, secure his "fair share of the system's rewards."[17]

As compelling as these readings are, they do not account for the material conditions that made *Pimp* possible. In particular, they do not account for the way Holloway House appropriated street culture to serve the aims of sleaze. When the book came out in March, it fell between two works of erotica, *De Figuris Veneris* and *Venus in India*, and two tabloid exposés, *The Lopinson Case* and *Skouras: King of Fox Studios*. There was very little to connect these titles except for the fact that they lent narrative shape to lurid scenes of sex, violence, and corruption. In this, they exemplified Holloway House's repackaging the obscene as classic erotica, reportage, or, in Slim's case, the confession. Like Barbara Payton, Slim penned a contrite introduction to the memoir:

In this book I will take you the reader with me into the secret inner world of the pimp. I will lay bare my life and thoughts as a pimp. The account of my brutality and cunning as a pimp will fill many of you with revulsion, however if one intelligent valuable young man or woman can be saved from the destructive slime then the displeasure I have given will have been outweighed by that individual's use of his potential in a socially constructive manner.[18]

This note has been interpreted by Gifford as proof that Slim wanted *Pimp* to be read as a morality tale with a clear message: do not follow my example.[19] But the confessional note was a well-worn strategy in the sleaze trade, an alibi pornographers used to ply their craft under the nose of censors. True, the narrator warns the reader against following in his footsteps ("can be saved from the destructive slime"), but he also piques his interest by guaranteeing him access to something forbidden or taboo ("the secret inner world of the pimp"). The point was to enter into that world.

Morriss was drawn to Slim's story because it put a new spin on antidomestic ideology. For him, the black pimp was the ultimate sleaze hero: a man who had no illusions about women, marriage, or romance, and who saw sex in strictly instrumental terms. For example, when Blood's first prostitute, Phyllis, asks him to treat her like a "lady," his caustic retort gives voice to sleaze's basic tenets: "You stinking black Bitch, you're a fake. There's no such thing as a lady in our world. You either got to be a bitch or a faggot in drag. Now Bitch, which is it? Bitch, I'm not a gentleman, I'm a pimp!"[20] Slim thus offered a vision of a reclaimed manhood that Morriss would have been more than happy to exploit. The evidence for this can be seen on the front cover of the first edition of *Pimp* (figure 2.1). In the foreground stands a raven-haired woman, stripped down to her nightgown. She is in the line of sight of a black man whose face, shadowed in blue, looms in the background. The size and positioning of his half-obscured visage has the effect of overwhelming her smaller figure. Her downward mien, meanwhile, implies her submission to his, as well as the reader's, gaze. It is a tableau tailor-made for the sleaze set, a skull book adapted for white tastes.

Just how deep did the masquerade extend? As deep as the symbolic value of the Iceberg persona itself. We now know that Beck did not go by that nickname during his pimping days. Instead, he was known first as Slim Lancaster and later as Cavanaugh Slim.[21] Consequently, the pivotal moment in the book—in which the narrator earns his stone-cold reputation and thus entrée into the hustlers' fraternity—is made up. Before this became widely known, Candice Love Jackson was the only scholar to note something amiss in the episode. In a 2008 essay, she observed, "This incident is one of the most suspect in the text, because the onomastic journey of Iceberg Slim is consciously constructed to reflect the character's growth into a successful pimp and later into the reformed pimp-turned-writer." The coincidence is too neat, which is why she contended, and I agree, that "*Pimp* is best read as a novel"—namely, a "formulaic *bildungsroman*"—rather than documentary truth.[22] To that

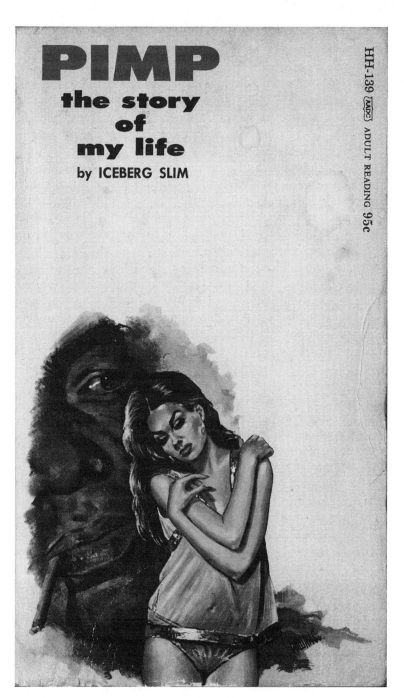

PIMP
the story
of
my life
by ICEBERG SLIM

HH-139 [AAB] ADULT READING 95¢

FIGURE 2.1 Front cover of *Pimp: The Story of My Life* (1967).

I would only add that a possible source for the moniker was Holloway House itself. In *I Am Not Ashamed*, Leo Guild, ghosting for Payton, penned, "I'd say a woman is like an iceberg. Only a facade shows. The rest is hidden and it takes months, even years to find out the mysteries of what's underneath."[23] By this point in the book, Payton is a fallen woman, a wino who exchanges favors for gifts and cash from black men. She is Iceberg's antecedent, and her (Guild's) metaphor may have made him her racial double.

Pimp, I am arguing, cannot be read exclusively as a black man's cry from the ghetto. Its conditions of production ensured that it served other purposes, wore different masks. Which is why Bentley Morriss had no problem advertising *Pimp* to his regular white male readership of the pinup magazines *Adam* and *Knight*. Beginning with the May 1967 issues, mail-order ads for the book ran under the banner "PIMP'S SECRET LIFE: Brutal Reality of a Sexual Jungle." The accompanying copy framed the book in terms at once lurid and ethnographic: "Few Pimps survive the perils of that savage sex underground lurking beneath the surface of every city. . . . Of the few who survived this jungle only one has had the rare combination of intelligence, perception and writing ability to tell the story, 'Iceberg Slim.' He is a real person, only the name is changed." What secrets did this mysterious author possess? The copy ended with a teaser: "raw, vicious, agonizing brutality and sex bondage."[24] With Watts's black rage conspicuously absent from this picture, Morriss showed how his appropriation of street culture was an essentially pornographic undertaking.

It was for his readers too. The July 1967 issue of *Adam* featured a review of *Pimp* by Bob Blackburn. Far from being concerned with Iceberg's fate, Blackburn was intent on learning from the master procurer. Observing that "most treatises on prostitution avoid emphasis on the pimp," focusing instead on the figure of the madam, Blackburn lauded Slim for "fill[ing] the gap, not necessarily nicely, but undeniably accurately." After praising the author's eye for detail, which made the book read like a how-to guide, Blackburn noted: "The most fascinating aspect of *Pimp* is the emergent relationship between Iceberg and his whores. It is a strange one, yet sexual. His stable treats him with adulation on the one hand and wariness on the other. He puts together a 'family' by playing the role of an ungodly Freudian father figure. He does exactly what 'Sweet' told him to: He *holds* his whores."[25] Here Blackburn seemed most intrigued by the last, possibly most important, nickname in Slim's repertoire: "Daddy"—something only the women under his control call him. That the narrator has a "sexual" relation-

ship with prostitutes yet controls them so completely as to be a "Freudian father figure" to them was not lamented by Blackburn. Rather, he
seemed amazed ("He *holds* his whores") by the notion that the narrator
could be a virile lover and respected father, phallic authority symbolized in the black pimp.

In the spirit of Norman Mailer's White Negro, the original readers
of *Pimp* might have wanted Slim to deliver them from their feminization—that is, to give voice to their own primal fantasies of sexual control and patriarchal domination. In his 1957 essay from *Dissent*, Mailer
lauded the "Negro" for living in a kind of continuous present, where
"life was war, nothing but war," and he "had stayed alive and begun
to grow by following the need of his body where he could." Bucking
the "sophisticated inhibitions of civilization," the Negro "kept for his
survival the art of the primitive." And it was through exposure to this
"art" that the White Negro could find himself in the Negro—that is,
in the urban black subculture that turned mainstream values on their
head. Mailer explained:

In the worst of perversion, promiscuity, pimpery, drug addiction, rape, razor-slash,
bottle-break, what-have-you, the Negro discovered and elaborated a morality of
the bottom, an ethical differentiation between the good and the bad in every human activity from the go-getter pimp (as opposed to the lazy one) to the relatively dependable pusher or prostitute. Add to this, the cunning of their language,
the abstract ambiguous alternatives in which from the danger of their oppression
they learned to speak . . . and it is not too difficult to believe that the language
of Hip which evolved was an artful language, tested and shaped by an intense
experience.[26]

Mailer made the swagger and styles of urban black masculinity fully
appropriable to the white male gaze. His was a primitivist exoticism
updated for the atomic age. And it was no coincidence that he cited the
pimp in his account. The pimp modeled the vitality of the present (as
a Negro) and the reversion to type (as a man) that Mailer upheld as an
ideal of white remasculinization.

Pimp itself was like a window into this world, with Iceberg's blackness serving as a mask through which white readers were allowed, or
given license, to feel closer to their manhood. The best proof of that
sort of engagement can be found at the very end of the book, where a
glossary contains a number of vernacular terms that appear throughout
the text. The definitions run the gamut from the satirically understated
to the technically astute. "Freak," for example, is defined as a "sexual

libertine," a gloss fit only for a square, while "cocktailed" names the process whereby "a marijuana butt [is placed] into the end of a conventional cigarette for smoking."[27] Regardless, the purpose of these flat-footed definitions is to domesticate, or render familiar, a language that was utterly foreign to the ears of Holloway House's readership. This point is further supported by the fact that the text of *Pimp* is littered with quotation marks that enclose vernacular terms and street nicknames—not only in their first citation but throughout. These marks make the text difficult to read in any straightforward way. They ostensibly signal when the reader might look to the glossary for some help, but their awkwardness actually goes to show how culturally separate the reader is from the world of Iceberg Slim.

The glossary was not Slim's idea—it was Milton Van Sickle's. He worried that readers could not get through *Pimp* without one. "At first," he admitted, "[I] couldn't understand what the hell he was talking about."[28] And neither would most white readers. Which is why Blackburn counseled in his review, "There is a handy glossary at the end of the book which, as usual, helps most if read first."[29] These were *Pimp*'s original readers: outsiders who wanted in, men who wanted to be men again. It would take a while for Slim to be reappropriated by the culture from which he sprang. For now, his mask played to whites.

The Second Coming

In its first foray into the black press, Holloway House advertised *Pimp* in the September 28, 1967, issue of the *Sentinel*. The ad used the same copy from *Adam* and *Knight*, with a notable addition at the bottom: "Author ICEBERG SLIM appearing on LOUIS LOMAX SHOW Sunday, October 1."[30] Though this televised interview has not survived, Lomax's involvement is enough to suggest how Morriss wanted to position his new author. Louis E. Lomax was a trailblazing black television journalist who espoused iconoclastic views on racial matters. In 1959, he and Mike Wallace collaborated on *The Hate That Hate Produced*, a documentary about Elijah Muhammad's Nation of Islam that denounced the group in no uncertain terms. Nearly a decade later, hosting his own show on KTTV Los Angeles, Lomax continued to sound skeptical about the push for civil rights. He admitted, "I wouldn't press for additional civil rights legislation; I would vigorously implement the legislation we've got and put on a massive job training program for Negroes and say: 'You're your own [*sic*], baby, you know I'm not your daddy. You've got to make it on your own.'" Of far more concern to Lomax was the fate of white women in America, a typical example of whom, he diagnosed, "has sold her soul for a mess of suburban pottage" and has "become a victim of washing machines and vacuum cleaners and now benzedrine, and the whole suburban boredom business." Trapped in the postwar cult of domesticity, the white woman, according to Lomax, "belongs to the most discriminated-against group in our society."[31]

Lomax's views made him the perfect mouthpiece for the fantasmatic investment in whiteness that structured *Pimp*. He would be joined in that effort by Holloway House's second black author: Robert H. deCoy, an actor and media personality from Los Angeles. Born in New Orleans in 1920, deCoy served in the army during World War II before earning his bachelor's degree from Huston-Tillotson College in 1948. He continued his studies in theater at Yale, where he was awarded an MFA in 1951. After stints teaching drama at West Virginia State College and working in news radio back in New Orleans, deCoy moved out West for good in 1953. In Los Angeles, he did media work for local news and radio while acting on stage and in the odd television show.[32] DeCoy's name was his career, which explains why it was a sensation when he published *The Nigger Bible* without using a pseudonym.

In the preface to the book, comedian and civil rights activist Dick Gregory called deCoy "one of the literary giants of our time." The *Bible* reflected his effort "to discard the traditional vestiges of Judeo-Christianity in order to find and reveal the spiritual truths of being black." If religion had instilled self-hatred in black people's collective psyche, then deCoy offered a different origin story, another "Genesis." Why, then, rely on a widely reviled slur to denote a new beginning? Because in deCoy's belief system "Nigger," unlike "Negro," had always been used as a noun, never an adjective. The distinction was meaningful, explained Gregory, for "no people can be adjectives, if that people are 'for real.'" To be real, then, African Americans needed to embrace their "Niggerness."[33] This was to be a spiritual transformation, yes, but also an ontological regrounding. And it was hardly a coincidence that Gregory vouched for deCoy on this count: his own 1964 autobiography was titled *Nigger*.

Part race manifesto, part street-corner sermon, *The Nigger Bible* is a heady mix of black self-help and social commentary. Predating Eldridge Cleaver's collection *Soul on Ice* by one year and H. Rap Brown's political autobiography *Die Nigger Die!* by two, the book can be read as an early Black Power treatise. Stylistically, though, deCoy takes his cue from James Baldwin's *The Fire Next Time* (1963). Most of *The Nigger Bible* consists of letters addressed to his "Nigger Son" or his "Nigger Children." This mode of address invites the reader to share in an intimate exchange at the same time that it appeals directly to youth as agents of social change. The word "Nigger" is key to both functions because of what it appears opposite to. "Throw Caution to the winds and refuse to Conform to the Concept of 'Negro' behavior," deCoy proclaims. Unlike "Niggers," who are what they are, "Negroes" suffer from racial false consciousness. Their desire to integrate into the "Judeo-Christian Social Structure" is "based on the mimicry and emulation of conduct of some other species in Creation, so distinctively different from themselves." But, deCoy points out, what they all come to understand is that "Negroes" are just "those Niggers who would waste their existence in the hopeless void of eventually dying as Christian Caucasians."[34] So it is that, against the churchgoing pretensions of the black bourgeoisie, deCoy offers pro-black teachings—parables and proverbs, epigrams and epistles—around which the next generation might orient a more authentic self. "Negroes" can have the Bible.

In its place, deCoy's *Bible* advances a mythos that, in theory, is centered on blackness. The mythos proceeds from a new "song of Genesis," which recounts how God took "Nature as his bridesmaid on a lovecouch, one of his planets named 'Earth,' for the conception of their children, called Mankind." According to deCoy, the initial, passionate coupling—God's "lumbering black penis" thrusting "into the pinkwhite infolds of Nature's tender belly"—literally formed the world's geography. Thus were God and Nature "divinely joined in the beginning, that their glory and splendor might last and remain so, until the end." But trouble arose when Nature was tempted to show up God's authority. "She smiled 'the smile of the bitch!'" and in the middle of the night, she "assumed the role of aggressor." From a position of being on top, she practically willed God to come again. "Mankind was conceived in this 'second round,'" deCoy preaches, as Nature proved to herself and to the heavens that "in moments of weariness, darkness and slumber, she could be and often was, the equal, if not the superior, of God."[35] In deCoy's Beginning there was not the Word but two rounds of sex with a white woman. In chasing the primordial pleasure of the first, the black man always ran up against complications and prohibitions instituted by the offspring of the second. The question for deCoy was whether black men would ever realize the authority of God again.

The value accorded to white womanhood here reverberates throughout *The Nigger Bible*. In one anecdote, deCoy advises, "When you take a white woman to a lovecouch, my Son, consider the common status you share. You are both but refugees, from two different cells of the same prison. You have filched the keys from the sleeping Warden and met in the darkened corridors. . . . Remember if you would be free, you must flee together." A black man and a white woman are imagined as fugitives from the white man's control. They "flee together" because, in the logic of the tale, their sexual union is subversive of the conditions that would oppress them. The theme is repeated in a letter to the "Black-Kind in My Life." Here deCoy confesses, "I had always believed that 'Justice was a White Woman.' I am a Nigger. So I was seldom allowed in her company." Barred from consorting with Justice, deCoy convinces himself that bedding her is the key to dignifying his racial identity. One night he has his opportunity. "Though I knew that Justice was, by no means, a Virgin," deCoy writes, "I thought that I saw her tremble, as a young bride in starvation for Love." In a repetition of the primal experience, black manhood conquers white womanhood, with the predictable result that interracial peace is reinstated in the world. For what deCoy learns after they have sex is that Justice "has 'Black-blood' in her veins," and specifically that she was "born of a mixed marriage between a black father and white mother."[36] He also learns that Justice has a twin sister, Liberty. The story ends with him stalking off to meet her. Symbolically, it is another attempt to recapture the union between God and Nature before she got on top of him—before the second congress.

If deCoy's *Bible* seemed more white erotic fantasy than black spiritual guide, it was because that is how it arrived at Holloway House's doors. Morriss, in fact, was not its original publisher. The January 26, 1967, issue of the *Sentinel* revealed that deCoy had been having a difficult time distributing a self-published book. At a press conference, he charged that the *Los Angeles Times* had stonewalled his efforts to advertise *The Nigger Bible* in the paper, and that a prominent Hollywood bookstore had refused to carry it. Regarding the former, deCoy brushed away the *Times*'s claim that the title of his book "was too controversial." "It was obvious," he said, "that [the] advertising department objected instead to the unorthodox content of the book rather than its title." After all, had not the *Times* run an ad for Dick Gregory's book two years earlier? As for the latter, deCoy objected to Pickwick Book Store's demand to take "40 percent on the sale of the $2 book." He countered that "his operation [would] allow only 35 percent commission," with the "five percent difference represent[ing] his margin of profit and promotional cost." Fed up with "ordinary book distribution outlets," deCoy said he planned to "hire Negro salesmen" to sell the *Bible* directly to bookstores and newsstands for the regular commission. Such an effort, he boasted, would "help alleviate unemployment among Negroes" in the area.[37] A seasoned media man, deCoy knew how to speak the language of Watts and its simmering aftermath.

But all of this was called into question a few months later after black readers made their thoughts on the *Bible* known. One week after *Jet* reported that deCoy's wife, the singer and actress Mittie Lawrence, had filed for divorce, deCoy requested "a permit to carry a weapon and for police protection" because he was "continuously harassed by telephone death threats" for his book.[38] Though this item did not clarify who was doing the harassing, the *Sentinel* ran a story with details of the backlash the same day. In the April 13, 1967, issue, Joe Bingham reported the bizarre account of a white life insurance executive, E. P. Jaffarian, being fired from his job in connection with his financing the *Bible*'s publication. The inciting incident was a debate between deCoy and fellow black newsman Booker Griffin, hosted at the Maverick's Flat, a private black club "in the Crenshaw-Leimert Park area." Jaffarian attended the discussion and, in the course of proceedings, revealed he was the book's backer. A white man had underwritten *The Nigger Bible*? What was his stake in it? The audience did not take kindly to either him or the author. Griffin and Jaffarian traded words, the former calling deCoy "a white man's nigger," the latter defending the author's "constitutional right to express himself and to be heard." After the event, members of the audience wrote letters to Jaffarian's employer, Prudential Insurance, protesting the controversial book. The company fired Jaffarian with little explanation except to say that he had been "a maverick."[39]

What this complicated backstory suggests is that deCoy's book was already a media event by the time it arrived at Holloway House. Even more, that it had become a media event precisely because the *Bible*'s racial politics were skewed, because deCoy's ideal reader appeared to be the White Negro. When asked about how he and deCoy had come to their business deal, Jaffarian was forthcoming. Tasked with hiring "new Negro insurance salesmen" for Prudential, Jaffarian was actually recruiting deCoy when the author brought the manuscript to his attention. He initially gave it to his wife to read; she thought it was "abominable." But after further prodding from deCoy, Jaffarian read it himself; he had the opposite reaction, calling it "astounding." "It opened my eyes to many things I had never known or dreamed of," he relayed to Bingham. From there he "put up the money as an investment" and saw to it that eleven thousand copies of the book were published.[40]

The self-published edition of *The Nigger Bible* is not substantially different from the Holloway House version. Despite a different layout, which cuts the total page length by over a third, the text is largely unchanged and the typeface is similar to Holloway House's. But there are meaningful differences. For example, the original does not include Dick Gregory's preface, which, in the later edition, serves as a hortatory preview of the book's contents. The original does include a dedication to Mittie Lawrence and to deCoy's four children: Sheri-Laine and Teri-Laine (with her), and Robert and Edwina (from a previous marriage).[41] It is a touching appeal to the subjects he addresses in the letters that follow. But without question the most notable difference is the front cover (figure 2.2). Maurice Scales's bold, black-and-white illustration of the title as a burning cross is arguably the most radical thing about this edition. The burning cross of course has a long history of being used as a symbol of white supremacist terror, particularly by the Ku Klux Klan. The illustration thus can be interpreted as critiquing the conjunction of religion and antiblack violence in the Judeo-Christian West.

Yet there are other elements of the book's design that point to appropriative interest of the sort I have been ascribing to the White Negro. First, the blurb on the back cover reads: "Written by an acknowledged Nigger, for and about the experiences of Niggers, addressed and directed exclusively to my Nigger people for whom it was purposely conceived."[42] DeCoy's statement is redundant, and while repeating the word "Nigger" could be interpreted as a form of political protest, it comes across as cloying for attention—anyone's attention. True, the repetition self-authorizes deCoy's voice as coextensive with "Niggerness," but that is hardly innocent to prying white eyes. Indeed, even though the blurb is the only part of the original cover design that Holloway House retains in its version, the front cover (figure 2.3) indicates a wider readership than deCoy's "people." The invocation of what "all men know but none has dared express" is meant to include white men who would be interested in deCoy's religio-racial heresy.

The second material feature is subtler but no less important. DeCoy named his self-publishing venture Blawhit, and the company's stamp appears on the inside of the back cover:

BLAWHIT INC.

PUBLISHERS—DISTRIBUTORS—PROMOTIONS

4321½ Leimert Blvd.

Los Angeles, California 90008

FIGURE 2.2 Front cover of *The Nigger Bible*, self-published (1967).

THE NIGGER BIBLE

The most controversial book of
our generation!

Slashes through hypocrisy
to reveal a seething, shocking view
all men know but none
has dared express

by Robert H. deCoy

FIGURE 2.3 Front cover of *The Nigger Bible*, published by Holloway House (1967).

This trace is evidence of the impress of deCoy's hand: it connotes not only the labor that went into the book's production but also the care with which deCoy handled his work. The street address, in the heart of South Central, only adds to the sense that this was a homegrown operation. However, the actual name of the enterprise seems to evoke something other than a voice of Watts. Take a closer look. If, like anyone who read the *Sentinel*, you knew Jaffarian was behind this book, you could easily see that "Blawhit" combines "black" and "white" into a neat, interracial portmanteau. Hence the White Negro is literally written into the name of deCoy's publishing company.

When Holloway House announced that it had picked up the rights to publish *The Nigger Bible*, deCoy was not treated as some prophet of the hood. He was, instead, hailed as the bad boy of American letters. Indeed, deCoy's reputation preceded him—so much so that Holloway House fast-tracked him to more infamy by nominating the *Bible* for that year's Pulitzer Prize. Of the pulp press's reprinting deal the *Sentinel* noted that deCoy "seems certain of a substantial national sale, this being a firm which is well established in the sale of controversial books."[43] As we have seen, that controversy was in large part manufactured by the Blawhit operation. It was not a function of one man's voice crying out from the ghetto. To be sure, deCoy espoused eccentric views on race, religion, and sexual relations. But those views got the airing they did because they conformed to what Jaffarian and later Morriss wanted. It was not just black men who could idealize white womanhood as Justice waiting to be had.

For all the indirect dealings that went into producing *The Nigger Bible*, Robert deCoy's name was the one verifiable truth about the book. However, Holloway House's reputation for masquerade compelled one black critic to question whether deCoy was who he claimed to be. Ron Welburn reviewed *The Nigger Bible* in the New York–based Black Arts journal *Liberator* in 1969. He began his piece on a wary note: "When the book was first released, the name deCoy triggered me to suspect anything." But "the author is for real," he conceded, "having been born in New Orleans and now a well-known commentator in West Coast media circles." Still, Welburn's suspicions were not completely allayed given that he was confronted with "another curiosity"—namely, "that deCoy's *Nigger Bible* is part of a Holloway House 'adult reading' catalog of predominantly sex-themed literature of various sorts." He did not make much of this fact, but the implication was that the book did not sit right. DeCoy's "epistolary rap," he wrote, was like a "tongue-in-cheek mixture of Soul talk and 17th-century scriptural prose." Welburn thought the account of the primal experience was "vividly told," and he commended the effort. Ultimately, though, he was not persuaded. Of the author he smirked, "He would surely be the real *decoy* amidst [Amiri] Baraka, [William Melvin] Kelley, [John A.] Williams, [Ishmael] Reed, [Lerone] Bennett, and [Harold] Cruse"—in other words, an imposter among the black male literary giants of the day.[44] For "real" black writers at least, deCoy had been found out.

Passing for Black, Passing for White

Iceberg Slim's second book, *Trick Baby: The Biography of a Con Man*, came out right after *The Nigger Bible*, in December 1967. Like *Pimp*, *Trick Baby* was categorized as "Biography" on the back cover. However, on the front cover and title page of this paperback, Holloway House revised the descriptor for Slim's debut. It now read: "ICEBERG SLIM Author of the Best-Selling Autobiography PIMP."[45] The change not only clarified the difference between the books' narrative voices—it indicated that Slim had arrived. The made-up moniker signified a whole new street legend, one that was bound up with Slim's status as a pulp author.

Part of that legend has Iceberg return as a character in *Trick Baby*'s frame narrative. In the preface and epilogue, we find him doing time in the Chicago House of Correction. It is October 1960, and Iceberg is about to meet his new cellmate. To his eyes, the man who walks through the door "could have been Errol Flynn's twin"—dashing but white. Sensing his discomfort, the man says: "Relax, Iceberg. I'm not white. I'm a Nigger hustler. My friends call me White Folks. My enemies call me Trick Baby." With two monikers under his belt, the man clearly signals that he knows how to play Iceberg's game. Sure enough, Iceberg recognizes him as "one of the slickest con men in Chicago."[46] After five days, the man begins to open up about his life. Iceberg is eager to listen, and the bulk of the narrative consists of what he hears. By stage-managing the narrative in this way, Slim legitimates Iceberg's standing as a real person at the same time that he focuses attention on another character entirely. Iceberg retreats to the shadows the moment Slim immerses us in somebody else's life.

That character has a fascinating backstory. Born John Patrick O'Brien Jr. in Kansas City, Missouri, in 1923, he is the only child of a black woman, Phala Grigsby, and a touring white jazzman whose name he bears. Johnny has fond memories of his father, but O'Brien Sr. abandons his family when he is only eight. Needing to support herself and her child on her own, Phala moves to Chicago to find work as a domestic. Growing up in the South Side, the light-skinned Johnny is alternately hectored and shunned by children in this predominantly black area of the city. They nickname him "Trick Baby," assuming that his mother was a prostitute who had gotten pregnant by one of her white "tricks," or johns. Despite Johnny's insistence to the contrary (his parents were married), the kids' teasing is relentless—"Nasty trick baby! Nasty trick baby!"[47]—and follows him wherever he goes. Thus, unlike Youngblood, Trick Baby is a nickname that bears stigma. It harkens to Johnny's shame over his family background and the fact that he simply does not fit in among other blacks. But the name is equally stigmatizing of Phala, whose imputed sexuality is cast as thoroughly exploitable. For Johnny to follow the condition of his mother would be perilous.

An event that takes place during his teenage years is the tipping point in the narrative. Phala, on her way home from a shift at the local cabaret, is drugged and then gang-raped by several men. The assault drives her mad, and she has to be committed to an asylum. Adrift and completely on his own, Johnny is on the brink of dissipation. But just when it seems Johnny has hit rock bottom, he meets Blue Howard, an old hand at the confidence game and a respected hustler in the South Side. Blue takes a liking to this lost son, and one of the first things he does is to give him a new nickname. He comes up with "White Folks." Johnny initially objects, saying that his moniker "ought to brag that [he is] a Nigger." But Blue counters with, "That's just what that monicker [sic] does for you. It's got a solid Nigger sound. There never was, and there never will be a genuine white hustler with that tag. It shouts that you're really a Nigger with white skin." After that explanation, Johnny becomes White Folks, symbolically leaving Phala (and Trick Baby stigma) behind while accepting Blue as a father figure. Crucially, Blue's justification for the alias relies not on first impressions but on ineffable qualities—it has a "sound," it "shouts"—that he associates with blackness. In order to get it, you almost have to be in it. The rechristening, then, is an invitation for Folks to become truer to himself: "Inside," Blue says, "you feel and think black like me."[48]

If, in *Trick Baby*, passing for black is about inhabiting an ethos or state of mind, passing for white only needs to go skin deep. In fact, Blue immediately realizes that Folks's white looks are all that matter when it comes to the confidence game. His scheme is simple: "To the Niggers, I say, 'Let's take that goddamn peckerwood's money.' You tell the white marks[,] 'Let's break that bastard nigger.'" In other words, it is a con that banks on people's racial prejudice toward the other partner. They pull off their first scam in textbook fashion. The mark is Otto, a German immigrant with whom Folks strikes up a conversation at a West Side (read: white ethnic) saloon. "We sat there talking about stupid niggers we had met, for about ten minutes," Folks recounts. After priming him with casual racism, he lures Otto to a nightspot where they can "buy . . . a piece of black ass."[49] Once there, Folks engages Blue in an impromptu coin-flip game. Throughout the game, which is rigged, Folks makes Otto believe he cannot lose, urging him to bet more. After several rounds Otto is up by a lot of money, and he entrusts it to Folks because he is making all the right moves. The trap is set. When Blue charges collusion and the white gamblers have to run away, Folks and Otto split up, leaving all the money with the con artist. Folks, the apprentice, proves that he can stay black by passing for white.

Trick Baby, like *Pimp*, is organized around the narrator's coming of age in the city. Bereft of his biological father, he navigates the black underworld with the help of a paternal substitute who can show him the ropes. Under that figure's tutelage, he learns how to be his own man—not by escaping the ghetto but by appropriating white money to it. Like Iceberg, Folks can be read as a trickster, someone who uses guile to put one over on the Man. And, like Sweet Jones, Blue may be read as the keeper of vernacular lore, someone whose anecdotes are "both functional—they help him survive and keep his audience happy—and allusive—they often echo earlier black fiction, and so help the griot tradition to keep on going on."[50]

Yet *Trick Baby*, no less than *Pimp*, was still very much a product of the trade in sleaze. Milton Van Sickle's glossary is reprised in this book for the benefit of readers like him. "Big Foot Country," we learn, is "the deep South United States," while "catch" means "to lure a victim into the first stage of a con game." Unsurprisingly, the squarest definition is reserved for "peckerwood," which, given the identity of the presumptive reader, is almost humorously understated: "contemptuous term referring to white men."[51] Another connection to white readers can be found in the way Holloway House advertised *Trick Baby* in its adjacent periodicals. An ad in the March 1968 issue of *Adam* reads, in part, "A WHITE NEGRO . . . IN THE DEADLY JUNGLE OF SOUTHSIDE CHICAGO!" Here Mailer's White Negro is folded into Holloway House's discourse. Specifically, his whiteness is accentuated as a counterpoint to the South Side "jungle," which codes black. One line clarifies the racial identity of the protagonist, yet it is factually inaccurate: "Only once did he pass himself off as white, to a wealthy white girl who was madly in love with him . . . but she hated 'coons.'"[52] We have seen how Folks passes for white as part of the confidence game Blue has taught him. Why, then, the misleading statement? Because it underscores the illicitness of an interracial love affair—a taboo that simultaneously stirs righteous feeling and prompts voyeuristic fascination. Whatever the reader thinks of such an affair, the White Negro is sure to be the point of fantasmatic identification for him in the book.

The case for reading *Trick Baby* along these lines is made by Slim himself, in the way he represents the woman in question. In the prime of his hustling career, Folks visits a Chicago nightclub where he beholds his feminine ideal: a woman he calls "Goddess." Her name is Camille Costain, and in addition to being older than Folks, she is married. That does not stop him from pursuing her, or calling her Goddess to her face. Slim's description of her features is embarrassingly unctuous: "Her angelic face had the gleam of rose-tinted porcelain," while "her hair was a platinum crown that coruscated in the pastel light." And his description of Folks is telling: "My enslaved eyes were chained to her as she glided away and sat down at the table next to mine." Here the man who has learned how to be proud of his blackness is suddenly, soddenly falling for whiteness. Indeed, when Folks, sitting across from the Goddess, thinks, "I sat there and played a mirror game with her,"[53] the implication is not only that the feeling is mutual but that they reflect each other's whiteness.

It has to be so because Camille is an unrepentant racist. As Folks courts her, passing for white but admitting that he lives in the South Side, she says what she thinks of black people: formerly white neighborhoods are now infested with "coon rot," and Folks's neighbors must be "savage niggers" and "disease-ridden coon girls." It is a wonder why this daughter of a wealthy Chicago manufacturer would even go out with him. Even more: why Folks would put up with her. "I wasn't too upset and angry about her nasty attitude toward my race," he reasons. "I'd sex her exquisite ears off the tender lesbian way [oral sex] and be so sweet to her she'd fall hard for me. Then I'd change her and make her realize how wrong she had been about us." Folks calls this his "racial cure." A trickster reversal, perhaps, except it does not pan out this way at all. During their first tryst, Folks performs sex the "tender lesbian way," but after they switch to having intercourse with her on top, she stops just at the moment he is about to climax. Camille has been in charge the whole time. It is deCoy's primal experience without the payoff. Yet the ache the Goddess leaves him with is the same: "I knew she was dangerous. And my first taste of her was powerful pleasure riddled with pain. But I knew I had to try her again."[54] The sleaze trope of a woman who pulverizes men only to stoke their desire is alive and well here. For Slim and deCoy, black men are always only ever chasing that first experience with a white woman.

Toward the end of the book, Camille invites Folks to meet her father, Bradford Wherry, and a police captain, Pete Packer, at the tony Palmer House hotel in downtown. The meeting is a scenario for Slim to stage competing white racisms: Wherry represents the liberal racism of patronizing condescension, while Packer (who hails from California) represents the reactionary racism of overt repression. As Folks is forced to sit through this dogmatic rehearsal of positions, he becomes conscious that his silence is untenable. When Wherry turns to Folks to ask for his opinion, he stands up and spits in his face. He does not reveal his racial background (he is silent in front of Wherry and Packer, after all), but Folks does leave in a huff. Gifford reads this scene as the book's consciousness-raising moment. "*Trick Baby*'s big reveal," he contends, "is that the true confidence game in America is white racism." Between liberals and reactionaries, Folks is stuck facing "the longest con of all, the deliberate and systematic oppression of black people."[55] But what Gifford does not account for is that Folks comes to regret acting out in this way. The episode forces Folks to confess his mixed-race heritage to Camille. No surprise: she leaves him. But the breakup sends him into a tailspin of despair, for Camille is still his Goddess. He laments, "She was a beautiful thing that had made my life glamorous, and classy. I was just a Nigger hustler from a sewer on Thirty-ninth Street without her." The "big reveal," then, is not that racism exists but that Folks's victory is pyrrhic: "Why did you let them trick you into exposing yourself as a nigger?"[56]

Trick Baby is a tragic mulatto script adapted to the sleaze set. It restigmatizes blackness at the very moment it laments Folks's loss of a white identity. Which makes the epilogue—our return to the frame narrative—all the more troubling. Iceberg is where we left him, listening intently to Folks's story. When he is done, Slim observes that his cellmate is about to be released in a few hours. He inquires, "What are your plans?" Folks lays them out: "I'm going to lose myself in the white world. I'm going to break every classy white broad's heart that gives me a second gander. I'm going to eat and sleep and fuck with nothing but white people for the rest of my life." In migrating to the other side of the color line, Folks is determined "to be the happiest white Nigger sonuvabitch there ever was."[57] These words from a heartbroken Folks cannot help but ring hollow. He has passed for white before, of course. This time, however, the ruse will not be part of a con that Folks perpetrates before returning to blackness. Instead, it will be a strategy of assimilation that allows him to permanently lose himself in whiteness.

Behind Slim's masks of defiance and transgression was an appeal to the white reader to understand and possibly even to relate him. This point was highlighted under rather bizarre circumstances when Slim appeared on the *Joe Pyne Show* on January 17, 1968. Pyne was no ordinary television host. An unabashed chauvinist and staunch conservative, he is regarded as the forerunner to today's shock jocks. Robert J. Erler describes the show's format as a classic bait and switch: Pyne would invite guests on whose views sharply diverged from the mainstream, and then he would assail them mercilessly for those views. He became a national celebrity around the time of the Watts riots when he and a militant black guest pulled out pistols they had brought to the interview.[58] Other Holloway House authors had appeared on *Pyne*, so it was hardly unusual for Slim to do so. What was unusual was Slim's choice of self-presentation. He wore a black mask that covered his entire face, with holes cut out for his dark glasses and his mouth. The pseudonymous author was shielded by a cumbersome-looking anonymity. He had succeeded in turning his first television appearance into an actual masquerade.

And that is how Pyne introduced him: "Our guest masquerades under the name Iceberg Slim." Decked out in a black suit, white shirt, and black necktie, Slim appeared to be looking down as Pyne read his prepared remarks. "Now he leads a respectable family life," the host explained, "and for this reason he continues to hide his identity." The audience remained quiet until Pyne revealed Slim's reason for being on the show: "He returns now to tell us about the most incredible con man he ever knew. A blond-haired, blue-eyed Negro called White Folks." Those watching in studio let out audible groans and gasps of disbelief; one or two guffawed. "You're not putting us on, are you, Slim?" Pyne asked, cigarette dangling from his fingers. "No, that's . . . that's, uh . . . that's factual," Slim responded with some hesitation. Did it matter that he was hardly believable? That he looked completely exposed under the beaming studio lights? Probably not. Slim was selling the audience a screen for their own projected desires. He was passing for whatever they wanted him to be.

Slim quickly gave up the pretense of writing biography, pitching *Trick Baby* as "an incredible adventure story of the con as it's played in the street." But the part that fascinated Pyne the most was the author's language: "There's one thing I know about reading your books, and that is, that, uh, it's always important to have a glossary in the back of your book because he does use these terms that, really, if you hadn't been a member of the underworld, you, you've never heard them." As the interview went on, Pyne kept interrupting Slim to dwell on this or that term. Indeed, he acted like the white audience's glossary lookup. "Now here again we have to use the terminology and translate," went one exchange. "'Cut in' means that—this is when he meets for the first time, he generally arranges the meeting to appear accidental, such as on the train or on the street in some way. The victim never realizes that the meeting was all by design, that it was a fully planned 'cut in.' Go ahead." The host ended up having so much fun with the excursions that, at one point, he was able to throw his own vernacular joke into the ring. Riffing on the con's mark, or target, Pyne deadpanned, "By the way he's named after an old con man named Marx. Did you know that? . . . [He] worked at the profitable con games of all types for many years." Even the archconservative could have his turn playing a White Negro.

The mask Slim wore on television was not intended to whiten him out. He could not be mistaken for Folks. However, in their own ways, the two were powerful objects of whites' fantasmatic identification— figures from the black underworld who embodied the masculine traits they felt they did not have. As the white paper on Pyne's interview desk danced in the reflection of Slim's dark glasses, viewers were confronted with a fleeting image of why the pimp-turned-author commanded their attention. Time ran out before Slim could address the Goddess beyond a cursory summary of her role in the narrative. But the interview was still a success: he had helped the (white) audience see how they, too, could pass for black.

Emory "Butch" Holmes II, a black editor who worked for Bentley Morriss and Ralph Weinstock in the 1970s, once described Holloway House's relationship with black writers in explicitly Mailerian terms:

What I understood about Holloway House even early on was that they had chosen an area of American life that was on the bottom of things. It was on the bottom of one's shoe. It was on the bottom of the economic ladder. It was on the bottom of all thought, all hope, and all redemption. It was like Norman Mailer said in the [sic] "The White Negro." Negroes have morality, but it is the morality of the bottom. The bottom. What they did was, they published literature that you had to go to the bottom to find. You had to go to the dark side of the moon to discover this literature or these images.[59]

Though Holmes did not use the term, sleaze would be an accurate descriptor for his take on Morriss and Weinstock's interest in black authors. That interest had nothing to do with black readers, much less the denizens of Watts. It was, instead, defined by the White Negro's fascination with blackness. The fact of racial difference was sleaze's limit point of experience, the horizon where white readers could identify with a low-down, antidomestic alternative to mainstream society. Like Mailer, Morriss and Weinstock valued blackness in purely functional terms—what it could do, or not, for whites.

The critical consensus that would define Iceberg Slim as a necessarily subversive writer ignores the print network in which he and Robert deCoy were originally published. There was enough trickster-like dissembling to go around in both authors' works from 1967. Nonetheless, as I have emphasized throughout this chapter, even these seemingly autochthonous representations were thoroughly mediated by Holloway House's stake in the marketplace for sleaze, which at the time catered to white men. To the extent that sleaze fostered a vibrant culture of dissembling unto itself, whatever Slim or deCoy wrote was invariably inflected by it. The masks they wore in fiction were offset by the masks all sleaze writers wore as a matter of sticking it to women.

THREE

Black Sleaze

In February 1968 *New York Times Book Review* critic Mel Watkins hit the pavement to survey what people were reading in the city's "black ghettos." He was led to do so after noticing a surge in race-related books on the market. Publishers, Watkins wrote, were waking up to the fact that "the slum dweller's supposed tendency to ignore the printed word" had been a function of "the prohibitive cost of hardback books and the lack of books dealing directly with the realities of ghetto life."[1] At last the paperback revolution had come to urban America.

Reflecting the social and political cleavages of the time, Watkins's survey noted a clear divergence between what older and younger people were reading. The former, he wrote, "have reacted to the accessibility of paperbacks with increased purchasing of best sellers and potboilers with heavy concentrations of sex and sensationalism." The latter, meanwhile, who Watkins identified as "those having attended or graduated from high school since the Supreme Court decision of 1954 [*Brown v. Board of Education*]," showed a preference for "politically and sociologically oriented books with an emphasis on black and radical viewpoints." No surprise, then, that these readers flocked to the works of W. E. B. Du Bois, Richard Wright, LeRoi Jones, and especially Malcolm X, whose collection of statements and speeches, *Malcolm X Speaks* (1965), was proving to be a fine complement to his *Autobiography*. All of which was in stark contrast to what Watkins found in the hands of older readers. Along with Pierre Salinger's *With Kennedy* and Jacqueline Susann's *Valley of the Dolls* (both 1966), "two novels . . . chronicling the adventures of a ghetto con man" stood out: *Pimp* and *Trick Baby*.[2]

Why this divide in taste? Watkins pointed out that it was not simply a matter of age. He noted a "lack of book outlets within the ghetto which provide a wide variety of titles" to readers. It was, then, a matter of class, geography, and tacitly racist distribution practices. Black readers seemed to lurch between extremes—radical literature to trash fiction—only because that is what book distributors (and the publishers that used their services) sent to their communities. For the average black reader, that meant having few retail outlets where he or she could pick up entertaining and affordable middlebrow titles. Instead, Watkins concluded, "one is likely to find on display only a few books— all with provocative cover illustrations and titles such as 'Shanty Town Girl' and 'The Diary of a Masseuse.'" A Brooklyn high-schooler he interviewed said that "in her neighborhood it was impossible to buy a book her father would allow her to bring home."[3] Thus, despite enjoying some of the fruits of the paperback revolution, many urban blacks still lived in a kind of book desert, at least when it came to accessing quality literature.

This state of affairs helps explain why white-oriented sleaze found a receptive audience among urban blacks. Lowbrow was what they were afforded, and that was much of what they got. With regard to Iceberg Slim, then, it was not because of some inherent cultural mystique that initially drew black readers to his work. Instead, racist distribution patterns ensured that Slim would become a best-selling author in black neighborhoods. Bentley Morriss's All America Distributors Corporation would have made Holloway House paperbacks a staple in these urban spaces well before Iceberg stepped onto the scene. In fact, Holloway House was far from the only company banking on white readers' appetite for racially exploitative fare. *Pimp* and *Trick Baby* had a lot of company when it came to *black sleaze*.

Black sleaze is the term I apply to white-oriented pulp whose prose style, plot structure, and cover design made a lurid spectacle of blackness, and specifically racialized sexuality. As a subgenre of the sleaze and pinup trades, black sleaze was titillating enough to cause a stir but not so graphic as to cause a scandal. It would be several years before explicit pornography took over the adult reading market, ushering in an era when, in John Harrison's assessment, "softcore hardened and the sleaze became sick."[4] For now, sleaze's tongue-in-cheek play of concealment and revelation still held sway, offering readers an excuse to delight in material that combined elements of erotica, sexology, autobiography, and porn. Until Slim came along, this was a domain set up almost exclusively for white hacks.

What black sleaze lacked in explicitness it certainly made up for in a voyeuristic gaze. As I detailed in the previous chapter, a key component of Slim's appeal was his claim to be offering an insider's view of life on the street. Through his prefatory matter and his reflexive status as a character in his own fiction, Slim positioned himself as an intermediary between the underground and the mainstream. As such, he lent readers the impression that what they were accessing through his books was forbidden, secret, and otherwise taboo—yet all the more real because of that. This kind of gesture was a staple of the sleaze enterprise, which tended to locate literary stimulation in the gaps between what could be said and what risked censure. When applied to race, however, sleaze's voyeurism presented a host of problems. What did it matter that Slim was black if the genre in which he wrote was tailor-made for white consumption? What were the implications of ghetto residents having access to black sleaze but not much else?

One year after his reading survey, Watkins published a piece on the vogue for black-oriented fare in the literary marketplace—something he called a "bona fide cultural and commercial phenomenon." Paperbacks again were the key to the surge in demand. Watkins noted approvingly that, owing to "the adoption of many titles by educational institutions," many socially and politically conscious books had doubled their sales in just a couple of years. That went for *The Autobiography of Malcolm X*, *Malcolm X Speaks*, Kenneth B. Clark's *Dark Ghetto* (1965), E. U. Essien-Udom's *Black Nationalism* (1962), LeRoi Jones's two-play collection *"Dutchman" and "The Slave"* (1964)—"the list could be extended tenfold." Yet reigning over all of these titles was the king of black sleaze: Kyle Onstott's *Mandingo* (1957), a historical novel about slave breeding whose Fawcett paperback had sold upward of three million copies. The decade-long popularity of that book had spawned a whole series: Falconhurst, named after the plantation on which much of the narrative takes place. Now on its second author (Lance Horner) and having seen its sixth title, *Heir to Falconhurst*, appear in 1968, the franchise boasted thirteen million copies in print, and it was still going strong.[5] Iceberg Slim did not merit mention in the piece.

This, then, was the distribution context in which Holloway House had to compete if it hoped to extend Slim's shelf life. The late 1960s paperback market seemed like it was able to reward books of immediate social and political relevance—much of which was of high intellectual merit—but its greatest spoils still went to sleaze, including the white authors of black sleaze. Before blaxploitation became a show-business fad in the 1970s, the literary marketplace had modeled how racially lurid fare could harness millions in white dollars—and bring black consumers along in the process.

In this chapter, I track Holloway House's efforts to gain a toehold in the black sleaze market between 1968 and 1970. Racial divisions deepened during this period. The assassination of Dr. Martin Luther King Jr. on April 4, 1968, dealt a fatal blow to the mass movement for civil rights. The assassination of Senator Robert F. Kennedy a mere two months later dashed any hope that the movement could be revived. With the demise of integrationist idealism, it fell to radicals, nationalists, and militants confederated under the banner of Black Power to confront white backlash against progressive social gains. The backlash only intensified, however, when Richard M. Nixon, having successfully run on a platform of "law and order," assumed the presidency in January 1969.

During this tumultuous period, Morriss and Ralph Weinstock remained safely ensconced in La-La Land, churning out more books for the White Negro's titillation. That black readers were purchasing their books in significant numbers was a major bonus but not an essential part of their strategy. Indeed, like any pulp operation that relied on hackwork, Morriss and Weinstock recycled formulas to keep their business humming. They did not have to look far for the labor to pull this off: Slim, Robert deCoy, and Leo Guild were called on to help establish Holloway House's place in the market for black sleaze.

Black Man's Burden

The assassination of Dr. King was too consequential an event for Holloway House to ignore. Yet, given the readership they were targeting, Morriss and Weinstock wanted to avoid even appearing to support the racial militancy that had surged in the wake of his death. They were able to navigate these competing impulses by turning to Louis Lomax—the veteran black journalist who had granted Slim his first interview as a published author. Based on copyright filings, it seems Lomax had been working on a book about Malcolm X when Dr. King was killed. At that point, Lomax decided or was advised to make room in his book for an analysis of the reverend's life and untimely death. The added material made sense given that, as Lomax wrote in the introduction, he "respected them both, and was a friend to both."[6] Despite the delay, when *To Kill a Black Man* came out in the fall, it became the first major book to compare the civil rights era's two most influential leaders.

Lomax's analysis was assured, but it was also antiradical, abjuring what were, at the time, ever more forceful calls for revolution. A son of the Great Migration, Lomax held firm to what seemed like an anachronistic plea for interracial understanding. To make his case, Lomax included a transcript of his and Mike Wallace's conversation with Elijah Muhammad and Malcolm X in *The Hate That Hate Produced*, where the newsmen were critical of black nationalism in general and the Nation of Islam in particular. To be fair, Lomax doubted that "King's effusive, though eloquent, proffering of love was a correct assessment of reality in an America contorted by a tradition of hate." In the final analysis, however, he embraced a King-like "ethic of brotherhood" in the way he chose to represent Malcolm's eventual turn away from the Nation: "The irony of Malcolm was that he embraced the notion of love at a time in history when it became fashionable for black men to openly express their hate."[7] By "hate," Lomax meant "antiwhite" sentiment coming out of the nationalist cause—the mirror image of white supremacy's "tradition of hate." Malcolm, by contrast, had turned to "love" as a means of escaping the narrow confines of racial chauvinism. When *Knight* printed excerpts of *To Kill a Black Man* in March 1969, Lomax's statement on Malcolm X fell in the penultimate paragraph while his defense of an "ethic of brotherhood" concluded the piece.[8]

This conservative response to the rise of black nationalism sat uneasily alongside the fact that race had become a hot commodity in the sleaze industry. The success of *Pimp* led to copycats like Paperback Library's *High Rider* (1969) and *Black Sister* (1970), about a pimp and a madam, respectively. Both novels were by Leo Guild, writing under the pseudonym Vance Donovan. Dell's *The Lords of Hell* (1967), meanwhile, claimed to be "the first attempt to describe the life of a Negro pimp, his relationship to the women in his stable and to his family."[9] It was as if the journalistic exposé had taken its talking points from Slim. Even writers not known for dealing with race got in on the act, as evidenced by Midwood (ahem) publishing science-fiction and fantasy hack Andrew J. Offutt's *Black Man's Harem* (1970) under the pen name John Cleve.[10] Finally, Greenleaf Classics, a major sleaze publisher based in San Diego, tried to outdo its California cousin in nearly every category. Its catalog swelled to include erotic fiction such as *Blacks' Beauty* and *Sally in Black Bondage* (both 1969), as well as one of the few such books to have been written by a black man: Frank Marshall Davis's

Sex Rebel: Black (Memoirs of a Gash Gourmet) (1968), using the pseudonym Bob Greene. The catalog also accommodated titles in that favored Holloway House genre, sexology. With casebooks such as *White Slaves* (1968), *Black Woman, White Woman* (1969), and *White Women and Black Lovers* (1969), Greenleaf hoped to cover all the permutations.

Then there was Falconhurst and its numerous imitators. The cash crop at the titular Alabama plantation was not cotton but slaves. This conceit allowed Onstott—a former dog breeder who had turned his expertise toward fictional black bodies—to exploit racialized sexuality under the guise of writing a historical novel. In the first and only scholarly study of the Falconhurst phenomenon, Earl F. Bargainnier writes that "the addition of sex to the fictional world of the Old South [was] the single greatest change in the image of that time and place" to appear since the days of the old plantation romance. Indeed, Onstott and later Horner made sure that Falconhurst was rife with "incest rape, nymphomania, homosexuality, lesbianism, masturbation of another person, defloration of virgins, fellatio, orgiastic exhibitions, group sex, sadistic sex, and general promiscuity."[11] Onstott and Horner understood quite well that the conceit of slave breeding opened up a world of sexual discourse where anything goes.

Mandingo was bound to be imitated. According to sleaze historian Paul Talbot, by the late 1960s, Falconhurst had "spawned a new pulp genre known alternately as 'slave fiction,' 'slaver novels,' 'slave gothics,' 'plantation novels' and 'bodice-rippers.'"[12] The so-called slavers combined historical claims on the antebellum South with soft-core scenes fit for the sexual revolution. That the former was utterly dubious was beside the point: Americans evidently liked their literary porn tinged with racial tension. Sample titles from 1968 and 1969 read like a veritable rogues' library: *Beast* (1969), *The Black and the Damned* (1969), *Plantation Breed* (1969), *Slave* (1968).

We can assume that black women's sexual exploitation was an expected feature of these novels, and one of the main reasons why they were popular among white men. But what would those readers have found appealing about representations of black studs—not just humans reduced to breeding status but fine specimens of masculine virility? The climax, indeed the exact midpoint, of *Black Vengeance*, a 1968 slaver by Norman Gant, the pen name of George Wolk, sheds light on that question. The setting: Curaçao. The situation: while plotting his escape from the island, a maroon is confronted by a young white woman from the plantation. The actors: a muscular black man and a delicate white virgin. Brash, the maroon, is initially worried that An-neke, the young woman, will expose him to her family. But Anneke has other things on her mind: "Her white hand came up to his thick lips and quieted them. It was the first time they had touched since they had been children. It released a savage fury in him the extent of which he had never suspected." The rest of the scene succumbs to a narrative frenzy: "Brash felt the fullness of her young body and lifted her off the ground to place her on the dry dirt before the mouth of the cave, ripping her green dress from her body and her underthings off as she reached for him and cried out in pleasure." Amid the writhing, Gant reminds the reader of the deeper meaning of this union: "They knew that they had only that one night to wrest from their fates enough pas-sion to satisfy their youths." It is, in other words, a release of pent-up sexual tension that is powerful enough to cut through the taboo of their attraction. However, the fact that it is a one-off means the ma-roon is far from safe. Indeed, Anneke has barely let out "happy cries [that] broke the tropical night" before Brash starts to suspect she will regret her actions. It is only a matter of time, he thinks, before she sees him again as a "brutal savage."[13]

A product of the aptly named sleaze house Lancer, *Black Vengeance* was the second in Gant's slaver series, which had started earlier that year with *Chane*. This scene was hardly unique: versions of it could be found in nearly every book of black sleaze from the late 1960s. Why? Because at a time when racial militancy was on the rise, white read-ers found comfort, even a certain reassurance, in soft-core interracial porn—a liberal version of the old plantation romance.[14] This is not to say black readers avoided these books, for even the *New York Times* could see that they read them. But it is to note that sleaze merchants were indifferent to their tastes when it came to producing such fare. The taboo, of course, was as old as slavery itself: black men were forbid-den from consorting with white women. By reviving the myth of the buck for a white male readership, black sleaze generated frisson—the pleasure in breaking sexual taboos—from this familiar racial script. Each book delivered an interracial kick, but it was the rare one indeed that showed a black-white coupling that could be sustained.

It was through sex, then, not social or political movement, that white readers could sympathize with black men in these radicalizing times. The dynamics of such homosocial sympathy were illustrated in an essay from the September 1969 issue of *Knight*. The title page for Norman Spinrad's "Darktown Strutters' Ball" showed a black male fig-

FIGURE 3.1 Illustration from "Darktown Strutters' Ball," in *Knight* (September 1969). Courtesy of Sirkay Publishing.

ure behind bars (figure 3.1). Except these were no ordinary bars—they were the red stripes in the flag of the United States of America. With such a powerful image, one would expect a searing statement on racial injustice in America. Instead, Spinrad began with two "nightmare" scenarios:

NIGHTMARE NUMBER ONE

Your wife is walking home alone one night through a "deteriorating" slum neighborhood. She is forced to traverse the mouth of a dark and ominous alley. As she passes the entrance to the alley, a huge black arm encircles her throat and drags her back into the inky darkness. A giant slavering Negro rips off her clothes with a few sweeps of his gorilla-like paws, slams her down on the cold concrete, and as she begs futilely for mercy he rapes her.

NIGHTMARE NUMBER TWO

Same as nightmare number one, except she digs it.[15]

Spinrad's sordid exercise in racial liberalism ("deteriorating") conjured the image of the rapacious black brute only to query whether white women might be turned on by the scenario. What if they were? How different would that make the brute from the reader? Perhaps it was time for white men to entertain the fantasy.

The piece aimed to do just that. Taking a page from slaver paperbacks, Spinrad left present-day reality to escape in a faux ethnography of the past. He conjectured that the sexual hang-ups instilled in men's psyches by slavery explained how the races got along (or didn't) since. Spinrad implied that black men's desires had been stifled, their sense of masculine pride quashed, and their image in the white mind maligned because of the putative threat they posed to white women. Now, however, was the time for racial reconciliation. In terms reminiscent of Mailer's White Negro, Spinrad yoked the brute, or "nigger," and the white man, or "puritan," together in a bond of masculine identification:

Why does the puritan fear the nigger?

Because the nigger is his own created mirror-image; the nigger is what he would be if only he dared.

Why does the puritan hate the nigger?

Because the nigger represents to him all his hidden sinful desires. He hates the nigger because he hates himself for wanting to be a "nigger."

Thus, in addition to the guilt White America feels for having enslaved human beings, in addition to the guilt White America feels for having created the stereotype of the "nigger," is a deep vein of inadmissible guilt for the secret desire to be like the "niggers."[16]

In short, to the extent the black man acted out scenarios the white man ("puritan") had made illegal or impermissible, he merited sympathy, or an acknowledgment that he and the reader were linked by fate.

Only by this logic, and only in the realm of pinups and sleaze, could interracial sex be tolerated. What Mailer considered a vital part of the underground jazz scene in 1957 had become the full-blown ethos of a culture industry.

In light of these developments, it made sense for Robert deCoy to publish with Holloway House again. *The Nigger Bible*'s discourse on interracialism was of a piece with black sleaze's, even though the former defied easy generic categorization. For his follow-up, deCoy chose to write a biography of Jack Johnson, the celebrated, and reviled, black prizefighter from the first part of the twentieth century. Johnson was the perfect subject for a Holloway House paperback: unsparing in the ring and brash in his personal affairs, he had flouted Jim Crow like almost no black man had done before him or since. The only thing whites had hated more than reading about Johnson's victories over white boxers was seeing how his taste for fine clothes and fancy cars endeared him to white women. This during a time when interracial sex, and even the appearance of interracial intimacy, was strictly verboten. *The Big Black Fire*, deCoy's biography of the sportsman, appeared in 1969.

The book is a hack job. Another scholar has pointed out that it is "riddled with quotation marks but no citations," leaving the reader to wonder exactly what, or whom, deCoy is citing. The lack of citations is especially vexing insofar as oft-repeated tales, such as Johnson's wrapping his penis in gauze before a fight to lend the appearance of heft, can be traced to deCoy but are unattributed to any source.[17] Yet verifiability may not be the ultimate goal here. Johnson's life story emerges as a kind of vehicle for *The Big Black Fire*'s real interest: talking about interracial sex. Indeed, the biography assigns an inordinate amount of weight to Johnson's musings on white womanhood. When, early in his career, a reporter asks him why he would breach this social taboo, Johnson is quoted as saying, "Because, they enhance me more than my women do. And in return, I allow them to bask in the limelight, temporarily." At times, it seems as though deCoy reads Johnson's entire life through this lens—an extended meditation on the meaning of white femininity for the black man. Editorializing for a bit, he writes, "The Negro male and the Caucasian woman are supposed to duck and dart around in darkness, with the threat of death and condemnation for being seen together. But Jack 'wasn't having none of that, for sure.'"[18] Here deCoy's tone is almost wistful: if only more of us could be like Jack Johnson.

By "us" I mean white readers identifying with a particular condition of black masculinity—barred from getting what it wants. Even going under the assumption that black readers could access *The Big Black*

Fire, the broader prerogatives of black sleaze compel deCoy to address a white audience. There is no better proof of this than when deCoy cites *The Nigger Bible* in the biography. Chapter 15, for example, is titled after a line from the book, "Justice Is a White Woman"; it uses that personified figure to dwell on Johnson's prosecution under the Mann Act, or so-called white slavery law, in 1913. DeCoy frames Johnson's legal battle as a kind of psychosexual drama with Justice. The scenario goes like this: Having been found guilty of interstate crimes, Johnson started to refer to her as "'Mis' Justice." Now, in the interregnum before sentencing, he had "two weeks to win the beautiful white hand of Justice"—even though "folks told him that he didn't stand a chance of winning the lady." Johnson's mother stepped in to give him sage advice, warning that if he did not succeed in "appealing for Justice," it would be "the end of [him] as a man."[19] This is speculative history, to say the least—an application of the *Bible*'s framework to Johnson's biography. But that, of course, is the point: what deCoy forgoes in accuracy he more than makes up for in interracial sexual tension.

The Big Black Fire concludes with another citation of deCoy's previous work. Heaping praise on the former heavyweight champion, deCoy goes so far as to claim that he is the inspiration for the following quotation:

When you take a white woman to a love-couch, my Son, consider the common status you share. You are both refugees from different cells of the same prison. You have filched the keys from the sleeping Warden and met in the darkened corridors, along the cell blocks of time. Remember if you would be free, you must flee together. The consequences are terrible upon recaptured escapees.[20]

Recontextualized in this chapter, deCoy's biblical allegory of "freedom" is revealed for the base sexual fantasy that it is. If *The Big Black Fire* is a hack job, its source material is *The Nigger Bible* and its formula is that of black sleaze.

The Limits of Sympathy

In October 1967 Congress enacted Public Law 90-100, which led to the creation of the Commission on Obscenity and Pornography. The governmental body's purpose was "to determine whether such materials are harmful to the public, and particularly to minors, and whether more effective methods should be devised to control the transmission of such materials." But in order to draw those conclusions, the commission first had to figure out exactly what they were dealing with. So Congress also asked it "to ascertain the methods employed in the distribution of obscene and pornographic materials and to explore the nature and volume of traffic in such materials."[21] Chaired by constitutional law scholar William B. Lockhart, the commission began its work in July 1968, conducted research over the next two years, and published a final *Report* in September 1970. That document became the first comprehensive study of the adult-oriented culture industry in the United States.

The *Report* concluded that the traffic in sex media was big business, generating $537–$574 million in sales each year. Much of that figure came from sexually explicit motion pictures, which harnessed a whopping $450–$460 million in box office receipts. Yet "adults only" books and periodicals also had a well-defined stake in the industry. In this category, books at retail ($45–$55 million), periodicals at retail ($25–$35 million), and mail-order media ($12–$14 million) totaled almost $105 million in sales at the high end.[22]

But these figures did not tell the entire story. The *Report* went on to suggest that the market for sleaze paperbacks and pinup magazines was bigger—much bigger—than this. Because not included in the aforementioned tallies were mass-market books and periodicals that, while not branded "adults only," contained content of a sexual nature. Of course, it was impossible to determine exact sales figures for sex media that did not label themselves as such. So the commission simply noted that mass-market paperback sales "exceeded $340 million in 1968," and that an eyeball survey of best seller lists between January 1969 and July 1970 counted eighteen books of a sexual nature that made it into the top twenty for more than one month. As for mass-market periodicals, the commission isolated three types that targeted men: "barber shop" or male-oriented "action" magazines ($12 million); "men's sophisticates" or straightforward "girlie" magazines ($31 million); and "specialty" magazines such as *Playboy*, which combined nude pictorials with content of some literary and cultural cachet ($66 million for *Playboy*, a quarter of that for all others combined).[23] A conservative estimate, then, would put sex media in the mass market at double the sales of books and periodicals in the "adults only" market.

This second set of figures demonstrated that what had been the domain of the sexual underground in the 1950s was now a fixture in American popular culture. And the trend of moving the formerly illicit into the mainstream showed no signs of slowing down. The commission noted, "There is an overlap of sexually oriented materials between the mass and the 'adult' markets; some publishers produced materials for both, and many other publishers constantly seek to expand distribution of their 'secondary' product into the mass market."[24] This described Morriss and Weinstock's larger business operation to a tee. For while Holloway House paperbacks still carried the label "Adult Reading," *Adam* and *Knight* were men's sophisticates (to use the *Report*'s terminology) that took advantage of the era's liberalizing sexual mores in the mass market. These magazines were the key to building an audience for their books.

Framed in this way, we can better appreciate how Holloway House's black writers—Slim, Lomax, and deCoy—were enlisted in a literary project not of their own making. Treatments of race in *Adam, Knight,* and other men's magazines were tethered to the white voyeuristic gaze. As long as that was the case—or, better, as long as Morriss and Weinstock believed that to be the case—there would be no change to how Holloway House produced race-oriented fiction.

So it is that after publishing a string of black-authored paperbacks, Holloway House followed up on *The Big Black Fire* with *The Girl Who Loved Black* (1969), another sleaze "biography" by the erstwhile Leo Guild. It was less a reversion to type than an elaboration of formulas in currency with black sleaze. In the same issue of *Knight* that carried Norman Spinrad's screed, an advertisement for the new book blared: "A Beautiful White Girl's Passion For A Negro Pimp!!!" (figure 3.2). Here the figure of the "beautiful white girl," signifying purity and innocence, contrasted with that of the "Negro pimp," signifying the opposite. It was a fairly crass effort to exploit racial and sexual stereotypes. And yet the term connecting the two figures, "passion," confused matters somewhat. Could a girl who felt such passion be innocent after all? The male model displayed on the book's cover certainly did look appealing—less a threat than an object of sexual fantasy. Maybe this black man deserved to be loved rather than feared. That notion was entirely plausible given the smaller tagline that appeared above the plot synopsis: "Behind The Scenes View of Hollywood Racial Prejudice."[25]

The Girl Who Loved Black is quintessential black sleaze: interracial porn that plays on, but ultimately forecloses, the idea that black and white should be equal. Sandy Hyland (a name Guild assures us is a pseudonym) is a twenty-year-old virgin with blonde hair, long legs, and a face that is "open and smiling"—a veritable icon of white purity. But Sandy waitresses at a drive-in in a section of Los Angeles that, in Guild's clumsy phrase, "exuded poverty." Predictably enough, that fact

A Beautiful White Girl's Passion For A Negro Pimp!!!

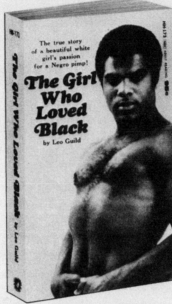

FIRST U.S.A. EDITION

95¢

Behind The Scenes View Of Hollywood Racial Prejudice

Sandy Hyland (a pseudonym) is a beautiful white girl currently under contract to one of Hollywood's largest motion picture studios. A talented singer and film actress, her only hangup was that she loved a Negro . . . a Negro pimp to be exact.

The studio subjected Sandy to every pressure they could exert to break up the affair . . . and Sandy, in desperation, fled the arms of her black lover and married a white man to protect her career.

Here is a behind the scenes view of Hollywood at its ugliest . . . racial prejudice . . . financial pressures . . . lust at its lowest and at its most "sophisticated" levels. The shocking, true story of The Girl who Loved Black.

64

FIGURE 3.2 Advertisement for *The Girl Who Loved Black*, in *Knight* (September 1969).

is meant to suggest that Sandy comes into contact with more black people than the average white person. True, she is far from being a child of privilege. Sandy grew up in a mixed-race neighborhood and is working her way through school—"a secretarial course at night"—that would land her a better job.[26] Yet these details are merely window dressing for the primary confrontation: the wide-eyed, virginal white girl with the sexually experienced black man.

The man who comes into her life is named Robert Krebb. Hacks do not put much effort into naming their characters, and one wonders if Guild simply took "Robert Beck" and reversed (with a difference) the letters of the last name. When Robert pulls into the drive-in in his 1965 Cadillac convertible, he certainly cuts a figure similar to the youthful Iceberg's: "The man at the wheel was a rather good-looking young Negro wearing sun glasses and sporting a thin black mustache." Regardless, Sandy is intrigued by the big-tipper. On his second visit to the drive-in, Robert comes on stronger and asks her out. After she politely declines, he asks, "Is it because I'm a nigger?" Flabbergasted, Sandy exclaims, "Of course not," and overcompensates by taking a ride in Robert's car. There she begins a tortuous self-assessment of white guilt, musing, "[I] really didn't care that he was black," and, "What would it be like to be taken by this good-looking black?" Sensing that he has her, Robert says, "You know I may be a nigger but I feel and react like any other man. I can love and hate too. I'm not only a sex machine."[27] Their ride ends with tension lingering in the air, but Guild has set up the basic coordinates of his narrative: the well-meaning white girl will explore her deepest desires with a black man forced to the margins of society.

Sandy's inevitable seduction by Robert is crudely rendered, but Guild draws the reader in through his representation of interracial commingling: "She pulled him back to her. He undressed her skillfully, never being aware that things were coming off until she had nothing on and then suddenly he was nude, too. She was shocked by the blackness of his body made blacker by the night. It was the white of her and the black of him. What a marked contrast." This "contrast" proves as alluring to Sandy as anything else about the more experienced Robert—though, to be sure, it can only help that he has, by his own account, "a big wang."[28] Like deCoy and the slaver novelists, Guild generates sexual excitement out of the sleaze imperative to break taboos. This deflowering scene is not just about taking away Sandy's virginity; it is, more powerfully, about removing the color prejudice that would prevent her from experiencing the pleasures of a black lover.

Robert, as the ad for *The Girl Who Loved Black* made clear, is a pimp; his interest in Sandy is strictly transactional. Seducing her is but the first step in priming her to start turning tricks for him. Sandy's first time doing that is involuntary: Robert invites a paying john over, and, with the lights off, he fools Sally into thinking she is making love to him when she in fact is putting out as a prostitute. That heinous double cross incenses Sandy, and she tries to move on with her life. But no matter what she does, Sandy simply cannot quit Robert. The long middle section of the book sees her move up the career ladder—from underpaid secretary to overpaid assistant to professional singer—and muddle through a succession of underwhelming white lovers, two of whom become her husbands. All the while, Sandy keeps coming back to Robert for sex. Her desire for him is so strong that at various points (while all of the above is happening) she turns tricks for him, recruits a girl for his stable, and bails him out of jail. Perhaps most important, Sandy becomes a version of Robert. She comes to view sex as a transaction, and all her career moves result from dealing in quid pro quos with men in power. Thus, in both sex and economics, Robert does Sandy a tremendous amount of good. He is the red-blooded American male readers want to be, as opposed to the whining, neurotic, and usually impotent white lovers whom Sandy is compelled to put up with.

Guild secures homosocial sympathy for Robert through a hackneyed device: the unmitigated racists who at various points find out about Sandy's long-standing affair with him. That would include her father: "Young lady don't you dare bring disgrace on our family by getting involved with a black. They're far beneath you." Her mother: "They're all in the whore business. All the men." Her first husband: "They're just inferior people. Dirty, thieving, illegal people." And her agent: "I tell you, black boys like that have to end up badly and they'll carry anyone down that's around them. . . . You're playing with a lot of people that have faith in you. You'll drag us all down."[29] Taken together, these instances constitute the "Hollywood Racial Prejudice" that the ad for *The Girl Who Loved Black* promised to expose. Guild relies on them to activate sentiments that would be familiar to any reader of slaver novels. The presumed reader would not only express shock at such rank color prejudice; he would also feel righteous in condemning it. This is why black sleaze was at root a genre of racial liberalism.[30]

Of course, the fact that this device was a cliché—a ready-made way to paper over thornier issues—suggests that there are clear limits to the genre's ability to sympathize with black manhood. In *The Girl Who*

Loved Black, those limits are marked by Sandy's own racism, which (unlike the unvarnished racists) is expressed in roundabout ways. On one hand, there is the *we can't change the world* defense: "What if Robert and I had children and they were black?" Sandy speculates. "I'd kill myself. It would be terrible." The blatant prejudice of this statement is explained away by the vague notion that one cannot act on individual convictions because the world is such a nasty place. Sandy's associates are constantly reminding her of this: "Maybe fifty years from now it'll be okay, but not now," says her black girlfriend Earline; "The world's not ready for it yet," says her white boss Bob. On the other hand, there is the *it's not about race* defense. Mulling over how she should have responded to her parents' openly racist statements, Sandy has an epiphany: "What she should have done was tell her parents exactly the truth. How she dug Robert's body and how, when she was in bed with him, she was in heaven. It had nothing to do with marriage or permanence or social justice. It had to do merely with sex and thrill but she didn't have the guts to discuss that with her parents."[31] Note that with both defenses Guild assiduously avoids any recognition of racism as bound up with white privilege. In the first scenario, racism exists, but Sandy can't do anything about it. In the second, Sandy insists that her actions should not be construed as racially motivated. Racism, then, is other people's problem, not her own.

That, of course, absolved the reader of coming to terms with his own racism. In the world of sleaze, black manhood could perform white sexual fantasy, or it could assuage white racial guilt. It could not be an embodied personal or political identity. This point was driven home with particular force when Holloway House hack Paul Gillette worked on a piece for scandal rag *Cloak 'n' Dagger* in 1964. In February of that year, Cassius Clay had defeated Sonny Liston to become heavyweight champion of the world. Shortly thereafter, Clay insisted on going by the name Cassius X—in effect a public declaration of his commitment to Malcolm X and the Nation of Islam. White people were incensed, offended that the boxer would use his platform to bring attention to a group they deemed "antiwhite." Gillette was tasked with penning an editorial response to Cassius X's actions. The first draft of the "open letter" seethed:

The editors of CLOAK 'N' DAGGER have probed into the association of the new heavyweight champ and come up with some startling facts—facts which, no doubt, will jolt the champ himself.
    They're all contained herein—

And, if Mr. Clay takes heed, he can still prove to the American public that he's a MAN—not just a MOUTH!

Gillette's final copy for the opening salvo was less threatening but equally patronizing:

It is high time to face facts, Cassius—to grow up before it is too late!
   Get rid of your hate-mongering advisors!
   Leave politics to others and busy your self [sic] with what you know best: Boxing!
   Prove that your becoming the World Champ was not a freak of fate![32]

We know how that ended: Cassius X became Muhammad Ali. But it is revealing to see what happened when an actual, not fictional, black man stood up to the way white people framed his success. In the sleaze trade, his very manhood ("prove to the American public," "grow up before it is too late") had to be questioned.

By contrast, Robert never steps out of line in *The Girl Who Loved Black*. He knows his place, and Guild makes sure he stays in it. In fact, by the end of the novel the roles are reversed. At the height of her popularity, Sandy, on her second marriage, visits Robert, who feels indebted to her for bailing him out of jail. She initiates sex in a way that demonstrates her control of the situation: "She unbuttoned his shirt and took [it] off from the back. She just undressed him, as if he were a little boy, until he was nude." Robert is rendered diminutive by Sandy's advances. The tacit explanation for his feeling small is this: What if he was to resist? Would anyone believe that a white starlet actually wanted to sleep with a black pimp? Unsurprisingly, after their romp, Sandy proposes an arrangement: she will "send [Robert] a check every once in a while" in exchange for his sexual services. "Don't shake your head," she coos—or, more accurately, warns. He assents to the arrangement. Victorious, Sandy assures him: "I get love from Sammy. That's my husband. He loves me day and night but it doesn't do me any good. From you I get the joy. It's just a trick, a twist of fate."[33] Sandy's sympathy for Robert only extends so far as he fulfills his role as a boy toy. The pun in the final line is exactly right: Robert has been reduced to a "trick."

This arrangement is short-lived. In the very next chapter, after several weeks of seeing Sandy, we learn that Robert has been brutally beaten by a rival pimp. There are suspicions that the whole thing was set up by Sandy's agent, concerned that their affair would ruin her career. The circumstances of the beating are never fully explained, and

Robert succumbs to the injuries and dies. Sandy is devastated, but she is able to move on with her life rather quickly. For what her arrangement with Robert has clarified is that she still has the power to call on "several studs" to service her needs while she remains tied to Sammy.[34] "Stud," I would argue, is how Sandy truly saw Robert when he was alive: a racialized sexual object no more human than the enslaved breeders one could find on Falconhurst plantation.

Lose Your Mother

It had been two years since *Pimp* had come out, and Slim showed no signs of moving out of the spotlight. Though he certainly had his share of black readers, Slim still understood that his persona depended on wearing the mask for the voyeuristic white gaze. His June 1969 interview with the men's magazine *Rogue* was a case in point. Slim had sat for a three-hour-long conversation with Richard B. Milner, a white anthropologist researching a book on black pimps. Selections from that conversation appeared as the lead piece in the magazine's special issue devoted to "sex and violence in America." In framing the interview, Milner noted that *Pimp* had already sold half a million copies, making Slim a "legend" among "pimps and prostitutes" across the country. He also pointed out that "the history of pimping in America [was] intimately tied to the oppressive conditions of Negro ghetto life." But Milner quickly pivoted away from that subject to ask a question at the forefront of his mind: "What makes a good pimp?"[35] The White Negro wished to be instructed.

Slim spoke convincingly, if not harrowingly, of the pimp's ability to brainwash a prostitute. "There's never that much air for the whore," he said. "Because if you give her that much air, you've started the process of 'blowing,' losing the whore." When an intrigued Milner asked whether this insight could be applied to "all women," Slim replied in the affirmative:

You know, I am almost certain that the principles of good pimping apply to all man and woman relationships. Now let's cancel out, of course, the physical and overt thing that the pimp used to do. But the cruelty must be there in a successful relationship between a man and a woman, even if it's only subtle psychological cruelty. You must appeal to that degree of masochism within even a square broad. Of course, the degree depends on their sensitivity and culture and background. But they all like a *little* cruelty.[36]

The only way to sustain a woman's romantic interest, apparently, was to treat her just badly enough to make her believe she could be loved but, ultimately, did not deserve to be loved. In thus expounding on the nature of female desire, Slim turned the pimp's credo into a tactic of seduction. It was a Sadean skin game fit for any man to put into practice.

In addition to dispensing advice, Slim stated for the first time what would become a personal credo: "The best pimps I know are the pimps that were abandoned by their old ladies—left in garbage cans and in alleys when they were little, tiny—that never knew any affection for love." Based on that observation from the field, he concluded, "To be a great pimp . . . you've really got to hate your mother."[37] For Slim, the most self-possessed men were those who had turned a lack of maternal love into a spur for male cruelty. Such armchair psychology resonated in interesting ways with the issue's final article, a nasty "put-down" titled "The American Woman Is a Waste of Good Flesh." The main point of J. C. Thomas's screed was to insist on the relevance of the previous decade's discourse of male victimization. Praising Philip Wylie's *Generation of Vipers*, which I discussed in chapter 1, Thomas glossed the representative figure of "momism" as "an all-smothering, all-possessive, all-encompassing, and all-powerful disseminator of authority." Momism had come to define social relations "partly through the American male's letting down his guard once too often," Thomas said, and it would continue to do so unless "the American man"—and here he addressed the reader directly—let women know "that you, and *only* you, are running this show."[38] At first glance, it would seem Thomas was arguing the opposite of Slim: there was too much motherly devotion in society, and that was sapping the vitalism of the American male. In fact, though, they were arguing two sides of the same coin: the matriarchalization of American culture was the dominant trend against which the exceptional male rebelled, disclaiming any need for care or "affection." Real men needed only to rely on themselves.

Slim's appearance in *Rogue* was tied to the release of his new book, *Mama Black Widow*. The interview prepared the reader for what was to come. If *Pimp* had been an exercise in cruelty, this novel would be a study of grievance—a literary sociology of momism in black. For the book, Slim subordinated the male ego-gratifying conventions of sleaze to the task of writing a genuine cautionary tale.[39] His warning: this is what happens to black masculinity when momism is allowed to go unchecked.

Like *Trick Baby*, *Mama Black Widow* is a novel masquerading as biography. Slim reprises the frame narrative in which his fictional persona appears as an interlocutor to the protagonist. It is February 1969. Iceberg is visiting Otis Tilson, "an incredibly comely and tragic homosexual queen" with whom he was acquainted during his pimping days in Chicago. Entering Otis's "third rate" hotel room, Iceberg encounters a "tall young black stud with a natural hair-do and a hostile face"—Otis's jealous lover. After the man stalks out, Otis brags, "He's . . . fatally in love with my old hot yellow asshole and also is afraid I might suck a new cock." Otis is a bigger, broader personality than White Folks, and his memoir would seem to demand extra reassurance that it is true. So just as Richard Milner sat down with Slim for a taped conversation, Iceberg takes out his tape recorder and lets Otis do the talking. His aim, he tells his subject, is "to lift your whole story off the tape and put it in the book, gutsy and like it is."[40] Leo Guild could not have written it better.

With the tape rolling, Otis reveals his reason for telling Iceberg his story: "I'm doing it for my poor dead Papa and myself and the thousands of black men like him in ghetto torture chambers who have been and will be niggerized and deballed by the white power structure and its thrill-kill police."[41] Otis's fiery statement is boilerplate Black Power rhetoric. The notion that racial oppression is best understood as the symbolic castration of black men would have rhymed with ideologies promulgated by cultural nationalists and revolutionary socialists alike. But *Mama Black Widow* does not, in fact, tell that story. Instead, it recounts the life of a transvestite trying to free himself from the clutches of his domineering mother, Sedalia. She is a classic Wyliean figure: selfish, predatory, controlling—if Slim had not used the black widow metaphor, he would have said "bitch." (He kind of does in chapter 1's clever title, "Mama You Mother . . . !") Over the course of the narrative, Slim shows how responsibility for the demise of the Tilson family should be laid squarely at her feet. Mama is so cruel and uncompromising that her abuse directly or indirectly leads to the deaths of her husband and two daughters and to the incarceration of her other son. Otis, a mama's boy par excellence, is the only family member to survive. Yet the price he pays is to live as a "niggerized and deballed" black man—the stereotypical "invert" of armchair psychology.[42]

Otis's first-person narrative spans almost fifty years (1919–68). It tracks the Tilsons' sharecropping life in Meridian, Mississippi, their migration to Chicago, and their eventual destruction by events set in motion by Mama. An important theme in the novel is the withering of "traditional" black masculinity—represented by Papa's God-fearing, wage-earning, and humble life in the South—in the black ghettos of the North.[43] Before the Tilsons migrate to Chicago in 1936, Papa, or

Frank, ekes out a living on a white-owned cotton plantation. But when an inheritance grants them the opportunity to move out of the South, everyone "except Papa was thrilled and excited at the prospect of going to the enchanted North." Otis reveals that the decision to migrate is Mama's, and that it is informed less by what would be good for the family and more by her pursuit of the fast life, which her cousin Bunny already enjoys. Predictably, Papa suffers the consequences of Mama's selfish actions soon after they arrive in Chicago. Highlighting his "smallness" in the city, Papa's hand-me-down clothes are described as too big—they make him "look like a child masquerading in his father's storm coat and boots." That metaphor rhymes with the fact that Papa cannot get a job because of the color prejudice exercised by the trade unions; they "didn't accept blacks as members or apprentices," Otis recalls.[44] Thus locked out of a breadwinning role—the primary means by which husbands and fathers could identify as men—Papa's pride is damaged and he begins to drink heavily.

As soon as Slim broaches the root cause of Papa's ruination, he steps back and, again, points the finger at Mama. The narrative turns decisively against her when she begins to work in Papa's stead. Papa is determined not to "fail" his family, but financial necessity demands that Mama seek work as a domestic to bring in some income. Once this shift in breadwinning roles transpires, Slim carries the parents' traits to the extreme, rendering Mama unabashedly narcissistic and Papa irredeemably pathetic. Mama starts going out with a local minister, not caring to hide her indiscretions from Papa, who is forced to stand by in "slaw jaw shock and awful anguish." Mama retorts to her daughter Bessie, "Ah'm the onlyess wuk hoss 'roun heah, and Ah'm gonna pleshu mahsef lak Ah don at uh bankit afta chuch." Papa's social and sexual redundancy is sealed the night he tries coming on to Mama, asking, "Whut's wrong wif uh man pattin' whut's his'n[?]" Her response is a symbolic death blow: "Niggah, git you paws offen me. Ah ain't gappin' mah laigs fer you. Uh man foots th bills fer whuts his'n. Mabbe yu is uh drunkard and mabbe you uh tramp. You sumpthin, but for sho you ain't no man."[45] According to Sedalia's logic, Frank's loss of breadwinning status negates his role as a husband and father. Papa moves out of the Tilson apartment shortly thereafter and lives on his own until his death in 1941.

In response to Frank's demise, the novel's moral center and Papa's only friend, a black man named Soldier Boy, gives voice to the crisis of black masculinity that both white racism and Mama have engendered. In a monologue notable for its clear-headed social commentary in "proper" English, Soldier Boy solemnly reflects, "There are many black women who understand that black men living in this hell hole life where the white man has a strangle hold on the life line, goods and services, need their black women fighting the enemy with them, not unwittingly helping the enemy to uproot the black family. Black women who don't understand this and crush their men are pathetic fools."[46] Soldier Boy's monologue is as damning an indictment of black motherhood as anything Wylie wrote about momism. By colluding with "the enemy," he says, black women rob men of their dignity and respect. Imagining the situation in militaristic terms, the aptly named Soldier Boy describes how black men are in a sense betrayed from within their own homes, thanks to women who simply won't let them be men.

Soldier Boy is a mouthpiece not only for momism but for ideas promulgated by the US Department of Labor's study *The Negro Family: The Case for National Action*, also known as the Moynihan Report.[47] Released in 1965, the report controversially tied high rates of black poverty to "the deterioration of the Negro family." Proceeding from the notion that the male-headed household is "the basic social unit of American life" and the basis for middle-class stability, Moynihan suggested that African Americans' female-headed households retarded their social advancement. He touched on historical causes for the current situation, including how slavery and segregation had interrupted black men's taking up their "natural" position as the head of the household. But the most important cause, Moynihan argued, came from within the black family itself: women who wore the proverbial pants. In a chapter titled "The Tangle of Pathology," he wrote:

There is, presumably, no special reason why a society in which males are dominant in family relationships is to be preferred to a matriarchal arrangement.

However, it is clearly a disadvantage for a minority group to be operating on one principle, while the great majority of the population, and the one with the most advantages to begin with, is operating on another. This is the present situation of the Negro. Ours is a society which presumes male leadership in public and private affairs. The arrangements of society facilitate such leadership and reward it. A subculture, such as that of the Negro American, in which this is not the pattern, is placed at a distinct disadvantage.[48]

Moynihan's was an all-out attack on black single mothers and women breadwinners, but by couching his ideas in the language of norms, he made black poverty sound eminently reasonable, a function of social maladjustment. So long as American political economy was patriarchally organized, he argued, black households led by women would operate at a "distinct disadvantage." His report thus turned structural inequality into a family affair, narrowing the public's understanding of racial oppression into a primal struggle between mother and her kin.

Husbands were not the only ones liable to suffer from a "deviant" matriarchal family structure. In keeping with Moynihan's study, Slim's "black widow" can refer both to an arachnid and to a black woman who has made her husband disappear. But her "strangling web" of abuse profoundly affects her children too. Frank Jr. rebels against the image of his weak father and takes to the streets as a small-time hoodlum. Bessie bides her time outside of school by hanging out with a neighbor, Sally, who introduces her to the world of urban prostitution. Carol, the sibling to whom Otis can relate the best, has a steady waitressing job and begins dating a white ethnic German; when she gets pregnant by him, however, Mama lashes out at her, forcing a miscarriage that results in Carol hemorrhaging to death. Her brazen wielding of phallic power has a more intricate effect on Otis: she turns him inside out, implanting in his psyche an alter ego who dresses up in drag and has sex with men. Otis names her Sally "in contemptible memory of the 'come [sic] dump' that had led big dumb Bessie to ruin."[49] In other words, Otis has internalized Mama's prohibition of the father's social and sexual agency. As such, he repeats the psychic experience of male "passivity" by identifying as a woman and having gay sex. This is Slim's idea of a very bad masquerade.

Because gay sex is so tightly bound up with emasculation in the narrative, Otis never experiences it as desire; it is, rather, a compulsion. He readily acknowledges as much at the beginning of the novel: "Each time I'd want to die as I lay there alone with the pungent slime oozing from me. I'd cry my heart out in the lonely darkness in remorse for the abuse, humiliation and shame of it all, and guilt that I had set the bitch inside me free." Otis is perspicacious enough to realize this, yet he is helpless in preventing his masochistic drive from overtaking him. In fact, shortly after this moment of clarity, he submits to his alter ego completely, and it is Sally who then has him dress up as Tilly, his drag persona. A double inversion of black masculinity, Tilly becomes the vehicle for Slim to confirm Otis's subjective pulverization. At a house party for sexual outcasts, Tilly, throwing caution to the wind, goes to bed with a stranger named Big Lovell, also known as Lovee. Lovee's huge stature, "gorilla face," and "fat lips" all fail to warn her of his potential monstrosity. Sure enough, Lovee turns out to be a hustler. He steals Tilly's money, beats her to a pulp, and penetrates her with a penis that appears to grow with each adjective Slim uses to describe it: "terri-fying—horselike—monstrous—deformed—impossible!" The brutality of the attack—"horrible rending pain exploded through the raw core of my being like I had been halved by an axe"—drives home for Otis how truly debased his condition is. Yet rather than blame or seek revenge on Lovee for raping him (a postcoital moment gives him the chance to plunge a knife into the man's heart, but he cannot bring himself to do it), Otis, as predicted, feels ashamed; it was "the treacherous bitch, Sally," he concludes, who let him down.[50]

Scholarly commentary on *Mama Black Widow* has tended to appreci-ate Slim's representation of Otis's sexual transitivity as both ahead of its time and sincere in its execution. Justin Gifford, for example, claims that the book is "one of the few African American novels during this period to deal explicitly with homosexual characters and themes." And Marlon B. Ross makes it sound like a black working-class version of James Baldwin's *Giovanni's Room* (1956): the book "tells the story of a black swishing sissy, Otis Tilson, as he tragically searches for love and tenderness in the harsh underworld of 'vice' criminality."[51] What these readings tend to overlook is the inextricability of stigma from a literary commodity whose conditions of possibility required it. For just as there was a mass market for black sleaze, so was there one for gay and lesbian sleaze. In this market, sexual transitivity was a device that prompted lurid fascination at sexual behavior that was deemed "abnormal." In 1964, Paul Gillette worked on another hack assignment in this vein. His editor at *Peril* wrote, "Please do a re-write of attached old story I had in Hush-Hush. Material is excellent but for Peril, please ROUGH IT UP, USE DIALOG and MORE DESCRIPTIONS. In short, make it less authentic and *more sensational*." The title of the piece would be "Creeps from Queers-ville: The Scandal of Those Transvestites." It was a fairly ordinary as-signment for Gillette: rework old material, accentuating elements that would elicit both interest and disgust. The editor even noted for good measure, "USE as dramatized lead the story with the black nightie on page 44 and then go ahead as you see fit."[52]

Slim uses the same device—the objectifying "dramatized lead"—in *Mama Black Widow*. Iceberg announces it when he begins interviewing Otis: "Start your story with Dorcas and that first time you lived with her as a stud." Daughter of the local undertaker, Dorcas is Otis's on-and-off-again female love interest, the girl he should marry if he were straight. Set in 1968, the novel's frame-within-a-frame narrative actu-ally exposes a by-now middle-aged Otis to be a failing stud. "What's wrong with me, Otis? Why is it so hard for you to make love to me?"

Dorcas complains. To which the narrator confesses: "I just lay there squeezing the limp flesh between my sweaty thighs and feeling desperate helplessness and panic." Slim outlines in excruciating detail the kind of mental acrobatics Otis must engage in so that he can have sex with Dorcas. He imagines that her "tits" are "jerking like monstrous male organs in climax"; excited, he "gnaw[s] and suck[s] at the heaving humps." But as soon as he is surrounded by her "fat softness," he feels himself "collapsing inside her."[53] The only way Otis is able to recover is to fantasize about an ex-lover, Mike, who we later learn is as serially abusive toward him as Lovee was that one night at the party.

The point of this introduction to Otis is not to feel sorry for him but to pathologize his "condition." To use the language of sleaze, it is a case study in "perversion." Indeed, I would contend that Dorcas's function throughout the novel is to remind the reader: *lose your mother or else.* From the moment he meets her, in May 1945, Otis seems to intuit that Dorcas is the only person who can free him from Mama's spell. But when he tries to explain to Sedalia why he is attracted to her—she is "nineteen and statuesque"—her reply cuts him down to size: "She's what?" Mama implies that this is an unnatural desire. A word like "statuesque" is something only the "smart and classy" Dorcas would use. "A slum fellow like you don't have a chance with a girl like that," she says. And yet Otis does have a chance with her. The problem is not Dorcas's middle-class background but what he openly confesses to Mama in the same conversation: "I can't escape because something like a bitch dog is hot inside me, filthy freakish and itching for guys." Mama pooh-poohs this admission and puts him back under her spell. She addresses Otis by the diminutive nickname that only she uses to speak to him: "Sweet Pea, love, honor and appreciate your Mama and make me happy like a man would and you will never be a man lover." Such false reassurance ensnares him even further in her web, leaving Otis to rue, "Dorcas is fuckish as hell. She wants to fuck me! But I didn't even get a little hard when we were together."[54]

Otis never does get over Mama: he continues to allow men to exploit and punish him, and his melodramatic romance with Dorcas withers on the vine. He makes one final stand toward the end of the book in the frame-within-a-frame narrative. After the sexual fiasco with Dorcas, he pays a visit to Sedalia and announces: "I should have amounted to something besides an aging cocksucker. If you hadn't killed and smothered every instinct and striving of manhood you ever saw in me. Mama, I'm leaving in the morning. I have to know what life is like without you." The next morning, as Otis is about to leave, Mama lashes out at him, nearly missing his throat with a pair of scissors. Otis leaves her abode as the words of Dr. King ring in his ears: "Free at last! Free at last! Great God Almighty I'm free at last!"[55]

Slim dates this scene to May 1968, one month after Dr. King's assassination. In the epilogue, Iceberg reappears in April 1969. Otis's joy, it turns out, was short-lived. Iceberg has just received word that Otis hanged himself "in a skid row hotel in New York City." Upon learning this news, he muses, "Perhaps the final solution to the torture of spirit and body that he endured could only be death."[56] Echoing the Nazi phrase for the systematic genocide of the Jewish people, Slim, the author, does not merely caution the reader about the perils of momism—he appeals to his better judgment to lose his mother.

In 1970 Holloway House released Delle Brehan's *Kicks Is Kicks*, an ostensible memoir by New York's top black woman dominatrix. Billed on its back cover as "a somber revelation of the warped manner in which some men seek love," the book promised to bring a bit of the slaver into the sex confessional. "Well-dressed businessmen beg for the privilege of groveling at her feet," the cover drooled, "for the exquisite humiliation of being stripped, tied, whipped, stepped on." These self-identified "slaves," it continued, flock to Delle and earn her "wealth and fame as the Black Bitch, the iron-willed Queen of Pain, who could break any man's pride and make him beg for mercy."[57] Interracial attraction, female dominance, the identification of white men with the position of the "slave": the positions might have been changed up, but *Kicks Is Kicks* was just the latest entry in Holloway House's catalog of black sleaze.

Kicks Is Kicks would have been sent out to retailers along with another book published in 1970, *Black Sexual Power*. As I mentioned in chapter 1, All America Distributors Corporation (AADC) oversaw distribution of the various print commodities Morriss owned, from *Adam* and *Knight* to Holloway House paperbacks. But AADC also had distribution deals with other sleaze entities. *Black Sexual Power*'s publisher—Century Books, an imprint of the mysteriously named corporation K.D.S.—was one of them. Though not a Holloway House title, *Black Sexual Power* drew from the same formulas on which Gillette and Guild had relied, this time to exploit black male sexuality. As figure 3.3 shows, the book's subject, Leroy Brown, was supposed to be "BIG, VIRILE, HANDSOME, AND BLACK," a sexual radical who sought to make "ONLY YOUNG WHITE WOMEN . . . HIS LOVE PARTNERS." To the extent that Brown's story had been "told to" Roger Blake, PhD, *Black Sexual Power* identified itself as

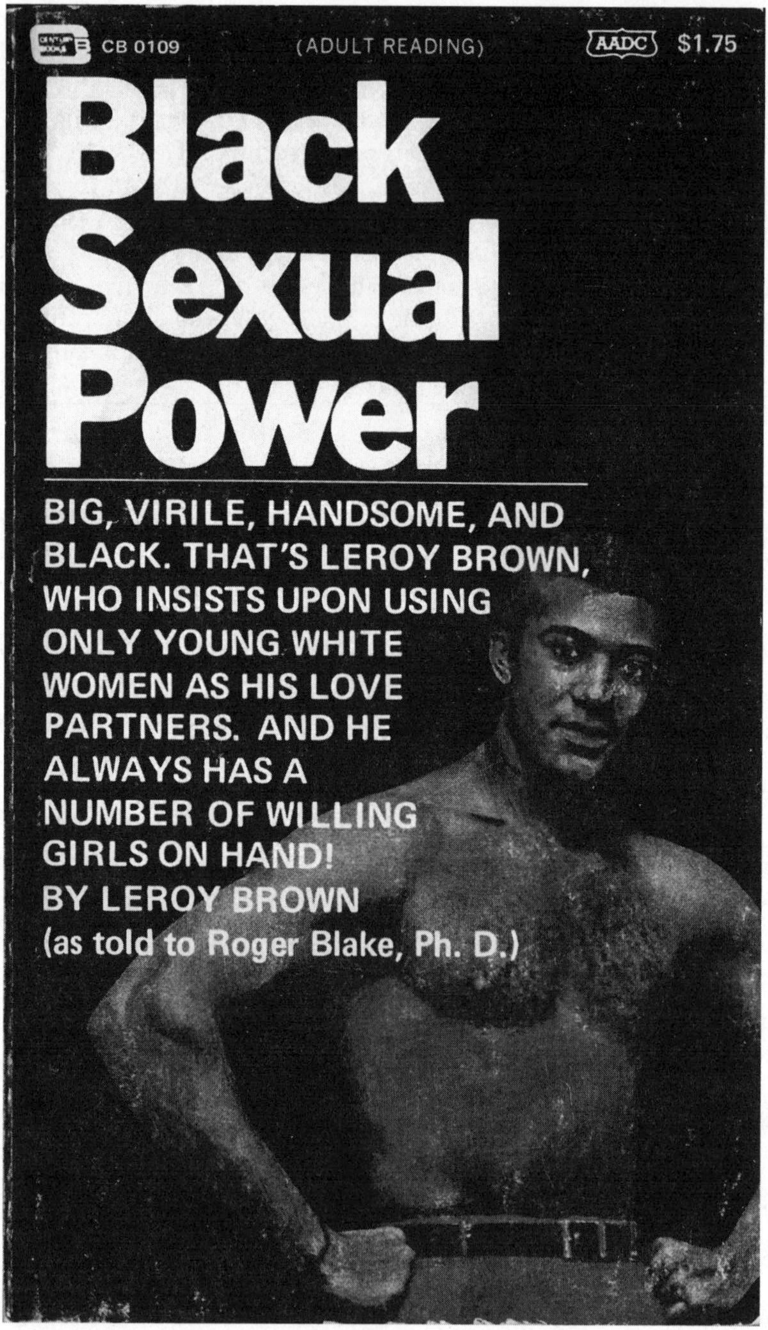

CB 0109 (ADULT READING) AADC $1.75

Black Sexual Power

BIG, VIRILE, HANDSOME, AND
BLACK. THAT'S LEROY BROWN,
WHO INSISTS UPON USING
ONLY YOUNG WHITE
WOMEN AS HIS LOVE
PARTNERS. AND HE
ALWAYS HAS A
NUMBER OF WILLING
GIRLS ON HAND!
BY LEROY BROWN
(as told to Roger Blake, Ph. D.)

FIGURE 3.3 Front cover of *Black Sexual Power* (1970).

one of the scores of sleaze books that used the excuse of exploring human behavior as a pretext for delighting in literary porn. That sexological frame was then filled in by black sleaze's core ideology: namely, that interracial sex acts did not augur actual racial revolution. To that point, the back cover reassured readers that Brown was "an upper-middle-class black man who 'knows his place'—except when it comes to sex!" And it quoted Brown saying as much: "I go in the back door, like a good nigger . . . but so what? I still make the white women hungry for my black body. MY black body!" Dr. Blake, the cover concluded, is Brown's "therapist," faithfully recounting his patient's exploits.[58]

A lot of lays without a hint of liberation: could there be any doubt that *Black Sexual Power* was a race liberal's sexual fantasy? "Leroy Brown" was no more real than any of the hundreds of personas Gillette assumed in his hack writing as a psychologist. What about its co-retailed sidekick *Kicks Is Kicks*? Delle Brehan has not been linked to any of Holloway House's known ghostwriters; the book is copyrighted under that name. Could Brehan have been a real person? Unlikely, for her narrative begins, "I want to be honest with you." In the world of sleaze, that confessional gesture practically announces the book's fictionality—something that the very next page seems to confirm. Describing how she "wrote" her memoirs, Brehan says she "got a tape recorder, put it all down and got a friend of mine who is a writer to put it on paper." Then, gratuitously, she explains, "I told him that if I came out soundin' lahk a li'l ole nigger gal who eats poke chops and doan axe no questions, I would brain him. If you do not believe I could do it, read on my friend. You will find that although I am only five foot five, there is something inside which gives me power."[59] Like Brown, Brehan refers to herself as a "nigger" before claiming some kind of "black sexual power." And thus, like Brown, she was a perfect fiction for the race liberal's imagination.[60]

That went for all black-authored books that Holloway House published and AADC distributed during this period. As I bring part 1 of this book to a close, it bears reiterating that Slim, Lomax, deCoy, and Brehan were originally consumed by white men expecting to encounter the obscene in black social life. The idea of black authorship was set up to reinforce that expectation—that is, to mirror what white men were looking for in sleaze. It mattered little whether a book was actually penned by a black person. In the final analysis, all race-oriented books coming out of Holloway House and AADC were projections of the white imagination.

It would take a large-scale reorientation of their publishing enterprise for Morriss and Weinstock to turn away from black sleaze and embrace black pulp fiction. That did happen over a key transitional period at Holloway House, which is the subject of part 2 of this book. But as I hope part 1 has implied, the reorientation came about only because it made good business sense.

PART TWO

Transitions

FOUR

Missing the Revolution

In 1969 Black Arts editor and essayist Larry Neal published his first collection of poems, *Black Boogaloo (Notes on Black Liberation)*, with the Journal of Black Poetry Press. Run by friend and fellow editor Joe Goncalves, the San Francisco–based press was one of the most important outlets for radical poetry during this period. Neal had just put out the movement-defining anthology *Black Fire* (1968) with co-editor LeRoi Jones (soon to be Amiri Baraka), and he was keen to have his work exemplify Black Arts's revolutionary commitments. In a collection brimming with militant feeling, one poem stood out for its second-person mode of address: "Brother Pimp." The poem's dedication left little doubt as to whom it was directed: "In memory of Iceberg Slim and others who have walked these streets."[1] By confining Slim to the past ("in memory"), Neal hoped readers would see the icon as a ghetto relic, a vestige of prerevolutionary times. He organized the poem around this temporal conceit.

As the poem begins, Slim (or a figure like him) is brought back to the present as a temporal foil for the black revolution:

Brother Pimp, you ain't shit;
and neither are we without you.
I used to dig your hip ways,
but you ain't shit yet;
and neither are we without you.
you just as bad as the honky,
only you dress better motherfucker,

only you drive your cadillac better mother-
fuck-er.[2]

Although the speaker passes harsh judgment against the pimp, he also
acknowledges that he "used to" look up to him. The presumable reason for his change of perspective is a political awakening—coming to
the realization that the pimp's mystique is rooted in exploitation. Crucially, this transformation is held out to the pimp himself: he "ain't
shit *yet*" (emphasis added), which implies that he could be "the shit" if
he were to reform his ways. If he does not, however, he risks reverting
to the debased condition of being a "mother- / fuck-er." By emphasizing the literal meaning of the obscenity, the enjambed hyphenation
makes incest constitutive to the pimp's masculinity. His allure ("dress
better," "cadillac"), the speaker implies, is a ruse covering up the fact
that he is fixated on his mother.

As severe as the poem is in its criticism, the speaker ultimately encourages the pimp to redirect his talents toward revolutionary causes.
In this sense, the "ain't-yet"-ness of the pimp's masculinity cuts both
ways: it defines his persona as incomplete or lacking at the same time
that it holds out hope for its reform. This is why the speaker grudgingly
admits:

you are genius black men of the streets,
have learned to survive.
we need you.
you are wise, aware of all games,
we need your minds.
you are the base of our thing.
you are the roots of our black power,
would-be brother.
you are the essence of style, that which
we gleaned from the raw underbelly of the city.

Here the speaker acknowledges that the pimp possesses characteris-
tics—vernacular style, street smarts, an indomitable will to survive—
that can be harnessed to political struggle. The phallic symbolism ("the
base of our thing") and conditional flattery all amount to a promise:
that the pimp may reclaim his masculinity by joining the cause. The
question is whether the pimp will decide to "pimp for the revolution, /
[or] pimp on the revolution."[3]

Acts of interpretation like Neal's helped distinguish *black pulp fic-*

tion, or male-oriented crime, espionage, and action-adventure novels written by black authors for black readers, from black sleaze. Neal may have had harsh words for Slim, but he legitimated that which Holloway House alone never could: the pimp's authentic place in African American culture. Here was a black reader who, despite significant qualms, could at least see himself in Slim. This was key, for as long as Neal acknowledged Slim as a "brother" and not simply as a screen for white fantasy, then there was hope for the pimp to redirect his subcultural knowledge toward the revolution. It took readers like Neal to help Bentley Morriss and Ralph Weinstock realize that black men were interested in their enterprise for something more than just tabloid eroticism. This was the opening Holloway House needed to reorient its catalog.

In part 2 of this book, I examine how Holloway House removed black-authored paperbacks from the sleaze market and positioned them in their own niche. This niche would eventually become the black literary underground. The next two chapters cover the years 1971 to 1973, a period when Morriss and Weinstock began dividing their catalog according to books that would sell to blacks and books that would continue to sell to whites. The publishing milieu for what we can now call black pulp fiction underwent a radical transformation during this time. The changes consequent to that shift merit extended consideration.

In this chapter, I consider Slim's role in turning Holloway House away from sleaze interracialism and toward the interests of black readers. His role, I argue, was to play out the contradiction at the heart of "Brother Pimp": disavow the past but leave enough room to capitalize on past glory. Concretely, this took the form of Slim stepping out from behind his pen name. In the early 1970s, the author—in media interviews and in an important book of nonfiction prose—sought to distinguish the "real" Robert Beck from Iceberg Slim. By doing so, he hoped to address black readers directly and lay bare the truth of his sordid past. He wanted to exorcise Iceberg Slim. The pen name, however, was inescapable—a necessary fiction, the actual source of his celebrity. Readers made clear that it legitimated Slim's status as a culture hero, identifying him as someone who, though perhaps not fit for emulation, was an authentic voice of bygone days. Neal could see himself in Iceberg Slim, not Robert Beck. Caught between these two imperatives—of disavowing yet needing the past—Slim in this period continually performed his stuckness in history. He was the key to authenticating Holloway House as a publisher of books for black readers, but the price for keeping his street credibility was to represent himself as perpetually missing the revolution.

Pimping out of Step

When black liberation came to Holloway House, it was not a political necessity so much as a business opportunity—a way for the company to rebrand in light of its growing black readership. *The Naked Soul of Iceberg Slim* (1971) would be the cornerstone of that effort. The main purpose of this collection of short prose pieces was to announce Slim's conversion, albeit belated, to Black Power. Appropriately enough, it began with a subtle response to the opening of Larry Neal's "Brother Pimp." *Naked Soul* was dedicated to "the heroic memory of Malcolm X, Jack Johnson, Melvin X, Jonathan Jackson; to Huey P. Newton, Bobby Seale, Ericka Huggins, George Jackson, Angela Davis; and to all street niggers and strugglers in and out of the joints."[4] By aligning revolutionary icons with "street niggers and strugglers," Slim was not only recouping his reputation—he was suggesting that the criminalization of political leaders and of ordinary black people were of a piece. He even underscored the point by stretching Neal's temporal conceit to include past ("heroic memory"), present, and presumable future. It was the kind of sentence one could hardly fathom Slim penning just a few years earlier.

Holloway House's investment in *Naked Soul* could be gleaned from the rambling introduction by Slim's editor Milton Van Sickle. The first sentence pulled off the mask: "Robert Beck—or Iceberg Slim as his people know him—is living evidence (for those who need it) that times have not changed—only the con." Van Sickle's use of the phrase "his people" once again gestured to an implied white reader. But that presumption was itself challenged by the idea that Beck, not Slim, was finally speaking his own mind. And on that count, what he had to say challenged white sensibilities:

Today the con is, "We must have Law and Order. Now civil rights legislation is being passed. Justice will come—but it takes time." (Tomorrow, the con will be something like, "You can't get anything by bloodshed. Take it easy. Justice will come.") The truth is, nothing has changed. The same Establishment against which Jack Johnson fought single handedly [sic] (see *The Big Black Fire* by Robert H. deCoy—the only biography of the greatest fighter prior to Muhammed [sic] Ali which captures the essence of the man and his times), the same Establishment that murdered Bessie Smith, the same Establishment that murdered Malcolm X and Melvin X—to say nothing of the nameless thousands every year in the collective ghetto of our nation—that is the Establishment of today—and it hasn't yielded one inch in all this time.[5]

If Slim's early fame rested on his reputation for bringing a new voice to the adult reading market, here, in 1971, he was being extolled for repeating a timeworn truth: that the "Establishment" had a vested interest in keeping black people down. In playing down Slim's sleaze origins and bringing deCoy along with him in the process, Van Sickle was actually rebranding Holloway House as a place where counterestablishment energies could be focalized.

Slim, in *Naked Soul*, lives up to the billing. The book is a wrenching confessional, a performance of abjection on par with *Mama Black Widow*, but made more poignant by use of the first-person voice. Slim's introspective "I" looks back on the past with a fair amount of regret. He warns readers that, "trauma for trauma, a pimp's life is perhaps the worst type of life anybody could live." Despite seeming evidence to the contrary—the fancy car and glamorous accouterments, pockets lined with cash—the pimp, he insists, cuts an anguished figure: he "is feared, hated, despised and walks a greased wire with the penitentiary on one side and his death on the other." The pimp, in sum, "lives his life with a stick of dynamite stuck in his rectum."[6] Slim's loaded image refers to the incredible stress under which the pimp operates; one false move and he is done. But it is also an apt symbol of the fragility of Iceberg's manhood. Struggling to keep everything in (line), the pimp is not so much cool as uptight.

Waste, it turns out, is the key to understanding the distinction *Naked Soul* draws between the youthful, preconscious Iceberg and the present-day, self-flagellating Beck. "I feel no envy for pimps—only pity that they waste their youth and intellect," he writes.[7] Of course, if Slim is to be taken seriously, then the judgment he must cast on his own life is that he has wasted his own youth and intellect. And this is the tricky proposition of *Naked Soul*: that Iceberg is a prime example of what not to do with one's talents. Instead, it is the example of black nationalists that urban youth in 1971 should follow. In order to make such a case, Slim frames the full sweep of his life as redeemable only by the virile, phallus-oriented politics of Black Power. Slim had just turned fifty-three in August of 1971, and throughout *Naked Soul* he uses his advanced age as a standard against which urban youth should define themselves. I call his staged performance of contrite authorship *redemptive anachronicity*.

A key part of this performance is Slim's attempt to reconcile with his estranged father, who abandoned him when he was a child. In a letter dated May 10, 1970, Slim addresses Papa and apologizes for cruelly rebuffing his previous requests for help. In hindsight, Slim sees how "America's racism . . . warped and twisted legions of innately good black men, causing the vital vine of black family stability and strength to be poisoned, hacked down by the pity, fear and hatred of black children." Slim regrets his earlier feelings of resentment. In his youth, he failed to appreciate how black men like his father were "forced to abdicate manhood in the racist, brute crucible that is America." But today, amidst the black revolt, Slim grasps how his plight is interlinked with that of previous generations. He can finally identify with his father. To be sure, this newfound sympathy is a direct result of Slim being labeled an old-timer himself. "Young black militants," he writes, feel resentful of "elderly and middle-age black men whose survival tactics—for themselves and their loved ones—seen through history's unflattering lens appear the antics of despicable Uncle Toms marinated in cowardice." There is no denying his past exploits, of course. All Slim can hope for is that these militants come to accept him in the same way he has chosen to embrace Papa. For "we older black men," he says, urban radicals are "the young rejuvenators of our balls"—their only hope of a properly masculine salvation.[8]

The turn toward militancy as a corrective to black men's social impotence is realized most fully in Slim's essay on visiting the headquarters of the Southern California Black Panther Party, which had come under attack by the Los Angeles Police Department on December 8, 1969. The first Panther Slim met "hesitated for a long moment before he smiled thinly and slapped his palm against [his own]." Neal's "Brother Pimp" is the hidden score for this initially wary but finally accepting gesture. After a few more exchanges, Slim notes with some amusement, "Unlike the hundreds of non-Panther black youngsters who had recognized me on the street and admired me as a kind of folk hero . . . the Panther youngsters were blind to my negative glamour and, in fact, expressed a polite disdain for my former profession and its phony flash of big cars, jewelry and clothes." Even when another man stepped up to challenge his reputation directly, Slim says he remained calm and "responded with love and understanding." He accepted the fact that he was an "old nigger surrounded by Black Panthers." The essay concludes with Slim remembering how he continued to take the "violent tongue thrashing" because it revealed a valuable lesson to him: not only were these young men the "antithesis of the distorted image carried in the collective mind of America's older, brainwashed blacks"; they were the "authentic champions and heroes of the black race." In awe of this revolutionary embodiment of black masculinity, Slim concedes, pathetically, that the

Panthers were "superior to that older generation of physical cowards of which I am a part."[9]

The protest novelist John A. Williams penned a lukewarm review of the book for San Francisco's African American newspaper the *Sun Reporter*. Surveying Slim's career, he wrote that the author was "untouchable as far as vivid expression" was concerned but that his style was a confounding "mixture of deep, deep street talk and high validictorian [sic] English." *Naked Soul* evinced a similar tension between content and tone. Williams wrote that, although Slim struck a "very militant" note, he came across "like a weary traveler who had missed his scheduled train and has hopped one that was a little too fast for a man his age." In other words, *Naked Soul* felt strained, pulled in two directions at once. Slim was trying "to face himself as a man of his people; to reveal himself body and soul completely naked," but his overwrought performance of anachronicity, which Williams diagnosed as coming from Slim's feeling "ashamed" of his past, only served to conceal his identity further. Thus, he wrote, readers were "cheated out of the real and true 'Naked Soul.'"[10]

Williams's review was directly contradicted by Holloway House's marketing of the paperback. The front cover of *Naked Soul* intended to unmask Beck, the man behind the Iceberg persona and the Slim pen name (figure 4.1). In stark contrast to the *Joe Pyne* appearance, the portrait of the author on this surface promised to bare all, to be "naked" in front of the eyes of the reader. The back of the book repeated Van Sickle's erroneous assertion that "Iceberg" had been Beck's "ghetto name," but even though this was a lie, its gesture of unmasking again painted the author in a positive light. Indeed, rather than focus on Slim's anachronicity, as Williams did, the rest of the copy accentuated Slim's redemption: "Don't cry for his soul because he's Black. Though Black is pain. Black is death. Black is despair. Black is the ghetto where he was born. . . . He cured himself of the ghetto rot. To write—as no other man ever has—about his people and his life. His name is Robert Beck."[11] Offering nary a word about Slim's support for black nationalism, Holloway House equivocated that the author's individual success could somehow stand in for collective liberation.

So which was it—Iceberg Slim or Robert Beck? Which persona would solidify the author's status among African American readers? Holloway House did not end up having to choose. It was precisely Slim's ability to straddle these divisions—reactionary versus revolutionary, pimp versus prophet—that made his discourse appealing to the black press. Up

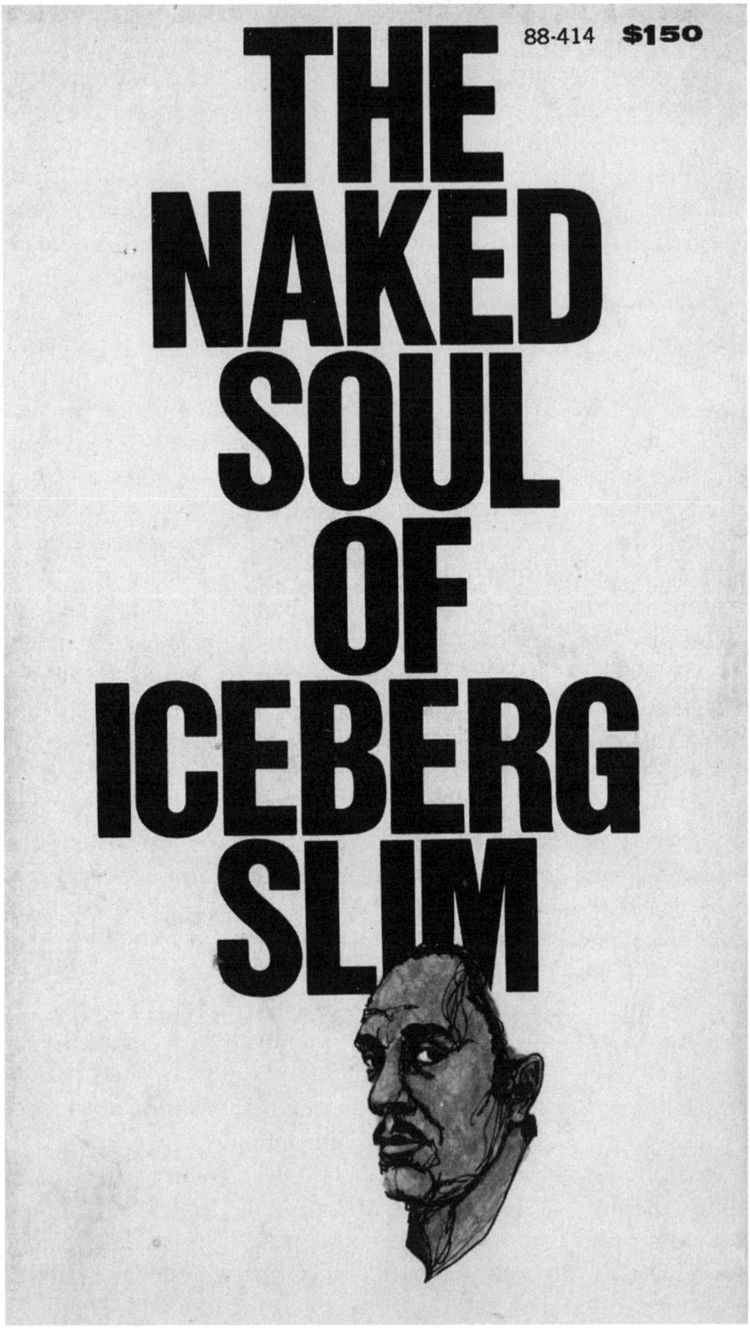

88-414 **$150**

THE NAKED SOUL OF ICEBERG SLIM

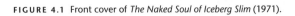

FIGURE 4.1 Front cover of *The Naked Soul of Iceberg Slim* (1971).

to this point, African American newspapers and magazines had passed over Holloway House paperbacks in reviewing contemporary literature. This made sense given that, as chapter 3 showed, the company's catalog had been bound up with the thinly veiled minstrelsy of black sleaze. *Naked Soul* was different. It stood out from the pack for its anti-masquerade masquerade. By promising to lift the veil on this mysterious author, the book advanced its own metadiscourse about the stakes of reading his work. This, in turn, made Slim inherently interesting to black media outlets. Whatever one thought of him, he was a lightning rod for debate and conversation. That his soul was divided became a talking point in itself.

All of which helps frame a defining appearance for the author on the African American–run television show *Black Journal*. The November 2, 1971, episode, "The Black Pimp," featured a long interview with Slim, highlighted clips of him lecturing to a college audience, and dramatized scenes from *Pimp*. Produced under the auspices of the public broadcasting company National Educational Television, *Black Journal* was a current affairs program that disseminated news about Black Power to urban communities. African Americans were the driving forces in front of and behind the show's camera.[12] For "The Black Pimp" episode, producers enlisted the Chicago Black Arts performance group Kuumba Workshop to stage the vignettes from *Pimp* that viewers then were meant to find appalling. The twelve-minute segment opened the broadcast that night, and Slim was introduced as Robert Beck.

Kuumba provided four actors for the episode, which was shot in Chicago. The workshop had been founded in 1968 by Francis and Val Gray Ward, a husband and wife team committed to the Black Arts scene locally and to radical theater and performance art nationally. The workshop's mission, as they defined it, was clear: "to accept any Black person committed to its ideals and principles of art, professional or not." Those "ideals and principles" lined up perfectly with Black Arts' overarching goal of "contributing to the Black liberation struggle through creative force."[13] In short, there was no better local group with whom Slim and the New York–based *Black Journal* team could collaborate to pull off "The Black Pimp." Kuumba had the credentials to legitimate Slim's coming out as Robert Beck to the media, and its participation formed a bridge between the author and the black community. Indeed, in an early story published about the project's filming, the *Chicago Defender* framed the planned episode in terms exactly resonant with Neal's poetic description of a radicalized (ex-)pimp: "Director [William] Gaddis and author Beck expressed admiration for the strength that is required for a black man to exist as a hustler, but hope that the film will show blacks that hustling is not in the best interest of blacks building a nation."[14] This was Slim's best shot at a major rebranding.

The majority of the episode contrasts an aging but still dapper Slim seated at a bar, answering questions posed by a *Black Journal* interviewer, with a young Iceberg, played by Kuumba actor Alade Johnston, manipulating and controlling his prostitutes (Mukai Bariki, Thelma Brown, Carolyn Jackson) to varying degrees of physical abuse. The dramatizations are adapted from *Pimp*, and they are uniformly disturbing: Iceberg lashes out at one for daring to walk out of his Cadillac, he bludgeons another with a telephone book for brushing off a date with a trick, and he smashes a bottle over the head of the third for taking time off from work to go to the bar. Slim's response to these scenes makes clear that he now disidentifies from Iceberg's actions. Referring to his former self as an "ill man," Slim laments that he had been duped into worshipping the "flash and glamour" of pimps in his youth, and that the life of the prostitutes he controlled had "to be holy hell." He stops short at fully apologizing for his wrongdoings, but the manner in which Slim's verbal observations are laid over or interspersed between damning images of sexual terrorism underscores the gulf that divides the speaking subject from his visual double (Johnston has very few lines in the show).

Indeed, by having Johnston play the young Iceberg—clad in showy, tight-fitting red leisure wear and sporting a boat of a white luxury vehicle—*Black Journal*'s producers materialized in televisual form what had been *Naked Soul*'s literary intent: to highlight, by glaring contrast, the distinction between Beck, the author, and Iceberg, the narrative persona.[15] This doubling effect lay at the heart of *Naked Soul*'s investment in redemptive anachronicity. Unsurprisingly, the same idea is brought to the fore as "The Black Pimp" moves to focus more intently on the contemporary author's vision for the future. With Kuumba's dramatizations still fresh in the mind, Slim intones, "Pimps and whores today are anachronisms in the face of the kind of thing that has occurred in black America since Malcolm X. Our enemies are both within and without." The reference to the nationalist leader was apt, given that Malcolm X was an early popularizer of the view that African Americans' exploitation of their communities ("within") was a problem equally in need of elimination as whites' oppression of blacks ("without"). Conveniently enough, the episode follows Slim from the bar to a lecture hall at Malcolm X College in Chicago, a two-year school that had been renamed from Crane Community College thanks to the efforts of local

Black Panthers. In front of a mixed-gender audience of students, most of whom are dressed in African-inspired garb, Slim offers himself up as someone who had once "brutalized and exploited our black queens" but who now espoused full political consciousness: "You have to have a realization that when you exploit your own kind, that you are in effect counterrevolutionary, that you are hobbling and crippling the struggle of black people for freedom and dignity."[16]

In the course of the interview, Slim also imparts specific advice to readers: *Pimp* is not to be considered a handbook on how to become a pimp. The interviewer prompts him by saying, "You know, Brother Beck, your autobiography *Pimp*, which you wrote, it may have encouraged a lot of young brothers to become pimps. How do you feel about this?" After a contemplative pause, Slim utters, "I think the fact that my autobiography *Pimp: The Story of My Life*, the book—I think it's very unfortunate that there have been many misguided young black men—who should know better—who miss the whole message in the book. And that was that I was a pretty bright guy and yet nothing good came to me except the penitentiary and a heroin habit and misery and the complete waste of my life." Slim's initial drawn-out response shows, to my mind, that he is trying to convince himself of the book's status as nonfiction. It is as though he must agree to the interviewer's description of his work before proceeding. Strained though it may be, once he does this Slim can summarize the book's "message" as warning "young black men" away from the streets. In this reading, *Pimp*'s disingenuous preface, which I discuss in chapter 2, is now the whole reason for reading the book.

All of this would seem to support the idea that Slim had turned a sharp corner and become Robert Beck, at least in the eyes of the public. "The Black Pimp" has the feel of an extended public service announcement, complete with a takeaway point for viewers to mull over: the writer formerly known as Iceberg Slim "encourages young black brothers to take a sister off the corner," booms a final voiceover. "Pimping is not where it's at." The segment then concludes with a final tableau, which shows the three presumably ex-prostitutes strolling down a street in Chicago. A funk song with conscious lyrics plays out the segment:

All you people out there that think you're cool
Let me tell you, you ain't got nobody fooled
. . . .
I don't feel we should use one another
We should be more like sisters and brothers.

Having relinquished control over the trio, Iceberg could now truly be called "Brother Beck."

Despite these gestures toward community uplift, there is one scene in "The Black Pimp" that exposes the hollow core of Slim's redemptive anachronicity. A middle-aged woman who averts her eyes from the camera is positioned just behind Slim at the bar during his interview. After the Kuumba dramatizations but before the Malcolm X lecture, the woman and Slim are shown seated across from each other in a booth at the bar. The black woman is seen only in profile, and she is wearing a gray wig and tinted glasses. In a staged, awkward introduction, it is revealed that she is Slim's former prostitute, whom he has not seen in fourteen years. He claims to have just run into her on the street, but that is hard to believe. She appears tense, uneasy. "Oh sure, glad to see you, behind that time," she says in response to his amazement at how long it has been. Perhaps noticing her tension, Slim reverts to type and tries to sweet-talk his way into her good graces; he does so by making a terrible assumption. After claiming he has no ulterior motive for being there (i.e., pimping her after all these years), Slim surmises, "If you're working . . ." (i.e., he would not stand in her way or make any judgments). The woman quickly corrects him: "Oh, I'm working. I'm a nurse's aide. Working there seven years." Slim's surprise is readily apparent—it is as though he could not imagine her to have moved on after what was surely a horrific experience. "Tell me, baby," he asks, "why did you square up?" The woman recounts what she has been through over the past fourteen years, including serving time in prison and watching too many girls in her situation getting cheated out of their money and murdered by johns—to say nothing of what the pimps have done to them.

The anonymous woman in this scene makes no appearance in the credits for the *Black Journal* episode. That is probably just as well. Trauma lies behind her very effort to remain anonymous while claiming dignity in the face of her exploiter. As she lights a cigarette and trails off with the observation, "That's the way life is, but everybody wakes up sooner or later," one has the sense that this is the truest thing anyone has said in the episode. For she now sees the man in front of her for who he is, while he remains stuck in an illusion of his own making. Her testimony compels us to come to terms with the fact that there is, finally, no Robert Beck. There is only Iceberg, the persona of legend, and Slim, the author beholden to his creation. Despite *Black Journal*'s best efforts to place a reformed Slim on the right side of history, Iceberg's notoriety carries the day.

Getting Played

In January 1971, *Time* magazine published an unsigned article in its "Behavior" column about the ethnographic fieldwork of a PhD candidate in anthropology at the University of California, Berkeley. Titled "The Pimping Game," the piece introduced readers to Christina Milner, "a shapely, 27-year-old redhead" who was studying the black "players and hos" she had met at the San Francisco nightclub where she worked as a go-go dancer. In sharing her findings with *Time*, Milner repeated hoary stereotypes, such as, "Because black men have traditionally had trouble finding legitimate jobs, they are used to the idea of being supported by women," and that "there is no loss of status in making money from sex" in the black community. But what lent these field notes their legitimacy were statements Iceberg Slim and other (ex-)pimps had made to Milner and her husband, Richard. The piece cited these figures as the progenitors of pop-Freudian insights such as, "To be a great pimp, I think you've really got to hate your mother," and, "Each ho thinks her man is God." The egoism inherent to the pimp's control over women was even cast as biblically inspired: "When Adam let Eve tempt him into taking the apple, he gave up his manhood, and today man is fighting to regain it." In thus framing the pimping lifestyle as one that sought to reclaim and consolidate masculinity for an oppressed demographic, the article substituted a local cultural fantasy for broad social fact. Pimps, it said in closing, had fashioned "a way of striking out at the white man by taking his money—and his women too. By 'gaming off' Whitey, the black pimp becomes a folk hero, the Jesse James of the ghetto."[17]

Time was the first in a series of mainstream publications heralding Slim as the voice of urban black culture. Slim initially seemed bothered by the fact that agents of cultural appropriation were responsible for securing this exceptional status for him. He quickly learned, however, that insofar as subcultural knowledge circulated as a form of symbolic capital, he could build up enough credit to offset claims that he was a political reactionary. He learned, in other words, the value of being a cultural spokesman, which, unlike the position of activist, did not mandate a progressive or forward-looking outlook. For its part, Holloway House welcomed any news of Slim's cultural import. As with black media coverage of his engagement with nationalism, the company stood to gain whenever his persona was promoted outside the sleaze market. Thus, even when reports were dubious, simplistic, or just plain wrong, the fact that Slim was treated as culturally authentic—that is, a native informant—served to reinforce the brand they were trying to create for their paperbacks.

Slim had time to include a barbed response to "The Pimping Game" in *Naked Soul*, which appeared over the summer of 1971. There he not only demeaned Christina Milner; he also denied ever having met her, much less agreed to be interviewed for her dissertation. Appropriately, Slim's response is staged as an imagined dialogue between him and Sweetsend Pappy Luke, an old prison acquaintance. The conversation allows Slim to ventriloquize, through one character, what might have been numerous street-level accusations that he had sold out. Pappy confronts Slim with a copy of the *Time* article, asking how he could "sucker off for that conniving white broad," letting her "dupe [him] into the fairytale bullshit" about the pimping lifestyle. Curiously, although Slim claims to not even know Milner, Pappy lectures him as though he is well aware of his mistake: "Your pimp brain can't grasp that the white broad stole something from you and those black pimps in San Francisco more precious than money." According to Pappy, Milner "stole" Slim's cultural patrimony, an account of "black people's labor, talent, folklore and creativity" that she could present to white audiences as the genuine article.[18] The result was bound to unduly romanticize ("fairytale bullshit") the pimping lifestyle in that Milner had effectively made Slim her "whore," "pimping" his knowledge to a crossover audience of racist onlookers.

Having defended the authenticity of his street knowledge (albeit through the voice of Pappy), Slim attempts to show how the whole sordid episode could be put to good use. The dialogue points out that the article caused consternation among middle-class blacks who had been keen on preserving their self-image among their white counterparts. Pappy references a black newspaper columnist's reaction to "The Pimping Game," in which the writer characterizes the subjects of Milner's study as "sick criminals and . . . a splotch on humanity." Upon hearing this, Slim loses respect for the writer, whom many considered the "Henry [Hank] Aaron of Journalism." To his ears, the man's criticism defends middle-class respectability over the flawed character traits of the black underclass; in so doing, he advances a position that runs counter to black liberation. Bemoaning the bourgeoisie's "intellectual glaucoma," Slim again announces his support for "black militant strugglers and street nigger losers way down there in the gutter"— the lumpen whom neither Milner nor the columnist seeks to truly understand.[19]

Slim was not being forthcoming: he of course knew the Milners—and was no doubt complicit in their popularization of the pimping lifestyle. When Slim's lawyer put the couple on notice that his client intended to sue them for damages, Richard sent back his published profile of the author, which, as chapter 3 notes, had appeared in the men's magazine *Rogue* in 1969. Richard included a copy of the release, signed by Slim, granting "unrestricted permission to reprint the interview."[20] Slim was not going to win that case. And yet, even though he seemed to regret collaborating with the Milners, Slim gained something valuable from them: the symbolic capital of cultural authenticity. By independently confirming his status as a native informant, Slim actually burnished his image as a man of the streets. This is why the key turn in the conversation with Pappy was the introduction of the black journalist. With this figure, Slim leveraged the culture he spoke for against the pretensions of the black bourgeoisie. Indeed, by the end of the piece, it was not the white anthropologist but the black journalist who emerged as the real enemy of black liberation.

Cultural authenticity was something for whites to fetishize when reading Slim and for Slim to mobilize when discussing intraracial class politics. This explains how one of the main essays from *Naked Soul*, "Rapping about the Pimp Game," could appear in the November 1971 issue of *Adam* magazine, offering white readers yet another look into a black underworld that had turned gender relations on its head. But it also explains how in February 1972 Slim could recount a talk he had given at San Jose State University, which started, "I would like to disclaim that I ain't no lecturer. I'm just a street nigger who's come here to rap with you and who's learning to be a writer. None of that pompous stuff." In front of this audience, Slim wanted to be taken seriously as a ghetto denizen. From this position, he could rail against the black bourgeoisie: "Ten or fifteen years ago, a black writer would talk out of both sides of his mouth, just as so-called black leaders [did]. They could delude and fascinate, hypnotize large segments of black people from grass roots [*sic*], ordinary black street people all the way up." Slim was not like these establishment figures; he wanted cut through the rhetoric and tell it like it is.[21]

This, in short, was how Slim eked out a narrow path between exoticization, on the one hand, and intraracial discourse, on the other. Depending on context, genre, audience, and medium, he appeared either as a subcultural guide or as a social agitator. And while Slim obviously spoke for himself in these interviews, Holloway House had a clear stake in his being marketed as a native informant. Since the company held the rights to his books, they stood to gain regardless of who read him.

So it is that, on the side of white fascination (à la the Milners), Slim was often cited in the social science literature on urban poverty and street culture. Selections from *Pimp*, for example, appeared in Gregory Armstrong's *Life at the Bottom* (1971). An anthology of sources documenting the previous decade's urban crisis, this big Bantam paperback complemented the best-selling Report on the National Advisory Commission on Civil Disorders, also known as the Kerner Report, which Bantam had published in 1968. In a similar vein, sociolinguist Thomas Kochman included the foreword to *Pimp* in his anthology *Rappin' and Stylin' Out*. The selection intended to illustrate how "the pimp lifestyle" had exerted a "pervasive influence on black urban male youth."[22] Rather than view this influence as a determinant of deviance, which traditional social science might have done, Kochman approached it as an example of cultural difference, a social norm that could not be judged by outsider standards or terminology.

Far from shying away from the attention, Slim learned to relish the symbolic capital whites accorded to him. In the October 1972 issue of *Playboy*, for example, Slim, acting as cultural spokesman, wrote a letter denouncing a short story by another black author: "As a long-term payer of extortionate dues on the black ghetto street scene, I got suspiciously odd vibes, and felt frustrated as hell, after my visit with the poltergeistic street-nigger people in James Alan McPherson's *The Silver Bullet* (PLAYBOY, July)." Slim might have left it at that, but he felt it necessary to demonstrate his bona fides over McPherson, then a newly minted Iowa Writers' Workshop MFA. In a bizarre tangent that took up most of the letter, Slim described an incident from his street-running days, when one of his prostitutes handed over his money:

Her enormous eye whites gleamed like phosphorous in her ebonic fox face as she leaped from an alley into my moving hog. She opened her legs wide and put both feet on the dash. For a long panting moment, she probed with frantic index and middle fingers deep inside her vagina. There was a juicy kissing sound when she finally pulled the soggy roll out. It was a grand in C-notes. It stank like a sonuvabitch (pimps develop cast-iron guts) as she laid it in my palm.[23]

What this tawdry, graphic episode had to do with McPherson's short story was anyone's guess—Slim certainly did not provide a clear explanation. But maybe that was the point. Slim only used the occasion of critiquing McPherson to demonstrate his street credentials in the most shocking way possible. That he conflated sexual explicitness with vernacular insight did not seem to matter. Slim was still, as ever, writing his mythos into existence.

Slim's street credibility served different purposes for black readers. In his book *Long Black Song* (1972), Houston A. Baker Jr. called for the appraisal of "ghetto language" as a complex artistic form: "In a situation where property ownership is rare, employment scarce, excitement minimal, and literacy sparse, but where talk is abundant, it seems natural that status is conferred according to verbal ability."[24] Recognizing the importance of this urban vernacular to the emerging field of African American literary study, Baker cited *Mama Black Widow* as one example of black men's efforts to subvert dire economic circumstances through cultural practice. Also in 1972, William Robinson, director of black studies at Rhode Island College, published the anthology *Nommo*. In it, Robinson gathered black and African diasporic authors whose writings drew connections between Black Power and African decolonization, or national and global struggles for black self-determination. Surprising or not, *Nommo* included excerpts not only from *Pimp* but also from Robert deCoy's *The Nigger Bible*. Perhaps whatever Slim and deCoy lacked in political consciousness they made up for in authenticating the masculine ethos of Robinson's revolutionary pan-African archive.

We can see, then, how the symbolic capital accorded to Slim by black readers was different in kind from that defined by whites. Take, for example, Preston Wilcox's review of *Naked Soul* in *Black World*. Almost a year after Williams had reviewed the book, Wilcox, an education activist and former confidant of Malcolm X, interpreted *Naked Soul* exactly as Slim had intended it for a black audience. Redemptive anachronicity could be heard in the way he commended Slim's confessional style: "Brother Slim acts out the answers to the hard questions which few men—Black or white—would dare ask of themselves. It is much easier to ask another muthafucka how he came to be one than it is to ask one's self why one continues to be one." But an appeal to authenticity could also be heard in the way Wilcox favored Slim's perspective over that of the black bourgeoisie. "Black caucasians," he concluded after reading the book, "would rather be used by white people than Black people." An even more provocative takeaway was, "You are not liberated if you cannot imagine a nun as being a call girl and a clergyman as a pimp."[25] Though it certainly sounded like sleaze, broaching the limits of taste in this manner constituted Wilcox's political point about black reading habits. Like many black radicals of the time, he goaded the middle class by using obscenities ("muthafucka") and making outrageous statements. The discourse was sort of a litmus test for authenticity: could you handle reading the language of the street?

The greatest challenge to Slim's own claim to authenticity appeared at the end of 1972, when Christina Milner's revised dissertation came out as a hardcover book, *Black Players*, from Little, Brown and Company. The publisher had had success with another revised dissertation in urban ethnography, Elliot Liebow's *Tally's Corner*, in 1967. With *Black Players*, Christina and Richard (now credited as coauthor) gave a more detailed and, perhaps inevitably, more lurid account of street culture than Liebow's work. The book would have fit right in with Holloway House's catalog. Coming in at over three hundred pages, *Black Players* evinced little critical distance from its subjects. Much of it was devoted to outlining the mechanics of pimping and to rehashing its racial politics—namely, that pimping black women to white men "reversed" the power hierarchy of slavery and, later, Jim Crow. The book also included, in the appendixes, "A Dictionary of Black Hustling Slang." This was, then, the sociological equivalent of *Pimp*: a street-level peep into the black underworld that only lacked the bildung, or narrative development, of the novel. After the Milners appeared on the weekly newsmagazine *60 Minutes*, sales of *Black Players* rocketed to three hundred thousand copies.[26]

Slim emerged as one of the Milners' key informants. Text from the 1969 *Rogue* interview was reworked into different parts of the study. More importantly, *Pimp* was routinely cited as a veritable sourcebook of the subculture. The Milners elided Holloway House's investment in *Pimp* as sleaze literature and presented the paperback as cultural fact. Indeed, they came up with their own way of inhabiting Slim's language of the skull book, which I addressed in chapter 2: *"Pimpin' by The Book* means following closely the traditions and techniques which have been transmitted orally until a few years ago when they were recorded for the first time in 1967 by Iceberg Slim, the pseudonymous author of *Pimp: The Story of My Life.* This book, which sets for a good deal of The Book, was read by the majority of pimps we met."[27] As a complement to the Milners' on-site ethnography, *Pimp* served as an authenticating window into the subculture of pimping. Their presumption that the book had an organic connection to oral tradition ("The Book") buffeted the Milners' efforts to highlight the radical otherness of Slim's and other ex-pimps' lives. That "the majority of pimps" they encountered had read the book implied that there was a genealogy linking The Book to *Pimp* to the act of pimping itself.

Predictably, white book critics hailed *Black Players* for exposing the reality of the black underworld in a way that piqued their interest. In the *Los Angeles Times*, Marvin Gelfand confessed that reading the book had been as "exciting as discovering a new tribe of cave people in the Philippines." The strange psychosexual dynamics of pimping and urban prostitution were a revelation to Gelfand, leading him to proclaim, "The Milners' scholarship is real—their glossary of the lingo of this subculture is almost worth the price of the book." The only faint criticism he had of *Black Players*—that it did not do a good job of teasing out the experiences of women prostitutes—was itself expressed in terms that marked his exoticization of the ethnographic subject: "the hos are fan magazine-reading, cigaret [*sic*] and potato chip–getting, Chivas Regal–pouring ciphers despite the Milners' best efforts."[28] Gelfand's attempt at thick description was symptomatic of *Black Players*'s overarching tone.

Yet, despite the appearance of these exoticizing accounts, in many respects Slim had already been shielded from the full force of the Milners' work. That was because in February 1972 the black lifestyle magazine *Sepia* had run a profile of Slim whose title, "The Inside Story of Black Pimps," would echo *Black Players*'s subtitle, "The Secret World of Black Pimps," just under a year later. It was hardly a coincidence. The profile, written by Bob Moore, had recycled all the text from the *Rogue* interview (and, thus, *Black Players*)—except it was composed in a way that accentuated his redemptive qualities. There was no indication that Moore's source material came from *Rogue*, or what relationship (if any) Moore had to Richard Milner. However things happened, the original prose framed Slim in a completely different light from Milner's voyeuristic gaze. Moore scoffed at how the pimp figure was "accepted as some kind of folk hero by the mindless and unknowing," and he contended that Slim agreed with his sentiment: "To him the humor is in the new aura of seeming esteem for pimps; the tragedy is that in his eyes pimping is racism in the raw." Thankfully, Moore wrote, he was now "a respectable family man" with a wife, a young son, and three younger daughters, and thus presumably immune to the allure of the street. As if to drive Slim's shame home, Moore sneered that *Pimp* was "revolting, obscene, repetitive and inevitably boring," and that this was to be expected given that it was "a big book in the gutter library of a West Coast publisher."[29]

Who could accuse Slim, after being abjected so pointedly, of romanticizing his former vocation? *Sepia* got the jump on *Black Players* and practically rendered him harmless. The photographs that appeared throughout the profile emphasized this point. For example, a still from *Black Journal* that showed the Iceberg character violently slapping down his prostitute was placed alongside a photograph that showed Slim autographing one of his books for a black girl. The message was clear: Slim was no longer the man he had once been; he now respected members of the opposite sex. An even more intriguing juxtaposition had a photograph of a shirtless Slim sitting at his typewriter next to a photograph of a shirtless Robert deCoy talking to Slim while the latter sat poolside. The message was less clear, though we might surmise that this homosocial display identified Slim's literary career as fueled by desire between black men. Unique to *Sepia*, these photographs ensured that Slim would remain an enigma as Holloway House sought to capitalize on his image.

White Folks and Black Readers

Pimp. Revolutionary. Writer. Dad. Iceberg Slim had started the decade hoping to unmask himself as Robert Beck, but his identity only seemed to fracture into smaller pieces the longer he stayed in the limelight. This was to be expected, perhaps, for the entire point of writing under a pseudonym is not to confuse one's "real" self with the fantasy of one's authorial persona. Slim had bucked the industry trend in order to make the case for his relevance in the age of black nationalism. The result was incoherent and largely out of his control. And so, by 1973, Slim had begun retracting the experiment of going by Beck. Readers, white and black, loved his writing for all the messy, complicated reasons that had made it adult reading in the first place. If his books were to enjoy an extended shelf life, it was Holloway House that needed to change, not Slim. This last point was driven home by the disaster that was Bentley Morriss and Ralph Weinstock's decision to turn one of his books into a film.

As blaxploitation took Hollywood by storm in the early 1970s, Holloway House realized that its modest catalog of street narratives could meet the high demand for race-oriented scripts. In 1972 Universal Pictures collaborated with a new production company, Cinema Entertainment, to adapt *Trick Baby* for the big screen.[30] Because it was the first Holloway House book to be made into a film, the adaption was a source of pride for a company that had connections to the film industry but remained on the margins of major Hollywood deals. Still, the producers were cagey in their reasoning for bringing out *Trick Baby* at the time.

Co-owner of Cinema Entertainment James Levitt said, "We did the picture, not because the black film was in an ascendency in popularity, but because Iceberg's story about the strong bond between two slippery con men had strong dramatic values and appeal."[31] If Levitt was a tad disingenuous in disclaiming his company's effort to make a quick buck from the blaxploitation fad, the actual marketing of *Trick Baby* made clear where his interests lay. One week after his statement appeared in the *Chicago Defender*, an illustrated advertisement for the film's Midwest premier popped up in the same newspaper. Underneath a tableau in which the barrel of a gun and a buxom figure feature prominently, the movie's tag line read, "Shake hands with 'Folks' and 'Blue.' And then count your fingers!"[32]

During production, Levitt and coproducer Marshal Backlar were faced with the problem of how to approximate Slim's eye for the social and physical landscape of the crumbling inner city. After deciding that audiences "needed a fresher setting" than Chicago "to convey the excitement of the con game," Backlar struggled with finding a location that he thought was culturally authentic. "Los Angeles is too familiar to movie audiences," Backlar said, and "San Francisco isn't typical." Eventually, Levitt said, they decided to shoot in Philadelphia, in part because its "ghetto, small as it is, had the feeling of an east coast black community. It had the look we needed."[33] Levitt might have been loath to admit that low-budget production costs required shooting in a nontraditional locale. (He also happened to be a Philadelphia native.) Still, Levitt's claim that he was after a certain "look" that would feel authentic is significant: blaxploitation filmmaking practices often conflated gritty urban settings with the "black experience" as such.

But if Levitt and Backlar were desperate to capture something essential about that experience in *Trick Baby*, they had an odd way of realizing Slim's story about a mixed-race hustler who, because he can pass for white, plays big-money cons on the Chicago elite. African American character actor Mel Stewart was tapped to portray the older and wiser swindler Blue Howard, but for the key role of White Folks the producers settled on a white actor, Kiel Martin, who had no stake in the racial politics of the narrative. Born fifteen years apart, Stewart and Martin were the perfect ages at the time to represent an aging Chicago hustler (out for the proverbial last big hit of his career) and his near-white mentee. But the tall, brown-haired, and green-eyed Martin was difficult to imagine as a mulatto "trick baby," and there was nothing in his background or acting history that suggested he could pull off Folks's street-bred masculinity. Martin's whiteness required that the producers play up his ability to perform blackness in a believable manner. The results were mixed.

Trick Baby begins by dramatizing the con that Folks and Blue play on Frascati (David Thomas), the old Italian man who wants to buy "hot," or stolen, diamonds on the cheap and resell them to a jeweler to make a staggering profit.[34] The film does well to set the scene for the con, cutting between images of Blue making himself and his motel room look unkempt and images of Folks persuading Frascati that the deal will exploit the black man's (staged) hard luck to turn a nice profit for them. At the motel Folks verbalizes the racist assumptions that the situation would seem to conjure for Frascati: he calls the desk clerk "boy," says Blue is "dumb," and, finally, refers to the dejected black man in front of him as "nigger." When Folks seems to lowball Blue by offering him $10,000 instead of the asking price of $50,000, he also convinces Frascati that they are getting the diamonds for a steal (i.e., they are essentially stealing from the stealer). The con is completed when Folks threatens Blue that he could have just walked away with the diamonds rather than have Frascati pay the lowered price. The "bargain" is sealed with Folks saying, "There's no reason why colored and white can't treat each fair." Frascati has not uttered a single word throughout the room scene, as Folks does the middleman's work of projecting racist fantasy onto an exploitable situation. This is what earns Frascati's confidence.

Immediately after Folks and Frascati leave, Blue takes off his shirt, gives himself a clean shave, and puts on his expensive suit and tie, undercutting the image of a destitute hustler that his persona conveyed. Composer James Bond's brass-heavy funk soundtrack starts up, giving the impression that the deal was orchestrated in some as yet undetected way. Folks is shown walking down the street, a broad smile on his face, while Blue steps out of the motel. If the connection has not been made yet, the film underscores Folks's "blackness" by having Martin perform a kind of racial authenticity in his gait, speech, and interactions with inner-city denizens. Martin's character slaps the hand of a black man on the sidewalk as Blue gets into his expensive car. Folks then shadowboxes with a black boy on the steps leading to a train line while Blue parks the vehicle in an apartment building lot. Finally, Folks holds the door open of the same building for a black woman and her child, saying, "How you doin', baby?" to the child. The next shot shows Blue and Folks emerging from adjacent elevators, slapping hands, embracing, and celebrating what the audience now understands was a successful con (figure 4.2).

The jump-cut editing that the film employs in this sequence labors

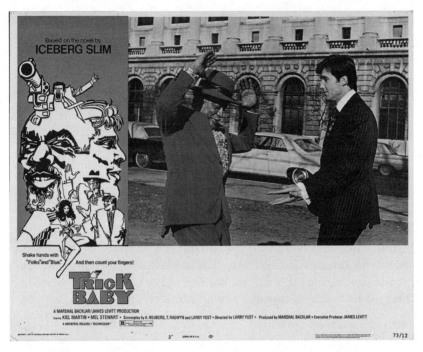

FIGURE 4.2 Lobby card featuring Mel Stewart and Kiel Martin in *Trick Baby* (1972).

to authenticate Folks's blackness, but in doing so it effectively caricatures race as so much pimp walking and jive talking. This is to say that Martin overplays blackness—offers only a hyperbolic and stereotyped image of it—on the way to convincing the audience that his character is really of the same world that Blue comes from. When Blue asks Folks how he feels about pulling off the con, his reply is given in a stilted vernacular: "Like the guy that's just laid the most beautiful broad in the world." A few moments later, this cool pose is echoed when Blue asks Folks what he plans on doing with his share of the money (having sold fifty dollars' worth of glass to Frascati). After ruling out leaving the city to lead a "simple" life, Folks jokes, "OK, I'll spend it all on hookers!" The effect of hearing these utterances is uncanny: they are intended to authenticate Martin's performance of blackness through a kind of urban minstrelsy, yet the actor's unconvincing delivery of them almost mitigates against their racist import. It is as though Martin's sincere but ultimately failed efforts to inhabit blackness render his take on Folks a caricature in its own right. Perhaps this is why another jump-cut sequence involving Blue and Folks making love to their respective partners loses all of its racialized significance. Whereas Slim wanted Folks's sleeping with a white woman to both confront and disturb racist fears of miscegenation, the film's clumsy equivalence of Blue's and Folks's sexual prowess only serves to represent two couples of the same "race" having sex. Figure 4.3 shows Folks with his love interest Susan, played by Beverly Ballard. There is nothing remotely subversive about this match.

Reviews of *Trick Baby* confirmed the film's underwhelming reception among audiences, even during this peak period of blaxploitation production. Writing in the *Los Angeles Times*, critic Kevin Thomas identified Martin's (mis)casting as *Trick Baby*'s "crucial problem," since his performance "fatally undermin[ed] the film's credibility" and narrative intentions.[35] Indeed, because White Folks's novelistic representation was so undercut by Martin's acting, black audiences familiar with Slim's story were bound to be disappointed. Writing in San Francisco's African American newspaper, the *Sun Reporter*, Rhonda J. Foston asked, "Can you imagine a half-Black, half-white man growing up in the ghetto, yet having no 'soul'? He has no bounce in his walk, no jive in his talk. He would be very well fit into white society. But then, without

FIGURE 4.3 Lobby card featuring Kiel Martin and Beverly Ballard in *Trick Baby* (1972).

this characteristic, there would be no plot, right?"[36] Foston's astute observation tacitly acknowledged the constructedness of racial authenticity (putting scare quotes around the word "soul," for example) at the same time that it suggested embodying a certain kind of black masculinity was part and parcel of "growing up in the ghetto."

Despite the film's seeming irrelevance to the black community, *Trick Baby* became the flash point of at least one notable anti-blaxploitation protest. Several weeks after the film's opening in Chicago, three black ministers tried to ban *Trick Baby* from public screening on the grounds that it was "racist and unfit to be seen by anyone." For them, Martin's turn as White Folks exemplified Hollywood's appropriation of black masculinity in the blaxploitation era: a white man in blackface sells that performance to African American audiences as the genuine article. Although the ministers' bid to ban the film was unsuccessful, they did give voice to widespread grievances about the nature of blaxploitation filmmaking as well as the suspicion that Hollywood was "exploiting black youth into idealizing violence and drugs and falling into the trap of already existing prejudices."[37]

As with any Hollywood marketing campaign, media buzz around the people behind *Trick Baby* spiked at the time of its release. This brought an unprecedented level of attention to Slim, even though his role on the film was limited to providing the source material for the screenplay. In the several interviews he gave during this period, Slim largely fell back on his authorial persona, reassuming the masquerade that had seen him through his first public appearances in 1967. But it was not a complete transformation. Slim held on to the symbolic capital he had gained in the two years since *Naked Soul* came out. He sprinkled socially conscious dictums and culturally astute observations throughout his interviews, leaving behind much of the anxiety of his early appearances. Ironically, the whitened-out *Trick Baby* afforded Slim the opportunity to settle into his public voice.

The most important step Slim took to affirm his literary reputation was to revive the legend about his nickname's origin. Recall from chapter 2 that Slim, in *Pimp*, had made up a story about how he got the name "Iceberg." After toying with the idea of going by Robert Beck, Slim determined that he would stick by that story even when appearing as himself. The *Los Angeles Sentinel* reported that the moniker referred to the fact that he had been a "cool cat with ice-water in his veins," while Boston's *Bay State Banner* and the *New York Amsterdam News* each retold the barroom legend, highlighting the fact that Slim had been high on cocaine when he was shot at.[38] It is important to note that these interviews were conducted with the black press. That fact, combined with the awfulness of the *Trick Baby* adaptation, suggests that Slim was eager to buttress his relationship with black readers even as Morriss and Weinstock seemed intent on whitening out his legacy completely.

Another step he took was to conceive his literary career as an extension of the street hustle. He confessed, "I see similarities between writing and conning people."[39] Specifically, writing was akin to the storytelling he would do as a pimp. In order to trap a prostitute through psychological means, the pimp's story must have "the mandatory tenets of literature": "You have to tell her something with iron-clad unity, no gaps in credibility, something that's vivid. You have to structure the scene, bring the characters to life so they can be visualized, get the dialogue to flow and have good alliteration. You have to communicate emotion and there must be at the beginning a definite affinity to the end."[40] This extraordinary outline—a veritable theory of pimping rhetoric—revealed a side of Slim that no white reader, and as of yet not even Holloway House, was keen to explore. This was the author explaining to black readers how he was translating his experience onto the page at the level of structure and style.

Finally, Slim did not disclaim the mark of authenticity that whites had assigned his work. He upheld it, but only under the condition that it was directed toward black self-esteem. The pimp, Slim explained, "is the only black figure who defies all of the restrictions placed on black people. He exploits white women, he thumbs his nose at the powers that be, and he's made himself immune by taking the risk of imprisonment and the rest of it. He enjoys maximum freedom within the society." Although the thrust of his rationale could just as well have fueled White Negro fantasies of ghetto life, Slim's specification of "black people" linked the pimp figure to African Americans' desire for authentic culture heroes. A different market for his books—a black-oriented market—would embrace the idea that pimps "are the only ones that are free of that oppression that most black men are under."[41]

The sum effect of these steps was that Slim relinquished the redemptive script and embraced his anachronicity in a far less abject manner. He even gave himself permission to wax a little nostalgic. Back in the day, pimps had been "suave, well dressed," set up in a "luxurious pad." More often than not, they had applied "charm" to bring women under their influence. By contrast, the new-school pimps used "dope to control their women." Because these men relied on drugs rather than their own cunning or talent to run their business, Slim was loath to call them "pimps." They were, instead, "scavengers."[42] Needless to say, Slim was glossing over the brutality and violence that *Pimp* itself documented in graphic terms. But that was the price of nostalgia: Slim now viewed his own past through rose-tinted glasses as he condemned those he simply could not save.

Out of these interviews emerged the image of Slim as a throwback culture hero, a reminder of what it took to succeed by the code of the street in the days before the whole city went to pot. Assuming that status allowed Slim to embody his contradictions rather than try to deny he was one thing or another. It also meant that he could directly address black readers—those who were proving to be his most loyal fans. According to a profile of him in the *Washington Post*, by early 1973 Slim's books had sold 3.5 million copies across the country. *Pimp* accounted for more than 1.75 million of those sales, having gone through nineteen printings since 1967.[43] These were not typical Holloway House numbers. They pointed to an untapped niche in the pulp paperback market, an audience that was not adequately covered by the dominion of sleaze. These readers did not need Slim's or his publisher's hedging to figure out the power of his words.

If there is one kernel of insight in *Black Players* that strikes me as relevant to Slim's fate as an author, it is this: "The pimp is not an organized revolutionary; he is an individual one."[44] Slim had hoped to curry favor with post–civil rights youth. It was among them that he identified not only new leaders of African Americans' collective liberation but also a certain masculine charisma, one that ostensibly supplanted the charms of the pimp with the political goals of the revolutionary. Yet the more Slim tried appealing to young people, the more he must have realized that he stood alone. No matter how contradictory his own rhetoric, and no matter how diluted his books became through further cultural appropriation, Slim emerged from the early 1970s with his past reputation intact. It turns out people did not read him to get down with the revolution. They read Slim to get out of it, to enter into a fantasy world where black men were already on top.

Still, Slim seemed a man torn. A part of his celebrity would forever be linked to Holloway House's dabbling in black sleaze. So tightly bound was his exceptional status to a particular claim to cultural authenticity that even when he addressed black audiences Slim spoke as if he were leading them on an underground safari. Though he might have sought a spiritual rebirth with the publication of *Naked Soul*, Slim in fact settled into a familiar groove once the book came out. True, black nationalism had pushed him to move beyond black sleaze in a decisive way. But the work of severing black pulp fiction from black sleaze would fall to another writer entirely—the subject of my next chapter.

FIVE

Return of the Mack

One month after writing a profile of Iceberg Slim for the *Washington Post*, journalist Hollie I. West sounded a skeptical note about pimping's crossover appeal. He observed that the sartorial tastes of black pimps, which included "lavender and pink suits" and "two-toned perforated shoes with super-stacked heels," had taken the fashion world by storm. People were getting their cars customized into "pimpmobile[s]," replete with "glittering striping, dual spares, elaborate scrollwork and amber sunroofs." And then there were the crossover books: the Milners' ethnography *Black Players*, photographer Bob Adelman's lavish documentary photography book *Gentleman of Leisure: A Year in the Life of a Pimp* (1972), and Slim's autobiographical novel, sales of which climbed to nearly two million copies.[1] The black pimp was mass culture's latest fad, and West, for one, was fed up with it.

The craze culminated in the release of *The Mack* (1973), a blaxploitation movie with ambitions of depicting the rise and fall of a black pimp. West thought it had "more tinsel than substance." Titled after the urban habitué known as the "mackerel man," a derivation from *maquereau*, the French word for pimp, *The Mack* featured classically trained actor Max Julien as the sweet-talking Goldie, an ex-con whose idea of turning his life around is to prostitute women rather than deal dope to kids. West understood why people would view Goldie as a culture hero: he fit the "romantic mold of trickster and outlaw," a veritable "Br'er Rabbit outwitting the Fox (the white trick)." For him, though, the film merited no such respect. Julien's turn as Goldie (which was as strained as Kiel Martin's take on White Folks in the blaxploitation version of *Trick Baby*) demonstrated "little of the equivocation and tension that marks human character." The plot element that hinged on Goldie's showing how much he cared for black children was "too facile to document either generosity or a sense of conscience." And when it came to dialogue, *The Mack* substituted authentic street talk for watered-down aphorisms such as, "A pimp is only as good as his product," and, "Anybody can control a woman's body, but the thing is to control her mind." A rare bright spot in the film was comedian Richard Pryor's cameo as Slim, a down-and-out hustler who injects authentic levity in an otherwise false storyline.[2]

I begin with West's review to underscore how much had changed since *Pimp* debuted in 1967. In just a few years, the figure of the black pimp had been transformed from outlaw to role model, a blight on racial community to an icon of cultural fashion. Far from ignoring this shift, Slim felt personally responsible for instigating it. *The Naked Soul of Iceberg Slim* was supposed to divert readers' fascination with Iceberg into support for Black Power. His lectures staged his contrition for all to see. But none of it worked—at least in the sense of radicalizing Slim's readers toward a cause. On the contrary, in the early 1970s pimp style emerged as mass culture's latest symbol of cool. West was right: wannabe pimps were everywhere, from Main Street to Madison Avenue. JCPenney and Sears even got in on the act, designing their own pimp-inspired fashion lines that were anodyne enough to be featured in their print catalogs. In short, the black pimp had become a quintessential American type. By 1973, he was as square as the White Negro next door.

For these reasons, it was not through Slim, or *Pimp*, for that matter, that black pulp fiction emerged out of the shadows of sleaze. No, what pushed Holloway House to define a black literary underground was an unknown quantity by the name of Donald Goines. As much as Slim had been paralyzed by the need to reconcile his past wrongs with his present commitments, Goines pushed forward with what he felt made Holloway House's books so enticing: their ability to offer what Richard Hoggart in *The Uses of Literacy* (1957) called "sensation-without-commitment." In the section of that landmark study devoted to British "sex-and-violence novels," Hoggart, after surveying the reading habits of "juke-box boys," "married people" (husbands), and "conscript servicemen," concluded that "the effect on a reader" of these books "is likely to be much more inward, to be more a matter of fantasies than of action."[3] The idea that sensation, or an especially visceral fantasy, need not have a "real-life" correlate in action, consequence, or commitment, could be said to obtain for any form of genre narrative. Slim's belief that it could be otherwise—that sober minds would read *Pimp* and not succumb to the sensation of masculine bravado—doomed him to anachronicity. But Goines, as I make clear in this chapter, believed the opposite. He wrote for Holloway House precisely in order to stoke sensation, and that was it. He wrote without apology.

Between 1971 and 1973, Goines published six books, surpassing Slim in output and reorienting Holloway House's catalog away from sleaze. He did this, in part, by writing as a hack. By that I do not mean to diminish Goines's vision or talent in any way. Instead, I use the term to designate a specific stance or orientation toward authorship and the literary marketplace. Where Slim got caught up in his own celebrity— a celebrity that had been premised on white fascination with the exoticism of the black underworld—Goines abjured such attention and wrote, wrote, and wrote some more simply to make a living. In so doing, Goines committed himself to the hack's literary career: motivated by the need to cash the next advance or royalty check, he was always chasing the next sensation to put into words. This commitment, I argue, helped Bentley Morriss and Ralph Weinstock understand exactly what made Holloway House's books distinct from black sleaze.

Once Goines pointed Morriss and Weinstock in that direction, they devised a new publication that would help cultivate an urban black readership. If Holloway House had started out as the book complement to *Adam* and *Sir Knight*, *Players* would be the men's magazine complement to the company's burgeoning list of black pulp fiction. Its debut in 1973 sealed Morriss and Weinstock's investment in a market niche that no longer was defined by sleaze.

Insider's Indifference

Donald Joseph Goines was born on December 15, 1936, in Chicago. Father Joseph and mother Myrtle were hardworking migrants from the South who had managed to open up their own cleaning store. Around 1940 the family, which included older sister Marie, relocated to Detroit and resumed the cleaning business. It was in the Motor City that, according to biographer Eddie B. Allen Jr., Goines started down a dark path. Unlike Slim, who in *Pimp* and elsewhere blamed his mother's decision to leave his surrogate father for his descent into delinquency, Goines fell in with the wrong crowd "in spite of the Catholic school education, the respectable mother and father, and the stability that came with being the heir to a family business." Restless, unruly, yet incredibly sharp, a fifteen-year-old Goines forged a fake birth certificate, adding two years to his actual age, and enlisted in the US Air Force. The country was in the thick of the Korean War.[4]

Though Goines had a relatively short tour, during which he saw no combat, his time in Asia (between Korea and Japan) would forever change his life. He experimented with drugs, developed a penchant for prostitutes, and became hooked on heroin—all while serving as a military police officer. This itinerary of vice was hardly exceptional for the off-base life of a US serviceman. But Goines was in his mid-teens: still a boy in age, he was exposed to things that hardened him into a man. He returned to Detroit after being honorably discharged at war's end, in 1956. It did not end up a happy homecoming. "Smack would be his companion for life," and in order to get his fix, Goines resorted to all manner of criminal activity. He spent the next decade and a half in and out of jail, serving time for charges ranging from bootlegging to attempted larceny. Allen states that had Goines not been locked up during the Detroit riots of 1967, he would have been busy identifying "opportunities to make some personal gain."[5]

It was in 1969, during a stint in Michigan's Jackson State Prison, that Goines encountered something that would change his life: Iceberg Slim's fiction. Goines could relate to *Pimp* and *Trick Baby* on a level that was alien to the typical Holloway House reader. He had lived those experiences and, indeed, was still very much a part of the underworld fraternity about which Slim had written so powerfully in his first two books. This point of identification was important for what would happen next. If black sleaze consisted of race-exploitative tales spun out of whole cloth by just about anyone, black pulp fiction would be the genuine article—stories by black people, for black people, specifically about the black urban experience. According to Allen, Goines recognized that "what Beck was doing . . . was a new kind of hustle. He'd been in the life, made it out of the joint. Now he was simply telling about it."[6] Goines wanted in on the game, so he submitted a book manuscript to Holloway House and was offered a contract shortly thereafter.

Goines had been out of prison for about a year when his first novel, *Dopefiend: The Story of a Black Junkie*, appeared in December 1971. The publication of this book would be a turning point in Holloway House's history. Up to this point, Morriss and Weinstock's communications circuit presumed a white sleaze readership from whom it could draw the necessary talent to produce most of its fare. That circuit was completely amenable to black sleaze (by the likes of Slim and Robert deCoy), which, in addressing itself to white men, leveraged urban black masculinity to contain the threat of domestic white femininity. Goines was different: he was not Holloway House's presumed reader, as he could relate to *Pimp* from the "inside," so to speak. By taking a chance on his writing, Morriss and Weinstock opened the door to a new pool of creative talent, one that emerged out of an urban black readership. This was still cultural appropriation, no doubt, but in this circuit, the white reader faded into the background.

Dopefiend's very first chapter marks it as distinct from sleaze. The reader is immersed in a space of appalling filth and degradation: the flat of a Detroit dope dealer who lets his strung-out customers use his pad as a "shooting gallery." "The floor of the apartment," Goines writes, "had pools of blood on it, from where addicts had tried to get a hit, but the works had stopped up, and they had pulled the needle out, leaving a flowing trail of blood that dropped down from their arms or necks and settled on the floor." In this description of setting, Goines does much to suggest the characterological desperation that has produced such filth. Sure enough, the reader finds Jean, a local junkie, hiking up her skirt trying to find a vein that will still be able to take a needle. She plunges one into her groin area and hits a "small abcess [*sic*]," out of which "a stream of blood, mixed with pus," begins to pour. But Goines, amazingly, is far from done. This entire disgusting milieu finds its perfect complement in the pusher himself: a portly pervert named Porky who has a penchant for watching addicts suffer. When women in particular find themselves short of money, his "fiendish mind" devises "abnormal acts for them to entertain him with." Porky begins touching himself as he fantasizes about the time he forced Jean to have sex with one of his "large German police dogs." His right-hand woman Smokey, a strung-out addict herself and "one of the dirtiest-hearted black bitches alive," completes the job as everyone else looks on.[7] This all happens in a matter of seven and a half pages: Goines's chapter 1.

With milieu established, *Dopefiend* spins out the tale a young couple, Teddy and Terry, as they descend into Porky's realm of depravity. At the outset Teddy is already addicted to heroin. For him Terry is but a means to get in Porky's good graces. Teddy lives with his hardworking mother and sister—both single moms trying to keep their family afloat. Terry, on the other hand, comes from a solidly middle-class black family, mirroring Goines's own background. The Wilsons live in an integrated neighborhood, where "her father kept the lawn beautiful, and her mother kept the inside of the house immaculate." It is thus Terry's precipitous fall that propels much of the narrative. Early in her addiction, she thinks to herself, "She wasn't a dopefiend, she was far too strong for that." However, as the addiction grows stronger, Terry resorts to increasingly desperate measures to pay for her habit. She steals money from her parents and clothes from the department store at which she works. Then, with fellow junkie Minnie, she defrauds the store—an act for which she is caught and fired. Finally, with Minnie's encouragement, she turns to prostituting, each trick giving her just enough money to pay for the next hit. Her young life has morphed into the slipperiest of slopes: "Well, I've come this far," Terry thinks before sleeping with her first client, "so there's no turning back now."[8]

By that point, Terry has cut out Teddy from her life. The precise moment of their break comes when Teddy fails to get an erection after shooting up and forcing himself on Terry. "To cover his shame at not being able to function as a young man should," Goines writes, "he exploded in a blind rage."[9] His sex drive replaced with a junk drive, Teddy can only muster the energy to rob, steal, and hustle the money he needs to pay for his next hit. His symbolic emasculation comes full circle when he steals his sister's welfare check, gets thrown in jail for trying to cash it, and has to be rescued by his mother (who asks her daughter to drop the charges). By the time Porky's henchmen shoot him dead for trying to double-cross him, Teddy is, in a sense, already gone.

Terry's fate is less certain but far more disturbing. Toward the end, in a fit of desperation, a pregnant Minnie submits to one of Porky's perverse shows. Reviving his memory of Jean's submission, Porky has her perform fellatio on his German shepherd. Minnie gets her fix, but at what cost? She hangs herself in her room. Goines seems to spare the reader the grisliest details of that act until Terry discovers the body:

The sight of Minnie hanging there was shocking enough, but when her eyes turned downward, away from the sight of her friend's contorted face, they fell on what looked to be a child's head protruding from between Minnie's naked legs. The head of the baby was covered with afterbirth, while only part of its body showed. The rest was still hung up somewhere inside the dead woman's body.

As if this doubled "hanging" were not horrifying enough, Goines has Terry fall on the ground—"her hands sliding through the waste that had escaped from Minnie's body"—gratuitously adding texture to that horror. The shock of this scene, we are led to believe, makes Terry go mad, and she is committed to a hospital. When the Wilsons visit their daughter over three months later, she is diagnosed with "chronic frustrational anxiety due to the traumatic experience of finding her friend dead" and apparently "feeling . . . deep emotional guilt" over it.[10]

Pimp had a handful of graphic episodes. *Mama Black Widow* was an exercise in black abjection. But nothing Slim ever wrote could approach the coldness and cruelty with which Goines approached this particular scene. That Minnie's violation was to a large extent foreshadowed by what had happened to Jean underscored just how total Goines's vision of depravity was. The reader was set up to fall right alongside Terry.

How was this not black sleaze? Goines was obviously in the business of writing sensational, even exploitative, literary fare. Yet *Dopefiend* did not fit with anything else Holloway House had published before. Slim's use of the first-person voice and the device of the frame narrative ensured that white readers could consume the black underworld from a safe distance. He wrote from the perspective of the outside looking in. Goines, by contrast, immersed the reader in his fictionalized ghetto, leaving little to no room for imaginative escape. His style was indifferent to the outsider's gaze; it simply sought to make the reader feel with the characters themselves.

Goines's aesthetic "sensationalism" was, in Hoggart's terms, "blatantly and crudely real." For Hoggart, the most striking "sex-and-violence novels" were those whose "almost subterranean appearance" came from "an unconscious desire among many readers for a sensationalism less artificial than that found in the more widely and publicly disseminated productions." In this sense, the most viscerally affecting pulp was to be distinguished from "the artificiality of so much mass-sensationalism."[11] The former, like *Dopefiend*, honed the reader's response to a degree that only invited the initiated; the latter, like a lot of pinup magazines and sleaze paperbacks, played with conventions with a wink and a nudge. There was an element of mass appeal even in Slim that Goines simply removed from his own writing.

Dopefiend, cannily enough, thematizes the difference between what its author sought to write and what was already available in the literary marketplace. In the opening scene, we are introduced to Porky sitting in a "huge armchair." Master of his domain, the "black and horribly fat man" seems as though he is in a den or some space designated for masculine repose. Porky could be, just for this fleeting moment, one of the dads who would have opened up a copy of *Adam* or *Knight* in the privacy of such a space. The narrator then observes, "He set aside the book he had been glancing through, laying it down in such a way that he could glance at the large technicolor pictures of a horse and woman faking an act of copulation."[12] The shock of this statement is twofold: first, that this is the kind of sleaze Porky would be looking at, and, second, that the narrator would bother to indicate that the figures in the pictures are "faking" it. Why is this fact relevant to the disgust we feel by the pictures themselves? Because, as we learn only two pages later, Porky has realized the act—of not just playacting interspecies "copulation" but bringing bestiality to life. Such is Goines's task: if sleaze can only gesture to depravity, he would animate the thing itself.

The final chapter of the novel harks back to this reflexive moment. With Teddy dead and Terry gone mad, we find Porky back in his lair, looking out over the street in summer. Muttering about the heat, Goines notes that Porky is "not really speaking to anyone in the room." Except he is speaking to the reader. Porky's flat is just as full of "young addicts" as it was in the beginning, and his predatory instincts identify Ronald and Tess, two teenagers, as new targets. "It was a game of life that he played with all the junkies," Goines writes, "only the cards were stacked against the junkies, and he was the dealer." And, like Porky, the reader knows exactly how this game will end for the likes of Ronald and Tess. This point, a metareflection on the nature of Goines's narrative, makes the final two lines all the more devastating: "He didn't use—no, of all his faults, that was one he didn't have. Porky was not a dopefiend."[13] By citing the title of his book as the last word in the book, Goines creates a kind of self-consuming artifact, a book of horrors whose true author is the pusher himself. In place of the bestiality paperback he has given us *Dopefiend*.

In one of the earliest pieces to try to bring Goines's underground reputation to light, Michael Covino, in 1987, described his style as having been "written from ground zero." By this he meant that Goines's prose was "the voice of the ghetto itself," and that his novels constituted "a fiction about people who largely don't read, written in their language." In one of the earliest academic pieces on Goines, Greg Goode, in 1984, found that Goines's books were "poorly written for the most part," and that his "descriptions, transitions, plots, and narrative voice [were] sandpaper rough." In reprints of Goines's paperbacks, Holloway House attributed the following to Goode from the same essay: "Almost single-handedly, Goines established the conventions and popular momentum for a new fiction genre, which could be called ghetto realism."[14] The first two quotations overlook the artfulness of Goines's crude writing: for Covino the prose is naturalized as paraliterate street talk, while for Goode it is subliterary in a very clumsy way. The third quotation dovetails with the argument of this section. It names a mode of writing, "ghetto realism," that, rather than appeal to an outsider's view of the black underworld, enacts an insider's sensation of heroin-fueled despair. Ghetto realism evokes Goines's effort to write the thing itself.

The irony is that the third quotation is made up. Kermit E. Campbell has shown that this line was tacked on to a lightly edited sentence from Goode's essay to make it seem like he had written it. But it is nowhere to be found in the original publication.[15] Goines's style may have stripped the veneer of romanticization off depictions of the black underworld, but that did not mean Holloway House would give up playing its tricks. When it came to marketing, the game was always one of masquerade.

Without Apology

When Holloway House brought out *Whoreson: The Story of a Ghetto Pimp* in February 1972, the book's design immediately signaled that Goines would be packaged differently from every author who had come before him. The difference lay in sameness: that is, the covers were laid out in identical fashion to *Dopefiend*'s. On the front (figure 5.1), title and subtitle were displayed in big block letters, underneath which appeared the author's name and a small icon representing the book's contents (in the case of *Whoreson*, a prostitute). On the back, a synopsis of the book's contents sat above the striking image of Goines himself—an illustration based on a photograph of the author. Visually, the design framed *Dopefiend* and *Whoreson* as two parts of a set. Not a serial (that would come later), but books of the same ilk. From very early on, then, Goines's legibility as an author was not dependent (as Slim's had been) on a splashy new illustration for each of his books. All it required was recognition that the black background of his covers—unique in Holloway House's catalog—indicated a fresh perspective on urban black masculinity.

Whoreson is Goines's response to the three novels—*Pimp, Trick Baby,* and *Mama Black Widow*—in which the Iceberg persona appears. By condensing the main themes of each into a single narrative, he in effect replaces Iceberg with his own first-person narrator. The novel relates the story of Whoreson Jones, the son of a Detroit prostitute named Jessie and a long-forgotten white john. Whoreson and Slim's White Folks have this backstory in common, but that is where the similarities end. Whoreson's coming-of-age narrative opens in 1940 with his

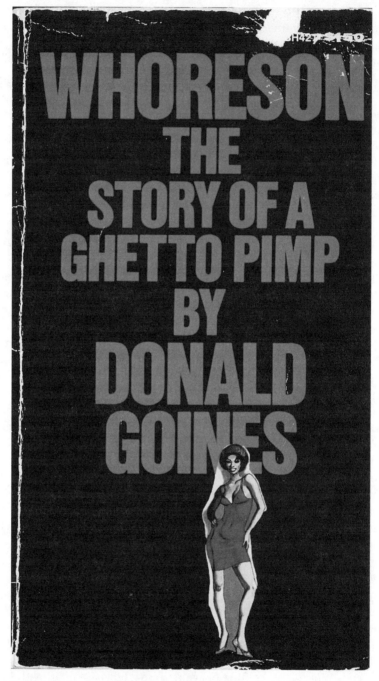

FIGURE 5.1 Front cover of *Whoreson: The Story of a Ghetto Pimp* (1971).

unceremonious birth. He recounts that he was born a "trick baby" in a prostitute hangout run by Big Mama, a surrogate mother to the girls. When the doctor asked Jessie what she wanted to name her son, she "laughed suddenly, a cold, nerve-tingling sound." For Jessie, the newborn was a reminder that she had been "badly misused by some man." As if to mark her baby with the stigma of her debasement, Jessie responded, "I've got just the name for the little sonofabitch—Whoreson, Whoreson Jones." Both the doctor and Big Mama urged her to change her mind. Jessie was unmoved: "I'm naming my son just what he is. I'm a whore and he's my son. If he grows up ashamed of me, to hell with him. That's what I'm wantin' to name him, and that's what it's goin' to be."[16] This scene provides a stark contrast to what we find in *Mama Black Widow*: whereas Otis Tilson's shame is internalized in the form of Sally, Whoreson's identity is constituted by shame when Jessie names him as such. This act of naming both externalizes shame as a social identity and brings the mother in line with the son's debasement. By coldly embracing her identity as a "whore," Jessie establishes a paradoxically close, tight-knit bond to this "sonofabitch."[17]

If Otis's kowtowing to his overbearing mother accounts for his internalized emasculation, Whoreson grows up in the image of Jessie, who in every aspect of her life legitimates a patriarchal social order. Indeed, Jessie's defiant identification as a prostitute leads other people in the ghetto to respect her: "Jessie had a way of walking that made people think a queen was going past." Unsurprisingly, Whoreson sees her as a role model: "To carry myself with such pride was my desire." Jessie's effort to help her son achieve this kind of respect takes the form of priming him, from a young age, to become her "little pimp." She schools Whoreson in the methods of effective pimping by offering herself as a kind of trial-run prostitute. "Pimping is an art," Jessie says, as she instructs her son on how to collect money from a woman every night—and by force if necessary.[18] Thus, in Goines's hands, the threat of black men's emasculation is defused when the phallus-wielding mother facilitates her son's survival in the ghetto by cultivating his sense of entitlement to other women.

This point is realized most fully when Whoreson decides to secure an established prostitute named Ruby in his employ. First, he makes Ruby believe he needs her help because he is new to the pimping game. After three weeks of earning her trust, Whoreson reveals his true design for her. He beats her down, strips her naked, and then whips her with his "pimp sticks," or coat hangers twisted into painful weapons of torture. Whoreson effectively breaks Ruby, as one would do to domesticate an animal, teaching her the meaning of "respect" as well as what it takes to be a "good whore." "I was born to pimp," he sneers. And so it proves, for this stunningly cruel act echoes a detail about Jessie that appears at the beginning of the novel. Jessie, we learn, had pimp sticks of her own, which she used on her son when he was "exceptionally bad." One time, after the police brought Whoreson and a friend home from school for engaging in gang-related activity, Jessie struck them so hard that "her large breasts strained to burst free from the sheer nightgown she wore."[19] Given the Oedipal script Goines lays out in the novel, Whoreson reroutes the sexualization of Jessie in this scene to fuel the brutalizing misogyny he displays as a pimp. With Ruby, then, we see how Whoreson is able to put maternal discipline (being beaten by pimp sticks) to use in asserting his entitlement to other women's bodies (using pimp sticks to beat her).[20]

The thrust of Whoreson's career is that everything he knows about being a man he learned from his mother. And while the plot takes other twists and turns, this simple fact abides: without Jessie's self-debasement, her son would not have been able to overcome the shame of his birth. Goines thus leaves the unresolved abjection to Slim. He supplants the neurotic Iceberg with an unapologetic mack. He introjects shame into his characters in such a way that they retain their capacity for action. Slim's characters are frequently undone by stigma, but in *Whoreson* Goines makes motherhood work for urban black masculinity.

If Goines effectively rewrote the Iceberg narratives in one fell swoop, his third novel, published in July 1972, took on the one thing Slim was desperate to hold on to: the rejuvenating promise of Black Power. *Black Gangster* relates the story of Melvin "Prince" Walker, a twenty-two-year-old ex-convict intent on taking over Detroit's underworld. Prince's gang, called the Rulers, operates under the guise of a black nationalist organization, the Freedom Now Liberation Movement (FNLM). Manipulating urban youth's desire for revolutionary action, Prince oversees a crime wave that claims the lives of supporters, policemen, and bystanders alike. But rather than cast Prince's cynical appropriation of Black Power in a strictly negative light, Goines positions him as a model of the post–civil rights black leader (hence his "royal" nickname). This leader does not shy away from the harsh realities of life in the ghetto; instead, he exploits those around him to get ahead and does so with all the power that inheres in leading a cult of personality. Goines does not condone Prince's ruthless behavior. But, as with Whoreson, he does foster an aura of inviolability around him—even though his actions point to his certain death.

Prince's appeal resides in his generic masculinism—Goines describes him sparingly as "tall, slim, and black"—and his capacity to adapt his criminal enterprise to the times. The "magnetism of his personality" endears Prince to the local community, and in short order, he commands a small army of black youth eager to do his bidding. The Rulers are organized like a proper black nationalist group, with "district leader[s]" and their subordinates, male members who wear "identical outfits," and a "main clubhouse," or headquarters. In truth, however, the FNLM is only a front for the Rulers' bootlegging and racketeering operations. These businesses in turn serve Prince's plan to become the indisputable kingpin of Detroit's underworld. Prince reveals the logic behind his plan to his confidants: "With all this black awareness coming to light, we're going to ride to the top of the hill on it. . . . Keep pounding it into the people's faces about police brutality, which there's always plenty of. All we got to do is keep it before the people's faces, and every time the pigs do something to a black man that stinks, we'll be on the case and cash in on it."[21] Prince's cynical calculus identifies in the movement for racial solidarity an opportunity to set up a criminal enterprise. By thus harnessing community outrage at police brutality, the FNLM deflects attention away from their self-serving practices.

Prince is a crime boss, and other people only get in the way of making money. This basic dynamic propels the narrative. The body count adds up quickly, as one violent act ordered by Prince—the assassination of a local rival—entails a series of reprisals and vendettas. Although the attempted hit does not find its mark, the attack leaves two innocent bystanders dead. The police follow up with the only witness who is willing to come forth with his testimony. Realizing the witness, an elderly black man, would likely pin the crime on the Rulers, Prince hires two professional assassins to slay him. The subsequent altercation at the man's house leaves him, his wife, and two policemen shot dead by the hit men. As the sequence of events unfolds, Goines's third-person voice casts a cold, indifferent gaze on the bloodshed. After the first attack, the narrator notes, "The scrawny kid who had given the alarm was on the floor shrieking, his mouth a gaping, blood hole." And in a pique of excess, the narrator adds, "The cigar butts and cigarettes that littered the floor now had something to swim around in. Blood. Pools of it."[22] In Prince's calculus, anyone who stands in his way is disposable.

Goines does not want Prince's cynicism to go unnoticed. When the leader takes the stage to address his followers, Goines writes, "For a moment he didn't have the slightest idea of what he would say." But then the con takes over and Prince is able to inspire them with boilerplate nationalist rhetoric: "We got to get off our knees. All that goddamn praying ain't where it's at, and singing We Will Overcome [*sic*] ain't about nothing either. Damn all that singing and prayin', what we need is some businesses for us to operate." Goines underscores Prince's insincerity in this moment of exhortation: he is being a "good showman," putting on a performance of revolutionary intent while inwardly "thank[ing] his lucky stars for the many political arguments he had had in prison." Yet, even after pointing out this ruse, Goines expresses admiration for the sheer audacity of it. "Dedication to a cause was beyond Prince's imagination," he continues, and this is not necessarily a bad thing, for "as far as Prince was concerned, there had always been ghettos, and there would always be ghettos." In view of that bedrock truth, Prince emerges as abiding the (only) law of the underworld: "If you were hungry, if you needed clothes, if your rent was overdue—take it. It was better to be a taker than one of those who got took!"[23] Prince thus cuts a paradoxical figure: he is both a ruthless exploiter and a model survivor, the kind of guy you would hate to look up to but look up to you must.

Rather than resolve this characterological tension, Goines, toward the end of the novel, displaces it onto an agentless fate. In the closing chapters, Prince himself is overshadowed by chaos reverberating throughout the inner city. Aided by Goines's intentionally flat descriptions of broken limbs, bullet-riddled bodies, and even a severed head, the reader becomes inured to violence in a way that generalizes it as a condition of life in the ghetto. In the process, Prince's responsibility for instigating the bloodbath recedes from view. As the novel enters into what might be called its *narrative death drive*, the connections between Prince's exploitation of the black community and the downfall of the Rulers are wholly obscured as his right-hand men are slaughtered by sadistic assassins, racist policemen, and armed-to-the-hilt mafiosi. Even his girlfriend Ruby becomes a stone-cold killer. Prince, meanwhile, goes the entire novel without ever lifting a weapon himself. He is the absent center of what turns out to be a maelstrom of violence.

Black Gangster was Goines's response to *The Naked Soul of Iceberg Slim*. Where Slim tripped over himself in that work trying to show common cause with nationalists and revolutionaries, Goines did the opposite: exposing a social movement as the front for a criminal enterprise. As politics, this is, of course, a deeply reactionary sentiment. But Goines was not writing politics. By this point in his career, he was writing black pulp, and his effort to script blood-and-thunder storylines was necessarily reductive about social issues where the emphasis needed to fall on propulsive action. Prince's cynical appropriation of the movement was thus exemplary of sensation-without-commitment—the sheer enjoyment of "bad behavior" without any apologies for morality or politics.

Settling into the rhythm of hackwork, Goines hit his stride in 1973. The novel that kicked off this extraordinarily productive period was *Street Players*. The protagonist is Earl "the Black Pearl" Williams, an inner-city pimp living large off the earnings of his stable. He has no backstory, and the plot, such as it is, revolves around the consequences of Earl falling for one of his prostitutes while kicking another out of his stable. What the narrative lacks in structure and focus it certainly makes up for in details about Earl's lavish lifestyle. When he brings a seventeen-year-old stable prospect, Vickie, to his penthouse apartment, the narrator describes the scene from her perspective: "The extra thick dark red wall-to-wall carpet gave her the sensation of sinking every time she took a step. The furnishings were French provincial, rich, ornate and colorful. The bedroom doors were modern French doors, with two adjoining doors hinged at the sides to open in the middle and long glass side-panes that were stained so that they matched the rest of the expensive decor." The world of *Street Players* is one in which things are more interesting than people. Here the apartment's furnishings function as symbolic capital (hence "French"), adding value to Earl's position in Vickie's eyes. Once situated in that calculus, though, there really is no way out. Just a few pages later, Earl takes the liberty of "caress[ing]" one of Vickie's "golden brown breasts." Assessing her body as if it were meat, he remarks, "Your tit is as hard as a rock. It won't take a trick long to figure out that he's getting something young and tender."[24] Vickie takes this as a compliment because Earl recognizes the value of the commodity she is able to display: her body. Like Iceberg and Whoreson before him, Earl has set the terms by which a woman can value what she already possesses. By the end of the night, Vickie has indeed landed her first trick.

In truth, almost all of *Street Players* feels like a coldhearted assessment of human capital. Vickie, needless to say, is highly prized by every white john who comes her way. Another addition to the stable, Doris, bemoans catching a case of the clap after having done too much with a john—it would be egregious to cite the bodily details here—just so that she could "surprise Earl with as much money as possible." The more experienced prostitutes fare no better. After crossing Earl, Fay sees her value tumble precipitously: she is thrown out of the apartment he set up for her and in which he had installed a custom-made bar. "I had a crew of carpenters come up here and build it right on that god-damn spot," he brags. And when Connie, Earl's most trusted woman, reconciles with him after a falling out, she announces her devotion by surprising him with the diamond ring and watch he was forced to pawn earlier in the story. By rescuing his "jewelry" from the pawn-shop, Connie achieves what amounts to the highest compliment Earl gives a woman: she is as good as his prized possessions. "You sure-nuff got the love I need, woman," he whispers gratefully.[25]

Much of this sounds like fodder for black sleaze. It reads that way because Goines draws on the same fount of misogyny and masculine entitlement that previous writers have. The difference, though, is that Goines's writing provides no escape from the setting in which his sto-ries take place. He refuses any frame narrative that would create dis-tance between reader and text, and he refuses any recourse to bour-geois sentimentality in both characterization and plot structure. Even his protagonists must pay the price for their hubris, with Whoreson being carted off to jail at the end of his book and Prince being shot to death by one of his hired guns at the end of his. In short, Goines does not care about white taste. In his world, women and men are ultimately reduced to things, whether prostitutes or dead matter.

The same goes for *Street Players*. The end of the novel sees Earl make his way into the bar after finding his feet again. A series of events drained his resources and sapped his confidence. But he has returned, thanks mainly to Connie's reconciliation, symbolically guaranteed by her gift of his personal property. The reader might expect the book to end on this note of resurrection, where the player is granted his come-back. After all, is Earl not the man we have been rooting for all along? Except lurking in the corner of the bar is the spurned Fay, still har-boring a grudge against her former pimp. "The sign of him now fully in control again was too much" for her, Goines ominously notes. Sure enough, on the final page of the novel, Fay shoots Earl to death: "The explosion was loud, but he never heard it. Her first shot tore the top of his head off. Her second one hit him in the face as he was tossed vio-lently back. The screams of the women never reached him as he fell to the floor."[26] And that is that. Earl is dispatched without ceremony or apology. His death is shocking but, perhaps, not surprising. A typical response might be: He had it coming. But only certain readers would be able to appreciate that point.

It was to those readers, urban black men, that Morriss and Weinstock turned their attention in the wake of Goines's success. They flooded the market with his books, signaling the arrival of black pulp fiction as a literary format. Goines had another novel come out that year (*White Man's Justice, Black Man's Grief*), and one more that, though filed with the copyright office in 1973, came out in January 1974 (*Black Girl Lost*). Another ten novels would appear between 1974 and 1975. Goines's work was almost singlehandedly pushing Holloway House's communications circuit onto a new track.

For He Who Is

He was greatly assisted in that effort by Morriss and Weinstock's new magazine. In July 1973, San Francisco's *Sun Reporter* crowed, "It's been long overdue and now it's here, a first rate, quality Playboy-type men's magazine for the black market." The title of the magazine would riff on Hugh Hefner's pinup success while paying homage to the urban milieu that had inspired it: *Players*. Morriss and Weinstock's intentions were made explicit in the *Reporter*'s extended coverage. The magazine would feature "content by blacks for blacks," including "interviews, articles, fiction and humor dealing with subjects of interest to a young, modern black audience, men ages 18 to 35." And given its "Playboy-type" angle, the cornerstone of the magazine would be "beautiful girls, the loveliest in the World."[27] Morriss and Weinstock had a new company on their hands: Players International Publications.

Nothing less than the *New York Times* saw fit to cover the announcement two days after it appeared in the black press. The *Times* story, however, began on an ominous note. One month earlier the US Supreme Court had decided *Miller v. California*, the most significant obscenity case since *Roth v. United States*. By a 5–4 vote, *Miller* upheld *Roth*'s contention that obscenity was not protected under the First Amendment. As such, ordinances against the production and distribution of pornography and related media were not deemed unconstitutional. In order to stay on the books, however, these laws had to meet a new standard that *Miller* laid out. The three-pronged test for this standard inquired

(a) whether "the average person, applying contemporary community standards" would find that the work, taken as a whole, appeals to the prurient interest [. . .]; (b) whether the work depicts or describes, in a patently offensive way, sexual conduct specifically defined by the applicable state law; and (c) whether the work, taken as a whole, lacks serious literary, artistic, political, or scientific value.[28]

The "community standards" criterion was taken directly from *Roth*: no surprise there. But the other two criteria were new, and the third in particular—focusing on "seriousness"—was viewed as a rather high bar to meet. The *Times* story began by noting that established men's magazines such as *Playboy* and *Penthouse* had been seized by local authorities in response to the Court's more stringent test.[29]

Yet it was precisely this test that gave *Players* the opportunity to outflank its counterparts. Representing the magazine, Weinstock told the *Times*, "We never planned to be radically provocative, while the others have to be. . . . That's the only way they can compete." By this Weinstock meant that *Players* would avoid the race to the bottom that *Playboy*'s Hefner and *Penthouse*'s Bob Guccione were running in order to increase sales. While the centerfold kings were constantly pushing the limits of what was permissible (especially when it came to showing models' pubic hair), Weinstock claimed he had no horse in the race. Instead, *Players* was primed to "give dignity and quality to the black female." The term "player," Weinstock noted, had once referred only to the street "pimp or hustler." But now, he said, it referred to "the good life," and it was that ideal to which the new magazine would be attuned.[30] Who would deny that African Americans deserved a taste of the good life as much as the next guy? The consumerist fantasy of masculine leisure had practically become a cornerstone of the American Dream. By thus making *Players* sound both tasteful and socially progressive—a natural extension of the "Black Is Beautiful" movement—Weinstock helped secure a place for black male pornography in the media landscape.

If that workaround was ingenious, the owners' choice of editor was inspired. As if to underscore the idea that *Players* was more than just a vehicle for male prurience, they chose a divorced mother and struggling writer from Watts to helm the magazine. Wanda Coleman, who later became an award-winning Los Angeles poet, edited the first six issues of *Players* (credited)[31] and was the driving force behind its early success. Like Goines, she submitted a manuscript over the transom, only to find that Morriss and Weinstock had bigger plans in store for her:

I was starving in the ghetto. I was living on 120th Street off San Pedro at the time. A friend said I should send my work to Holloway House, because I was trying to write this novel. This was the end of 1968, the beginning of 1969. I sent my so-called draft or proposal to Holloway House. I actually got a "come in and see us." I think it was a hand-written note. You get that rush, being a neophyte writer. I was pretty hopped-up about going all the way across town to Hollywood. When I got there, rather than talk to me about my novel, they started asking me a series of questions. I started telling them about my background, and they were really excited. This was Bentley Morriss and Ralph Weinstock. I met them both at the same time, and they asked if I could edit a men's magazine. And I said, "Sure." In other words, the idea was already there.[32]

Coleman, it turns out, walked into 8060 Melrose Avenue with hands-on experience in the field of men's magazines. As a girl, she had worked with her father and older brother on *Bronze Cuties*, something her father conceived as a black version of *Playboy*. There was nothing like it in the market at the time, even though pinup elements could be found in mainstream race-oriented magazines. According to Coleman, however, her father's plans fell through when Chicago's Johnson Publishing—owners of *Ebony*, *Negro Digest*, and *Jet*—nixed his distribution options.[33] Despite this past failure, the practical knowledge Coleman had gained from the experience made her the ideal person to take on this new venture.

Players lived up to the hype when it hit newsstands in October. With an eye-catching design and numerous color images, the magazine was printed on glossy stock—a luxury Morriss and Weinstock afforded no other periodical. In a tactile sense, this was to be a different kind of men's magazine. That message also came across in the issue's front cover (figure 5.2). A photograph of Ethiopian model Zeudi Araya topless and lying in the sand, her gaze fixed on the camera's eye, greeted readers. It was the perfect invitation in. Adding to the power of that come-hither look was a textual detail. On the same horizontal axis as Araya's eyebrows lay *Players*'s tagline: "FOR HE WHO IS." Why would this be used for a magazine targeting black men? The ontological tautology ("he" implies existence, or "is-ness") took on a different meaning for an audience that routinely felt their masculinity was diminished or denied by white supremacy. Here, then, black manhood was affirmed in itself—not simply by the word "he" but in the qualifying phrase "who is." The tagline granted black men the sort of subjective wholeness that readers of *Adam* and *Knight* might have taken for granted.[34]

Within the issue Coleman brought together a remarkable array of talent to realize the good life—not for the proverbial white bachelor, as had been done by Hefner to great effect,[35] but for the black man about town. A section called "Getting Down" brought the reader up to speed on the latest in black film, black books, and black music, featuring reviews by Leroy Robinson, Paul Carter Harrison, and Earl Ofari

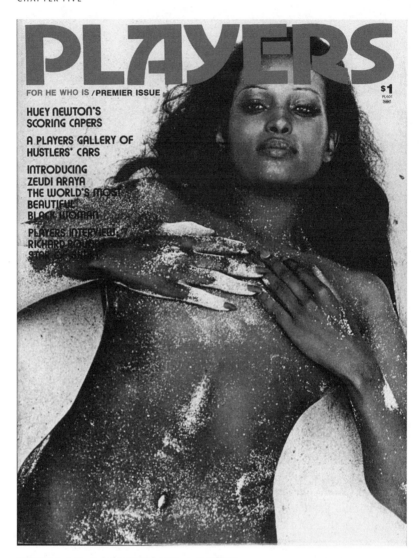

FIGURE 5.2 Front cover of *Players* (November 1973).

(Hutchinson), among others. Original fiction by Chris Wyse and Odie Hawkins was tastefully illustrated, the former by Robert M. Cunningham, a white artist who had gained fame for his work in *Sports Illustrated*, and the latter by Bob Smith, a black artist who would later start a successful black greeting card company.[36] And of course, as in *Playboy*, there were the playthings: photographs of nude women and advertisements for consumer goods laid out in full color for black men's enjoy-ment and consumption. In a clear sign that Morriss and Weinstock had done their homework, the featured goods ranged from Salem menthol cigarettes to Old Taylor bourbon whiskey, from Stevie Wonder's latest album *Innervisions* (1973) to the latest fashion from Eleganza and Flagg Bros. These objects of black male leisure were complemented by pictori-als of Araya, a former Miss Ethiopia, and one Nancy Foster, a Chicago transplant trying to make it big in Los Angeles. The models were shot in serene, natural settings—Araya on the beach, Foster in a meadow, and both lying supine in the grass—underscoring the "softness" of their appeal. Foster in particular approximated the ideal of the "girl next door" look made famous by Hefner in the pages of *Playboy*.

However, I hesitate to classify *Players* as a "black *Playboy*," as some scholars have done,[37] because the magazine advanced a unique edi-torial vision. Not for nothing did the press release announcing Cole-man's appointment as editor proudly proclaim, "Wanda Coleman is an attractive 26 year old black woman who was born and raised in Los Angeles and is still living in the South Central section known as Watts because 'I like being close to my people.'"[38] Coleman understood that her readers would not identify with the default white middle-class identity embodied by Hefner's idealized bachelor. She needed to ac-count for the fact that, as Slim and Goines illustrated in their fiction, black men aspiring to the good life would have possessed a wider range of class-inflected tastes and preferences than *Playboy*'s implied readers. The solution was for *Players* to be a bit more like *Adam*—less urbane than streetwise, more pimp than playboy.

From its inception the magazine was committed to the idea that pimps could dream big too. One uncredited cartoon showed two decked-out pimps walking down the street. The caption revealed what one says to the other: "Yeah . . . I'd like to be making some bread so I could afford to dress up sometimes."[39] The jarring juxtaposition—if this isn't dressed up, what is?—might have provoked laughter for those who knew that it would never be enough for a man so committed to ostentatious display. But subtending this commitment to luxurious ex-cess—which in the pages of *Playboy* would have seemed gauche—were characterological traits that *Players* framed as down-home "authentic." A pictorial layout titled "Hustlers' Cars" featured blaxploitation star James Cousar carrying on with two models who sometimes appeared with their tops off. Their tableaux showed off the high-end cars that "hustlers" liked to spend their money on. But the accompanying text clarified that the "hustle" to which the piece referred was one "for the man . . . behind a desk [who] keeps his shoes tied and don't want his 'business' in the streets." Indeed the text valorized hard work of the square kind: "All those nights moonlighting at the City Slicker BBQ Grill & Bar while pushing papers in the a.m. finally paid off." Yet despite the upwardly mobile thrust of the piece, certain details identified the humble origins of Cousar's figure. One segment read, "Cornbread and champagne for breakfast? Sittin' on a Bentley? Now ain't that just too too? Well, you can take the niggah out of the country, but you can't take the country out of the niggah, as grandma used to say." Other details, meanwhile, identified conspicuous consumption as essentially a street practice. Flanking a photograph of Cousar sandwiched between the topless models, one segment bragged: "Hey, all you old-breed cats out there, step aside! The new breed is not only taking over your territory, it's copping your wheels. We know the Cad has a certain tradition with you, but there's a new cat on the scene who's making waves."[40] Thus, for *Players*, value was not only determined by upmarket urbanity; it also was issued from the folk. Coleman understood the appeal, for black readers, of not forgetting where they came from.[41]

This editorial insight informed the last pictorial of the issue. Unlike the layouts for Araya and Foster, the one for "Ms. Robinson" consisted of photographs that were shot indoors, and specifically in what looked like a boudoir. The setting reflected the risqué nature of the model's sexuality. In an editorial move that would have been too sexualized for *Playboy*, Robinson was shown, not once but twice, lying down and clutching her breast, eyes shut in implied ecstasy. Another photograph showed her completely naked, legs slightly spread apart, lighting a cigarette in a holder. But the most obvious clue that this woman was more aware of her seductiveness than your typical (white) girl next door appeared in a photograph shot from behind a blurred object, which made the tableau seem voyeuristic. Robinson was shown—or overseen—applying makeup to the areola of her right breast. There were no illusions here: this was a woman who knew how to trade her sexuality. She was, in this sense, aligned with the pinups of Morriss and Weinstock's other magazines, not *Playboy*. Why would Coleman have included such a pictorial in the issue? As editor, she likely wrote the uncredited copy for this piece as well as that for "Hustlers' Cars." There were echoes of the previous text in Robinson's pictorial: "She's no bourgeois lady, or can't you tell? . . . You don't have to be middle class to enjoy the finer things in life. And what social class does she belong to? She's strictly in a class of her own."[42] As with the Cousar figure, Robinson was cast as having the best of both worlds: able to enjoy aspects of the good life while retaining her street authenticity.

Yet even in this particular fantasy there was a clear gender divide between what counted as racially "authentic." Although the piece made much of Robinson's ostensible independence, it attributed traits to her that, in effect, cast black women as the possession of black men. "In her opinion," the text read, "black women have always been liberated without the financial backing to make a success of it." With such a rosy (and benighted) outlook, Robinson was said to believe that, "lib or no lib, she's got what it takes to be successful." This easy accession to patriarchal authority implied that Robinson would eagerly trade the only thing she could call her own—her body—for the fruits of the good life. The text ended by teasing the black male ego with that possibility: "Ask her about 'revolution' and she'll tell you she prefers to discuss things other than automobiles. She's not about to take any handouts, but she doesn't see herself 'wearing the pants' either. She likes strong, self-confident men who know what they want and how to get it."[43] To be clear: women were playthings in every men's magazine, *Playboy* all the way down. The only difference was the discourse in which such objectification was couched. Early on *Players* showed signs that it was inspired both by Hefner's refined aesthetic and by the down-market ideologies of sleaze. To the extent that the latter was true, it is a mistake to claim that *Players*'s first readers "regarded . . . women not simply as tender bronze objects, but as women expressing themselves."[44] The medium required that female models be subordinated to the male gaze. Their "expressions" were never self-authorized. From the beginning, the project of *Players* was to stoke a particular fantasy of black masculine authority over women.

Another misconception about Coleman's editorship of *Players* has to do with the magazine's politics. Justin Gifford in particular has promoted the idea that the magazine exhibited "an informed black national and international consciousness" under her, and that "radical black thought was a key component of *Players'* style and ethos."[45] Yet, as the text for Robinson's pictorial hinted at, the magazine veritably scoffed at "revolution." Or, more properly, whenever black nationalism or Black Power appeared in these pages, it was as a foil to the more pertinent issue of fantasizing about black masculine authority. In the debut issue cartoonist Charles Johnson poked fun at the chauvinist ideology that revolutionary men, whether they liked to admit it or not, shared with *Players*'s readers. The cartoon (figure 5.3) depicted a funeral scene

"Lois was one revolutionary I'm sure going to miss!"

FIGURE 5.3 Cartoon by Charles Johnson from *Players* (November 1973). Courtesy of Players International Publications.

in which beret-wearing Panthers are mourning one of their own. The casket, however, had two pronounced bulges where the slain figure's chest would be. Combined with that detail, the caption revealed the irony behind the lead mourner's utterance: "Lois was one revolutionary I'm sure going to miss!"[46] In this, Johnson was not pointing out the hypocrisy of the Panthers so much as emphasizing the truth behind any politics: that men had, or deserved to have, sexual authority over women.[47]

Surprisingly, the most iconic figure of the black revolution also made an appearance in the debut issue. Huey P. Newton had just published his autobiography *Revolutionary Suicide* (1973), and Coleman managed to reprint one chapter of it in the magazine. On the surface this seemed to entail an endorsement of the ideas Newton put forth in his book, which deftly used his life story as a vehicle, or pretext, for theorizing a mass social movement in the present. Yet, in keeping with the editorial thrust of the magazine, the chapter Coleman decided to excerpt, titled "Scoring," covered Newton's prerevolutionary youth. The selection was not anathema to revolutionary discourse, but it read like an insider's guide to street cons, petty crimes, and court maneuvers aimed at getting one off the hook for doing time. ("I first studied law to become a better burglar," it began.[48]) Far from advocating political consciousness, "Scoring," on its own, could have been mistaken for a chapter from *Pimp* or *Trick Baby*.

Ultimately, rather than curry favor with revolutionary elements, Coleman and *Players* valorized the ideology of self-possession around which black pulp fiction was being defined. If *Players* was set up "to be a vehicle for [Morriss's] novelists,"[49] then it would have to reflect the world as Slim and Goines saw it. That came across in all aspects of the debut issue, including in an interview with Richard Roundtree, star of the wildly popular *Shaft* (1971) and a bona fide Hollywood sex symbol. The interviewer, Walter Burrell, asked the actor about "so-called black militant groups . . . telling the movie industry what is and is not good for the image of blacks on screen." To which Roundtree replied:

The game we play here is centered around the acquisition of that little man whose face is on that green piece of paper. If yellow people were what was happening in the film industry, you can rest assured that Hollywood would jump right on that theme. It has nothing to do with the color of the people's skin. It's a simple matter of exploiting for that dollar. We blacks happen to be the market now. What we have to do is capitalize on that. And today that doesn't mean riding in the front of the bus. It means owning the damn bus.[50]

Roundtree's advocacy of black capitalism ("owning the damn bus") over and against a model of civil rights integration ("riding in the front of the bus") was in line with the views of President Richard M. Nixon, who, as Robert E. Weems Jr. has shown, used the discourse of black property ownership to counteract class-conscious movements for racial equality.[51] Yet Roundtree's rhetoric could just as well have been taken from the pages of Slim or Goines. As I have shown in this book, the commitment to "exploiting for that dollar" knew no representational bounds in their fiction. If white men were willing to pay, the black pimp would let them have it. And when it came to the idea of exploiting other blacks, it was, in the words of Prince, "better to be a taker than one of those who got took!" There were no scruples in this literary underworld, and there were no real apologies either. Roundtree could hardly have been called a sellout—he was legitimating exactly what Slim and Goines had been saying all along.

The last stand of Holloway House's white readership was symbolized by Kiel Martin's turn as White Folks. *Trick Baby* the movie was an embarrassing, unintended parody of *Trick Baby* the book; it exposed the lie of black sleaze for what it was. The movie could be seen as Morriss and Weinstock's last-gasp effort to make the old paradigm work. It didn't. The only way forward, then, was to pitch race-oriented media to those who were sustaining it. This is how Holloway House came to rebrand itself as producing print commodities *by* black authors *for* black readers. What had started out in the domain of interracial titillation—of white men's messy, fraught, but still pleasurable identification with urban black men—was now identified with black readers themselves.

The shift made good business sense. By the early 1970s, sleaze was on its way out. *Miller* no doubt stoked fears about producing and distributing pornography, literary or otherwise. But in many respects the Supreme Court decision was belated: the sexual revolution had already taken root in American culture. Sleaze historian Stephen J. Gertz has argued that a combination of factors led to the demise of the "golden age" of adult paperbacks. With heightened regulation, salacious books became the province of adult bookshops. This allowed sleaze to continue apace, but it no longer enjoyed the broad reach postal distribution had granted to it. More profoundly, sleaze was a victim of its own success. The liberalization of sexual mores that adult paperbacks had helped bring about also ensured their demise. In short, sex was everywhere in the 1970s, *Miller* be damned. Mainstream publishers, for one, made porn respectable by bringing out high-minded (i.e., "serious") fare that contained lots of sex. The tidal shift, however, came with movie theaters that showed hard-core pornography. Like adult bookshops, these venues were strictly regulated. But the cinemas attracted exponentially more fans than the shops—a shift that signaled the irrevocable "move away from print media to visual" in men's popular entertainment.[52] Why would you read about naughty nurses when you could watch *Deep Throat* (1972) at the local theater? Hard-core porn was in, adult paperbacks out.

So while race-oriented paperbacks were being redefined as black pulp fiction in *Players*, Morriss and Weinstock struggled to rebrand white-targeted print commodities in their own right. For one, they drastically cut back on Holloway House books that were not race-oriented. The change was already apparent in 1970, when only a handful of titles appeared, the most notable of which was Jerry Le Blanc's sensation-alistic reporting on the Manson murders, *5 to Die*. Soon the Holloway House imprint would be identified almost exclusively with black books. In turn, Morriss and Weinstock started a completely new imprint, Mel-rose Square, to pick up the load of publishing content from the maga-zines. Unsurprisingly, the first titles were collections of cartoons taken directly from them: *For the Serviceman, For Newlyweds, Sick Humor for Healthy Minds*, and *Rx to Help You Get Well* (all 1971). But in 1973 Mel-rose Square, in keeping with the times, published *All about Swinging*, a guide to the popular practice of sexual partner-swapping. Featuring profiles of contemporary swinging couples, this how-to book also con-tained a handy glossary of terms, with entries for "Crisco party," "tin-kerbell," and "face, to give," for example.[53] By bringing back the glos-sary format that Milton Van Sickle had used for *Pimp* and *Trick Baby*, Melrose Square's *All about Swinging* demonstrated that swinging was the new subculture of interest for white readers. And so it proved: this book drew its content not from *Adam* or *Knight* but from a new venture, *Swingers World* magazine. A liberalizing sexual culture demanded in-creasing nichefication.

Morriss and Weinstock now had two segregated business models to juggle: one for black readers, another for white.[54] The twain rarely, if ever, met over the next decade, as the ventures became increasingly foreign to each other. All of this despite the fact that both operated out of a single office building in West Hollywood. The telltale sign that something was a Morriss and Weinstock property was its business address: 8060 Melrose Avenue. Yet *Players* and *Swingers World* were so different from each other that one would not have guessed they were produced by the same enterprise. The emergence of this stark differen-tiation—the separation of entertainment vehicles based on race—gave rise to the black literary underground.

PART THREE

Trajectories

SIX

Difference and Repetition

The early response to *Players* was enthusiastic. In the third issue, the first to feature letters to the editor, people wrote in to compliment Wanda Coleman on the new magazine for black men. "Glad to see a sister with an eye for what a brother likes," said one, while another confessed, "My prediction a few years back that this kind of venture would be attempted has come true. The beauty and irony of a black woman being it's [*sic*] editor is a good feeling, too!"[1] There was the inevitable description of the magazine as "your black *Playboy*," but another reader claimed that *Players* "already supersedes *Playboy* magazine" for its "outstanding photography and amorous articles."[2] The most interesting reference to Hugh Hefner's rival magazine came from someone who was "deep into the 'rabbit' program (stationary, key, etc.)." He was referring, in part, to the exclusive Playboy Clubs that required dues-paying members to hold a VIP key to gain entry. From merchandise to this nightclub franchise, Hefner had turned his magazine into a global brand in the 1960s and 1970s. But this reader was glad to finally see an alternative to the magazine that catered to white tastes. "Today I canceled my subscription (P-boy & VIP)," he admitted after picking up the *Players* debut.[3]

Even at this early stage, the letters showed that *Players* reached black men across class lines and social barriers. Writing from the Playboy Plaza Hotel in Miami, the former Playboy Club VIP offered this warning about taste: "Don't slip to a girlie mag level (*Gallery* & *Oui*), as this will only detract from your stature in the market." The reader encouraged *Players* to maintain its high standards, in part by "emphasiz[ing] the multi-nationality of Third World lovelies (Afro-Asians, Afro-Euros, Afro-Latinos, Hindustanis, Aboriginals and Afro-Hawaiians)"—a cosmopolitan, forward-looking perspective. (He already knew, of course, that Ethiopian model Zeudi Araya—"perfection!"—had graced the cover of the debut issue.) By way of conclusion, the reader offered this advice: "Stay International and off the Block."[4] But another letter articulated an alternative perspective. "Bros' and Sis,'" it began: "It's about time somebody got off their ass and gave us a no bullshit magazine. Congratulations to the Players from a player."[5] This reader, from New York, could have been a cosmopolitan playboy himself. But in both message and tone, he came across as someone who appreciated the magazine's appeal to "the Block." His note authenticated *Players*'s claim to the street.

The magazine's fourth issue featured an even more diverse band of readers. There was the Williams College student from New York who expressed his relief: "you can't imagine what a god send [*sic*] your mag was." He went on to describe Williamstown, Massachusetts, as a relatively homogeneous college town, home to "about ten black families," where most students were "upper middle class" regardless of race, and the average family income was $50,000 a year. Stressing how his urban background clashed with his new environs—"this is like being stranded in Siberia"—the student was grateful that he had a taste of the streets back home with *Players*.[6] The very next letter in the column was from an inmate in the George State Prison. Though he expressed reservations about "women's liberation," he claimed he was happy "to see a black woman excel in a male dominated enterprise." The magazine, he hoped, would help him and his fellow inmates keep "intelligently informed on the plight and struggles of the black men" on the outside.[7] And, finally, there was a critical letter from a man who thought *Players*'s focus on "automobiles, movies, and recordings" made it a magazine not for players but for "all blacks." He took exception to the craze about which I wrote in previous chapters: the way popular culture had become inundated with "ridiculous pictures of players' lives in both movies, books, and now television," and how even children could be seen "going to school in Super Fly suits and hats looking veritably like clowns." The reader had "lived the so-called 'life'" himself, and so felt compelled to stand up for old school standards. But his complaint made for unintended advertising insofar as his letter was captioned "Ex-Player" by the editorial team.[8]

Wanda Coleman and Bentley Morriss understood early on the potential of being able to reach such a diverse black readership. Aside from the odd short-lived effort,[9] no one had built up a men's magazine specifically geared toward black men—one that would offer a modern, fresh take on the consumer-stoking idea of black male leisure. In order to bring the idea to fruition, however, Morriss enforced a strict division of labor. In the 1960s Morriss had built a sleaze empire through Consolidated Advertising Directors, Inc., the business behind Knight and Sirkay Publishing. Now he was helming Publishers Service Incorporated (PSI), which was essentially the money arm of Players International Publications. And by "money" I mean advertising. Even at their peak, *Adam* and *Knight* were down-market publications; they traded in amateur photographs, dirty-joke records, adult comics, and sex toys. *Players* was a different matter entirely. Here was a magazine that could tap into upmarket advertising revenue based on the lifestyle aesthetic that it was selling. Holloway House's black-authored paperbacks had saved Morriss from the public's waning interest in sleaze, and *Players* was now primed to capitalize on his stake in the black consumer market.

In May 1973, before the first issue of *Players* came out, Coleman offered Morriss her suggestions on advertisers PSI should contact, based on a review of the latest issue of *Ebony* magazine. They included Kool cigarettes, General Motors, Justerini & Brooks (J&B) scotch, National Airlines, Ronrico ("puerto rican rum"), and Duke ("natural hair products"). Morriss's patronizing reply, attached to the original memo, began: "Thanks for the info. However, please don't think about this phase of the magazine at this time. Yes, we have reviewed and reviewed Ebony and all other publications in the field to pull potential, sample advertisers."[10] Coleman was justifiably worried that Morriss knew nothing about the "field" in question. In a memo to Coleman that, though undated, we can assume came from around the time she was preparing for *Players*'s debut, Ralph Weinstock wrote: "Bentley came up with a fabulous idea to get attention and publicity for Players magazine . . . are you ready for this . . . GERALDINE (FLIP WILSON IN DRAG) AS OUR CENTER SPREAD GIRL . . . perhaps we can get the writers and/or producers of the show interested . . . get us publicity generally and mention on the show specifically."[11] This was a horrible idea. It completely undercut the goal of establishing a print medium for black male leisure, and it thankfully never saw the light of day. But it probably signaled to Coleman just how much work needed to be done to keep *Players*'s white owners from sabotaging their own magazine.

The division of labor thus came down to this: Morriss would handle the money side of things, while, per his instructions, Coleman would "keep on the content of the mag—photos, sotries [sic], etc."[12] That more or less sums up how Morriss and Weinstock decided not only to run *Players* but to reorient the business of Holloway House. To black editors the directive was get content, and to black writers it was produce content—simple as that. Coleman's papers at UCLA's Charles E. Young Research Library demonstrate that these were intolerable conditions to work under. Yet, paradoxically, her and others' thoroughly exploited labor was the foundation for the emergence of a black literary underground. Morriss and Weinstock had listened to the communications circuit and made the decision that black men would be their readership base. But since neither of them, in truth, knew anything about black men, black women, black culture, or the black marketplace, they relied on a veritable army of black talent to help them make up the difference.

Get Content

Coleman was invested in *Players*'s success. In July 1973 she sent a memo to Weinstock asking that they plan ahead: "Let's sit down and talk about procedures some more, also the direction in which you plan to take players [sic], such as staffing, hiring of editors etc." Knowledgeable about the editorial and publishing schedule, Coleman correctly pointed out, "Assignments such as these require almost as much time as it's taken to develop PLAYERS. I think we not only need to map out a format pattern for PLAYERS, but a structure for PLAYERS INT. PUB."[13] She had a fairly clear sense of what needed to be done in order to get the magazine off the ground.

None of this was addressed, apparently, because a month later she attached this memo to another memo to Weinstock, adding, "Some sort of structuring will have to begin taking place with PLAYERS. It's impossible to keep moving at such a break-neck pace without some relief in the form of organization." Coleman requested basic office help in the form of a secretary. But she also wanted it to be known that she was being pulled in too many directions at once. "People keep throwing ideas at me without any organized procedure," she noted. "They come from everybody, not only from yourself and Mr. Morris [sic], and of course—Sid [Smith]—but the fellow over at the ware house [sic], to writers in the back woods [sic] of Tennessee."[14] With no editorial policy in place, everything felt ad hoc. Coleman would do all the grunt work—making industry contacts, commissioning writing and artwork, setting up photo shoots, approving budgets, and responding to all correspondence—only to have criticism thrown at her when the powers that be did not like something. Sid Smith, a black writer, was nominally an associate publisher, but he offered little in the way of help, functioning instead like a second Ralph Weinstock. Just under a year later, when Coleman again pleaded for office help—"are we going to get someone else in here?"—she addressed the Labor Day memo to Weinstock and Smith.[15]

What Coleman learned on the job was the she was editorial—all of it. In addition to putting the magazine together (executing the tasks mentioned above), Coleman came up with everything that was editorially exciting about *Players*. In order to build a national black readership, she devised a gossip roundup called "Drum," with check-ins from associate editors in New York, Los Angeles, Miami, and Philadelphia. Taking a page from *Ebony*'s profiles of success, she created a series called "Makin' It," one-paragraph profiles on black men and women who were flourishing in the post–civil rights culture industries.[16] Coleman also made sure the magazine featured high-quality graphic design. Even for a slight piece like Louis C. Young Jr.'s satire "Super-Fine Afrique Meets Pretty Boy Floyd" (figure 6.1), Coleman treated artwork, layout, and typography as different components of a clear aesthetic vision. Finally, Coleman had an eye for what it would mean to visualize a leisure aesthetic for black men. She followed up on "Hustlers' Cars" with pictorials devoted to furs ("Far Out Fuzzy Wuzzies," January 1974), kente-cloth fashion ("African Kings and Queens," March 1974), hustlers' hats ("Baaadasss Brims," May 1974), and travel to Jamaica and the Bahamas ("West Indies," January 1974). Though *Players* was not exactly *Playboy*, it did embrace the latter's crucial insight that men's fantasy world could be just as aspirational as women's. Did it matter that readers could not afford some of these luxuries? No. The point was to dream that they could.

When it came to fiction, Coleman was refreshingly eclectic, reflecting the diversity of *Players*'s readership. In the second issue (January 1974), she published Chris Wyse's story about a high-flying playboy's adventures in Saint Croix, inmate Charles Larsen's Goines-esque sketch of a struggling ex-heroin addict, and Watts Writers Workshop director Henry Dolan's Slim-like tale about a ghetto family, "Crazy Nigger." In later issues Coleman published more unknown freelancers as well as some rising stars in the black literary world, including Stanley Crouch, who went on to write a popular jazz column for *Players*, poet and pro-

FIGURE 6.1 Illustration from "Super-Fine Afrique Meets Pretty Boy Floyd," in *Players* (July 1974). Courtesy of Players International Publications.

fessor Everett Hoagland, who would win the Gwendolyn Brooks Literary Award for fiction from *Black World* magazine,[17] and, most notably, satirist Ishmael Reed—"probably the hottest black writer in country at the present time," she wrote in a memo[18]—whose *The Last Days of Louisiana Red* (1974) was excerpted in the eighth issue. These writers were of course featured alongside advertisements for the latest black pulps from Holloway House. The effect of which was not so jarring as one might think: *Players* tacitly acknowledged that black men's writing existed on a broad continuum, and that the literary public to which it appealed could make its own decisions about what (not) to read.

Coleman was able to do her own writing, too, but as editor of a woefully underfunded operation, that meant doing so pseudonymously and anonymously. Her papers at UCLA reveal that she used the pen name Andrew L. Tate to write content for *Players* that she could not secure from another source. "Ran into trouble in interview for number 4," she wrote Weinstock, referring to issue number 4, "so I'm doing it." The aforementioned Chris Wyse, she explained, "is not a very good interviewer and has alienated all the people he talked to—including the PR."[19] Coleman conducted that interview with film actor Yaphet Kotto, as well as one with Smokey Robinson, and published both under the Tate byline. As Tate, Coleman also penned reviews that, on occasion, pushed back against her employers. For example, she submitted a withering review of Goines's *White Man's Justice, Black Man's Grief,* ventriloquizing the author in part, "It's not always enough to say, 'Well I'm black and society has given me a raw deal and I don't deserve this fate.' Which may be true—but that's not made completely clear in *Black Man's Grief.*" Pointing to the fact that Goines's novel was caught between two minds—protesting the conditions of mass incarceration and depicting lurid spectacles of violence, some orchestrated by the wholly unsympathetic protagonist Chester Hines—Coleman offered the backhanded compliment that the reader would only put the book down "to get over your rage and/or nausea."[20]

To be sure, Coleman did most of her writing anonymously, as the person behind the magazine's editorial copy. Of all the copy she wrote, none was more important than that which was attached to the nude pictorials. For a brief spell in early 1974, Daphne Bolden came on to work as Coleman's assistant. A memo the editor sent to Bolden reveals how she went about writing "girl copy": "Read the girl copy in back issues of Playboy and Penthouse and imitate them when you start writing—imitate them as far as tone is concerned, or use the basic story line but make it black."[21] Everything hinged, of course, on that phrase "make it black." Though other men's magazines had staked out the baseline formula for writing girl copy—in terms of tone and storyline—Coleman and Bolden would add the small but crucial details that would make it black. Those details contained a world of difference.

Take, for example, the third issue's pictorial featuring nineteen-year-old model Cindy Cook.[22] Interlacing seven photographs featuring Cook in various states of undress was copy pitched in the voice of a brother on the block. "Let me mack it to you!" it read. "She's a young sophisticate on the rise looking for love, happiness and that bastard Success in the land of milk and money. No block action for this lady, no sir!" The gratuitous implication that Cook could be a prostitute but wasn't was, of course, one of the flavoring elements that ostensibly made the copy black. As the last chapter pointed out, *Players* aimed to be a medium of fantasy for the working man who also fancied himself a hustler. The complement to that hybrid figure was the female "sophisticate" who possessed a hustling mentality herself. Coleman obviously was not above playing into that rogue fantasy. On the other side of the centerfold the copy continued:

She's looking for a man, or a business manager, to steer her in the *right* direction. You cop jive? It's obvious that there's much the right man could do for her and she for he. She's a fine young filly who needs a man to fulfill her needs—hit me! And what does a man have to be like to qualify? I'll signify! He's got to have a head on his shoulders, clear vision, a mind for the future and an eye on opportunity. He's got to have it together too cold to be bold and have soul—I mean a man still in touch with his *root!*[23]

Here Coleman took the hustler fantasy as far as it would go. Cook's budding career in Los Angeles was framed as in need of "management," which itself slid into a discourse about finding the "right man." It was all code for pimping, of course, couched in half-baked efforts at rapping.

Soon the pictorials made no effort to conceal the models' profession. The fourth issue featured model Karry Onn (ahem), new to San Francisco, hailing from Kansas City, Kansas. Without any pretense of this being a country bumpkin narrative, the copy stated that Onn had moved to the Bay Area to pursue a "solid professional career" in the city's "topless clubs." It conceded that her "motive" was to "supplement her scholarship" at a local university and to "cover rent and other necessities." But Onn's ambition was strictly limited to the red-light district's club scene. The copy improbably stated that she could not be hired because her "dimensions (42-24-36)" had caused some club owners to be "disturbed by such pendulous action." The solution came when one owner recommended that she perform an act focusing on a different part of her body, which she did, dubbing it "The Total Orgasm."[24] The full-page photograph facing this text showed Onn miming the act, legs spread apart, hands resting on her thighs, her head turned to the side. A strategically placed blanket concealed her genitals, but the sexualized fantasy generated by the copy was already complete.

Was Coleman unhappy over having to write such copy for *Players*? We cannot know for sure, and her papers do not suggest anything definitive one way or the other. What that archive does show, however, is that the general view of black womanhood the magazine propagated as fantasy was built upon the very real exploitation of black women's labor at 8060 Melrose Avenue. Within a month of receiving the memo from Coleman, Daphne Bolden was already putting in her two weeks' notice. Her resignation memo made clear that, though she had been hired as an assistant editor, she was being forced to do tasks better described as "general clerical"—essentially all the things Coleman had asked relief from. Dispirited by the workload, the paltry salary, and the false pretenses under which she had been hired, Bolden left appalled by how much work had been left to the two black women in the office.[25] She was not alone. Michelle Kidd, a local black woman contributing editor, submitted a handwritten note, addressed to no one in particular (which is to say, everyone at the company), stating, "I, (Michelle Kidd) will have no further association with 'Player's [sic] Magazine' as you know a black geared magazine towards the black males between 18–35. . . . For not only is this magazine owned by 'whites' . . . it is use [sic] to exploit black creative [unreadable] of their talent—without paying *them*! Another rip off."[26] Coleman's complaints were long-standing, and in June 1974, she outlined the most egregious of them for Morriss, the real financial stakeholder in *Players*. There was a dearth of writing talent to draw from for the regular editorial features. That was connected to the lack of a budget that could afford to pay the kind of rates professional writers expected. And all of it had to do with Coleman having to overextend and overcommit herself to get each issue done, going so far as to ask for personal favors from photographers to cut down on the budget.[27] These were intolerable conditions to work under, and it was only going to get worse with *Players* projected to go monthly.

Coleman sent that memo after she had technically resigned from her position as editor on or around June 15. But, true to the way they had treated her all along, Morriss and Weinstock would not let her go with a clean break. Morriss brought in a "third party" to mediate, and it was through mediation that the harsh reality of the entire situation was made clear. Morriss was, in fact, the "*sole* owner of PLAYERS MAGAZINE and all sister publications," despite Weinstock's claims that they were business partners. Sid Smith was on board only because it had been his idea to start a black men's magazine in the first place, and he had to "practically blackmail himself into" working for the company. And all the work Coleman put into the magazine was uncompensated by design, for *Players*, from the beginning, had been "intended as a hit and run or fly by night (Michelle Kidd was polite when she called it 'experimental') proposition." The worst part was that, after mediation, Coleman would continue to work on *Players* not as editor but as an employee of PSI and Morriss for a trial period of ninety days.[28] In that time she helped put together issues 7 and 8, for which she did not receive credit. That went to her successor, candidates for which she interviewed in late July. Of the six she met with, she was least excited about one Joseph Nazel—"I don't dig the dude."[29] Nazel was the man Morriss and Weinstock selected to be the new editor.

Whether or not Coleman had misgivings about writing copy for nude pictorials, one thing seems clear: *Players* was turning her into a hack. Her employers were used to working with hacks in the sleaze trade; that was unlikely to change just because they made the transition to the black print market. Thus, while Coleman may have facilitated Morriss and Weinstock's appropriation of black men's popular taste, she also had her labor expropriated by a system that, ultimately, was only about maximizing profits. It was a hard lesson nearly every black writer, artist, or production team member had to learn upon agreeing to work for Morriss and Weinstock. Coleman understood that the basic infrastructure of sleaze lay behind even a new publication like *Players*, which is why when she quit for good in August 1974, she could not resist leaving Weinstock this parting memo: "If you want another KNIGHT in black face [*sic*], why don't you just say it."[30]

Copy That

While Coleman was struggling to get *Players* off the ground, editors at Holloway House were busy reorienting the catalog toward black pulp fiction. The issue is that Morriss and Weinstock needed more writers like Goines—hacks who could write action-driven fare at a clip. To their great fortune, one man stepped in to do the work of a dozen hacks. Replicating the extraordinary productivity of Paul Gillette was Joseph Nazel—the essential link connecting pulp paperbacks to *Players* magazine. Joseph Gober Nazel Jr. was born in Berkeley, California, in 1944 and grew up in Los Angeles, where his father worked in maintenance for the Walt Disney Company and his mother clerked for Los Angeles County. He would earn his undergraduate degree from the University of Southern California, crosstown rival of Morriss and Weinstock's alma mater, UCLA.[31] During a tour of Vietnam, Nazel was wounded "from a bullet that passed through his neck in combat," according to his Holloway House associate Emory Holmes II. Military service may have left him "embittered by the futility of war," but it did not stop Nazel from returning to Southern California and becoming an important figure in the region's black press. Before he took over at *Players*, he had "tumultuous stints" at the *Wave*, the *Sentinel*, and the *Watts Times*. His background in the fast-paced world of journalism informed the way he wrote his books. Holmes recalls, "Joseph could write a novel . . . in six weeks flat. And he did it while he was working full time as an (underpaid) editor."[32] By the time of his death, in 2006, he had authored over sixty books, nearly all of them published by Holloway House.

Nazel steered Holloway House away from black sleaze not by devising a radically new aesthetic but by copying genre formulas that were popular in the literary marketplace. Sometimes that meant piggybacking on a major cultural event, as was the case with his *The Black Exorcist* (1974), which took its cue from William Friedkin's 1973 blockbuster film *The Exorcist*, itself adapted from William Peter Blatty's 1971 novel of the same name. More commonly, it meant incorporating black male heroes into the tried-and-tested formulas of men's adventure paperbacks. The Iceman series (1974–87; eight novels, all but the last of which appeared in the first two years) and the James Rhodes series (1974–76; four novels) flooded the market with fast-paced, action-packed books that were light on detection and heavy on blood and thunder. With eleven books appearing in such a short period of time, Nazel did something that Gillette had done in the 1960s—he published the Rhodes series under the pseudonym Dom Gober. The coexistence of Nazel and Gober helped Holloway House market one man's writing as two men's series. But, as we will see, the formula on which Nazel relied the most—the conspiracy plot—lent his series an underlying unity that carried over multiple books.

Billion Dollar Death (1974) introduces us to Henry Highland West, a Harlem-born businessman who now owns and operates the Oasis, "a fantasyland of pleasure and recreation" set within "a self-contained city" near Las Vegas.[33] West, who grew up poor, is better known by his nickname: "the Iceman." The moniker signifies how he had to be "as cold and as hard as the streets he roamed." Orphaned by his early teenage years, he struck out on his own to become a self-made man through the means available to him: namely, pimping. The Iceman used his handsome features and magnetic charm to turn a small-time street-corner operation into "an organization that offered the most beautiful women in the world"; this, Nazel writes, "was the key" to his success. His former prostitutes are now security guards at the resort, "expert in the arts of love, and further trained in the arts of espionage."[34]

James Rhodes, the titular *Black Cop* (1974), would seem to be the polar opposite of the Iceman. Though he works for the Los Angeles Police Department, Rhodes comes across as someone who cares about his community. We are introduced to him during a stakeout with his white partner, Larry Turner. As Rhodes scans the street, he feels sorry for the "derelicts" and "motley array of cast-offs" who wander this predominantly black neighborhood. Nazel writes, "He was always bothered by what the white world had done to so many of his people. He was pissed!" When Rhodes voices his frustration openly, Turner retorts, "Shit, if it was up to me I'd bust them all down and throw the damn jail away. They're not worth a damn."[35] This show of hostility upsets Rhodes, and it takes an extraordinary effort for him not to lash out at Turner. He takes note of his partner's racism and recommits himself to better serving the community.

As different as the Iceman and Rhodes seem, they share features that point to their formulaic equivalence. For example, figures 6.2 and 6.3 show the physical resemblance between the Iceman and Rhodes. The similarities lie in their well-coiffed Afros, their thick mustaches, and even their gun holsters. The cover art also captures the fact that, according to Nazel, the men are of the same build: the Iceman, with "his six foot one, 185 pound frame," finding an echo in Rhodes and "his 185 pound hulk of solid muscle."[36] Beyond looking alike, the Iceman and Rhodes share the trait of being suspicious of the world around them. The Iceman, for example, describes seeing the world through "his cold shell, that impregnable veneer that insulated him."[37] Rhodes, meanwhile, "had learned the hard way that a good cop was one that never let his heart control his thoughts when he was on the beat." The incident in question saw Rhodes narrowly avoid death when he stopped to talk to a young suspect, who returned his sympathy with gunfire. Now Rhodes is careful not to let his guard down: "A cop had to be quicker than that. A cop had to be surer than that. . . . He had to face the icy blast the best that he knew how."[38]

Having emphasized the Iceman's and Rhodes's self-possession, Nazel follows the conspiracy plot to the letter and places them in situations that threaten their sense of control and security. Specifically, each

THE #1

BH440 $150

ICEMAN

BILLION DOLLAR DEATH

by JOSEPH NAZEL

Iceman's
survival is
threatened
by a
revolutionary
plot and
an all-out
confrontation
with
the Mafia!

FIGURE 6.2 Front cover of *Billion Dollar Death* (1974).

BLACK COP

BH461 **$150**

by
DOM GOBER

Heroin, racism and a
traitor plague an
undercover black cop
as he battles
the Syndicate and
his own
Department!

FIGURE 6.3 Front cover of *Black Cop* (1974).

protagonist has to undergo an epistemological crisis. In Rhodes's case, the crisis arrives when drug smugglers are tipped off to the stakeout. After a bloody shootout, in which Turner kills the lone man who surrenders, Rhodes is reduced to questioning what he knows: "He could be wrong. It bothered him. Nothing was certain any more. He was faced with too many possibilities. There was no way that he could be sure."[39] The Iceman's crisis is described in similar terms when an explosion in one of the Oasis's guesthouses disturbs his "peace of mind." Simply put, the Iceman cannot fathom why the Mafia boss Mario Valducci and one of the Oasis's buxom beauties have been blown to smithereens. He suspects there is "a weed in his garden of Eden posing as a rose." The Iceman tries in vain to grasp not only who might have gained from Valducci's execution but also how the bombing happened in the first place, right under his nose. "'There's been a break in security,' he said icily. 'How?'"[40] The question strikes at the core of his identity.

Nazel did not have to look far for inspiration for his conspiracy plots. Before he started writing for Holloway House, he had tried out a pulp series for Pinnacle Books, a fledging New York paperback firm.[41] Though he left Pinnacle after publishing only two books, the company introduced him to the key strategy of the hacks' trade: recycle formulas that sold. Pinnacle published genre fiction of all types, but in the early 1970s it was best known for its conspiracy thrillers featuring larger-than-life male protagonists. Nazel in effect copied plots from the Pinnacle catalog, replacing white men with black men in the lead roles. He had a lot of material to choose from: the original Executioner series, featuring Mack Bolan, by Don Pendleton (1969–80; thirty-seven books); the original Destroyer series, featuring Remo Williams, by Warren Murphy and Richard Sapir (1971–78; thirty-four books); the Butcher series, featuring Bucher (no first name), by Stuart James (house name for a syndicate of writers) (1971–82; thirty-five books); the Death Merchant series, featuring Richard Joseph Camellion, by Joseph Rosenberger (1971–88; seventy books); and the Penetrator series, featuring Mark Hardin, by Lionel Derrick (house name) (1973–84; fifty-three books). Needless to say, Nazel was not alone in copying. All of Pinnacle's authors were hacks: their plots were themselves derivative of midcentury pulp magazine stories—and of each other.

The formula these Pinnacle books followed was simple: put a strong, self-assured man in peril at the beginning, let the self-interested actions of any number of actors play themselves out in the middle, and assert the hero's primacy by having him put a decisive end to the actions and counteractions at the end. The conspiracy plot was perfectly suited to the formula. According to genre critic Jerry Palmer, the conspiracy thriller's "hero is always, initially, outmanoeuvred by the conspirators, for they have more knowledge of the circumstances than he does. The world that surrounds the thriller hero is always opaque."[42] After the hero goes through his epistemological crisis—which in *Billion Dollar Death* is likened to getting caught in a "tangled web woven by an unknown spider"[43]—the conspiracy plot makes it the reader's privilege to know more than the protagonist. At this stage, identification with the hero takes a backseat to the sheer pleasure of seeing an array of interests duke it out through power plays and double crosses. Just when everything seems to spin out of control, the protagonist returns to reassert his authority, and in the process reestablishes the epistemological certainty that the reader started off with. Pinnacle's book series featured cops, vigilantes, spies, and mercenaries in the title roles. These characters' motivations (to say nothing of their moral compasses) had little to no bearing on their popular appeal. What mattered were the thrills they provided. Pinnacle's adventure paperbacks turned what I referenced in the previous chapter as "sensation-without-commitment" into a durable literary formula.

True to the conspiracy plot, the key middle section of Nazel's books is given over to actors beyond the protagonist's ken. While Rhodes goes undercover on the streets, the people who run the drug ring plot their next pickup attempt. First, there is Bill Wilson, a black man who controls the flow of dope into the black neighborhoods of Los Angeles. Although he is committed to maintaining his side of the operation, Wilson is fed up playing second fiddle to his coconspirators: "Shit, he had done all the dirty work and the Syndicate was getting the biggest piece of the action." Helming the Syndicate is Morrie Slater, a white man who controls drug shipments to the city. Having "put the organization together damn near by himself,"[44] Slater negotiates with Wilson only because he needs him to run the drug-dealing operation in black neighborhoods. Both men would rather operate without the other, however, and they end up locked in a power struggle precisely while Rhodes is tracking them. Slater orders Turner (who is on his payroll) to dispose of his partner-cum-rival, but Wilson has his own plan for getting to him first. At this point in the book, the kingpins' mutual antagonism is of greater narrative import than Rhodes's antagonism toward them.

Billion Dollar Death multiplies conspiratorial antagonisms with globe-spanning implications. There is Angelo Pettreno, Mafia chief who tries to assassinate the Iceman because he suspects him of Valducci's murder; J.J. Brown, a washed-up singer who performs at the Oasis but resents the Iceman's success; a mysterious senator who seems to be in cahoots with Brown; and Umotu, prime minister of an unnamed African country who is not in Nevada on state business. As Nazel turns his attention to these characters, the narrative spins out into a handful of subplots. First, it is revealed that Umoto's intentions are traitorous: "Soon, if everything went as planned, he would be the new ruler of his tiny country. He would be the power." He is cooperating with the senator, who says that he "intend[s] to be the biggest, most powerful man in the entire world." The plan is to exchange US military weapons for Umotu's diamonds. The senator would then abscond to South America, where he could convert the precious stones into money—the titular billion dollars—that would help him "win a war."[45] What does J.J. have to do with any of this? The senator's end of the deal had gotten tied up with the Mafia somehow, and so he manipulated J.J.'s grudge against the Iceman to rid himself of Valducci, the man who would take his share of the profits. By the final tally, then, alongside Pettreno's efforts to kill the Iceman, there is a plot for an African coup, a scheme for world domination, and a story of revenge that explains Valducci's murder.

Now that the true power players have emerged, Nazel, following the conspiracy plot, ensures that his protagonists return to the foreground and reassert their authority. The Iceman, his female security team, and a posse of allies ambush all of the conspirators in the Nevada desert, where Pettreno, who had figured out the global conspiracy for himself, was trying to seize control of the whole operation. For their punishment, Umotu and the senator are sent (back) to Africa to face the consequences of trying to stage a coup against the king, while Pettreno and J.J. are dropped off on a remote mountaintop to languish in isolation. *Black Cop* is resolved when Rhodes's undercover disguise gains him entry to a clandestine meeting among the Syndicate's key players. A firefight ensues after Turner points out Rhodes's true identity to Slater. Rhodes is just too good of a shot to let the culprits get away: Wilson and Turner are mowed down to the delight of the reader. Slater skips out of view and seems to get away with it, only to be brought back in the final chapter when we discover he has been arrested.

Confirmation of the Iceman's and Rhodes's heroism was a foregone conclusion, of course. That is because the formula dictated it. The Executioner, the Destroyer, the Penetrator: whatever their moniker, Pinnacle's adventure heroes got lost in any number of conspiracy scenarios only to turn up at the end and assure readers they were back in control. That Nazel modeled his series on his former employer's output is clear.[46] The conspiracy plots that Pinnacle's hacks recycled from earlier sources and from each other inevitably found their way into Nazel's work. Even Henry Highland West's nickname can be traced to the Butcher series, whose protagonist went by the code name "Iceman." To be sure, copying Pinnacle's formula was neither extraordinary nor unethical—it was the name of the game. Pinnacle and Holloway House were, after all, in the same business: hiring hacks to write books that would appeal to men. Goines had pointed Morriss and Weinstock to the possibilities of writing black pulp outside the bounds of sleaze, and Joseph Nazel landed on a formula that would allow him to do that over and over again.

Die Another Day

Pinnacle's model of adventure paperback publishing brought about several changes to the Holloway House catalog. First, as discussed above, it propagated a formula for popular fiction that steered clear of sleaze tropes while still appealing to male readers. Though there were clearly sexist elements to adventure fiction (see the Iceman's harem-cum-security force), the formula was not beholden to antidomestic ideology to the extent that Holloway House's erotica and fake confessionals were. Second, Pinnacle underscored the value of publishing serial fiction as a strategy of the hacks' trade. Series with strong protagonists kept readers coming back for more, so long as the formula's rules were observed. Series' success also meant that a slew of black-authored titles now appeared in Holloway House's catalog where only a handful were present between 1967 and 1973. So the perception that Holloway House specialized in black pulp fiction was solidified by the publication of serial works. Finally, the Pinnacle model helped a slew of unknown writers gain a foothold in the publishing industry. It was the Goines effect on repeat: genuine outsiders, with no connections to Los Angeles or local media, submitting their action-packed stories over the transom.

One such author had a day job in Silicon Valley. Roosevelt Mallory was a television director in the Hewlett-Packard Data Systems training department. He had previously served as the company's "first professional computer instructor." Mallory's was a classic civil rights story: born on an Alabama sharecropping farm, he dropped out of high school, despite being "a top student and athlete," and enlisted in the armed services. In the Coast Guard, he became an electronics technician, which set him on his current career path, rising through the ranks at one of America's most established computing companies. Now, in early 1974, Mallory was celebrating the publication of *Harlem Hit* (1973), the first in a series of adventure novels starring an assassin for hire named Joseph Radcliff, a.k.a. the Hit-Master. In a feature story for Hewlett-Packard's company magazine, Mallory said he had created Radcliff after watching poorly scripted "hit-man movies featuring a black hero." He did not mention Pinnacle, but the Hit-Master seemed an uncanny echo of Don Pendleton's Mack Bolan, a.k.a. the Executioner: both are Vietnam veterans who, after the war, use their military training to take on organized crime and international terror networks. Mallory originally had ended *Harlem Hit* with Radcliff's death, but, at the urging of his publishers, he changed it so that his protagonist survived and the series could continue, which it did for three more titles, published through 1976. But the mild-mannered Mallory was quite unlike the gun-toting Radcliff, Hewlett-Packard assured its readers: his "real-life haunts" were "with his family; on a salmon fishing boat off the Golden Gate; a trout stream in the Sierra; some golf or skiing if his old football injuries permit."[47]

Coming from the opposite end of the social spectrum was James-Howard Readus (sometimes credited as James Howard Readus, without the hyphen). Like Goines, Readus decided to try his hand at writing in prison. Unlike Goines, he was forced to remain there while Holloway House published his books. Though not a series writer per se, Readus was clearly inspired by the Pinnacle model. His first novel, *The Death Merchants* (1974), was a one-off thriller that banked on the name recognition of Joseph Rosenberger's Death Merchant series. His next two novels, *The Black Assassin* and *The Big Hit* (both 1975), were potboilers in the same vein. Readus's hometown black newspaper, the *Indianapolis Recorder*, celebrated his achievements on the occasion of *The Big Hit*'s publication. The story speculated that the book "could well be about the author himself" insofar as it focused on "an angry, alienated, young black man" and took place in the "Northern Indiana underworld." But it also quoted a *Players* review of *The Black Assassin* that highlighted the real force of his aesthetic: "Fiction . . . but it might be true! A colossal conspiracy, spawned by business and military leaders, to methodically assassinate major political figures as the first black man moves slowly but surely toward the Presidency of the United States!"[48] This toggling between literary formula and what felt real lay at the heart not only of Readus's aesthetic but of black pulp paperbacks writ large.

That the *Recorder* could creditably cite *Players* as a reviewing source was no coincidence. The magazine's circulation ensured that there was a continuum between Holloway House's and black readers' interests. In turn, the *Recorder* authenticated Readus's status as a member of the community who had written books for that community's entertainment. The story affectionately referred to him as "a former Recorder carrier and resident of Indianapolis." It also mentioned he was currently incarcerated at the Indiana State Reformatory. And, perhaps most important, it devoted fully two-thirds of its allotted space to Readus's commentary on the need for prison reform both in Indiana and across the country. The *Recorder* treated him not just as an abstract author but as a living, breathing member of the community:

There's so much to be done in the area of "honest" prison reform right now, yet the pendulum is swinging in the opposite direction. For the hapless souls writhing in agony daily, nothing is being done. A lot of emphasis is being placed on tighter security, hiring more guards, and counterproductive stuff such as that. Contained within the Indiana Bill of Rights is a section that claims the philosophy of prison shall be based on reformation and not vindictive punishment. For a time I think there were token gestures in this direction but not any longer.[49]

Readus linked his fate to the prisoners who had perished in the Attica Prison riot of 1971 and to his fellow black inmates, who made up a majority of the reformatory's population. He was, in fact, bearing witness to the roots of what would come to be called mass incarceration. Even today, it reads as a riveting, deeply meaningful testament. By thus allowing Readus to speak on his own terms, the *Recorder* drew out the real-life concerns and experiences that lay behind black pulp fiction's growing popularity.

The Pinnacle formula proved to be such a handy template that it was only a matter a time before Goines himself came to rely on it. He had released four novels in quick succession in early 1974. *Black Girl Lost*, *Eldorado Red*, and *Never Die Alone* were stand-alone potboilers, while *Swamp Man* was a throwback to black sleaze, its lurid take on interracial rape in the deep South befitting slavers of the 1960s. At this point in his career, Goines was writing not for royalties but for advances that would pay for his next hit. Unfortunately, a stint in Los Angeles with his common-law wife, Shirley Sailor, and their two daughters had not been able to break the habit. Now, back in Detroit, with nine books under his belt, Goines had to consider what there was left to write about.[50]

The answer was the conspiracy plot. The March 1974 issue of *Players* featured an ad for his latest, a book called *Crime Partners*:

In this powerful first novel Al C. Clark lays bare the bloody, brutal world of crime in the black ghetto. CRIME PARTNERS is a gutsy, sometimes shocking story of Billy and Jackie, ex-prison buddies hot on the trigger to pull any job that pays the bread; of Benson, a black detective and his white partner Ryan, companions in the fight against black organized crime; and of Kenyatta, a ghetto chieftain torn between two ambitions: cleaning the ghetto of all drug traffic and gunning down all the white cops! This is a book that will grip you from first page to last![51]

The real Al C. Clark was Goines's childhood friend from Detroit. But as a pen name, Al C. Clark gave Goines the cover he needed to publish Pinnacle-style pulp fiction. Having worked with hacks his entire career, Morriss had suggested using a pen name: "We want to publish the books, but if you put out too many books of an author within a given period of time it has a sham about it. Would you consider putting a book out under a pseudonym?"[52] Goines not only ran with the idea—he devised an entire series out of it.

As Clark, he would go on to write a four-book sequence centered on Kenyatta, a Detroit gang leader bearing the name of Kenya's independence hero and first president, Jomo Kenyatta. The name conjured the revolutionary fervor of Third World liberation, and critics have read the series in that light, with Candice Love Jackson linking Kenyatta to the Black Panthers and Justin Gifford characterizing the books as "a theater to stage the radical possibilities of an organized subversion of white power."[53] But Goines was not one for such idealism. Drawing on the revenge plots of the Pinnacle formula, he created in Kenyatta his most uncompromising and tragically flawed character yet.

Kenyatta is introduced in *Crime Partners* (1974) when Billy and Jackie arrive at his lair and inquire about joining his "organization." They learn that Kenyatta's gang has been responsible for a string of assassinations of white police officers around Detroit. "How you think all them white cops that've been gettin' knocked off in this city got hit?" asks Kenyatta. "Do you know of any other niggers in this city with enough balls to knock off a cop?" Billy and Jackie balk at the idea of killing random cops, but Kenyatta clarifies that they would be expected to do just that if they wanted to join the group. As if to balance the scales a bit, he tells them that he is also committed to going after "every motherfuckin' hunky that has his hand in dope." Thus, between assassinating white cops and targeting white dope distributors, Kenyatta has defined his group's motto: "Kill the hunky. That's our rally cry. Death to Whitey."[54]

Structurally speaking, Kenyatta is positioned between conspiracies.

He is the shadowy figure terrorizing cops, but he is also the moral crusader trying to piece together the lattice of Detroit's dope network. The inclusion of Billy and Jackie here, and of Benson and Ryan throughout the series, is critical. Their narrative viewpoints provide readers a "check" on Kenyatta's conspiratorial mindset. So, for example, upon hearing Kenyatta's plan to rid Detroit's streets of both cops and dealers, Goines writes,

As he spoke, his voice rose with the power of his conviction. Jackie thought to himself that this brother is mad. He's stone crazy, he believes every fuckin' thing he's saying. There was no doubt in either man's mind of that. Kenyatta was serious about everything he said. The thought of him having over forty people believing in him was crazy in itself. That many people following in his path would give a madman quite a bit of power.[55]

Already the motives behind Kenyatta's actions are being questioned. It is not so much that Billy and Jackie question his sincerity—the "power of his conviction" is abundantly clear—as they question his sanity. That, of course, is a classic conspiracy trope, and Goines deploys it to keep the reader guessing whether Kenyatta is onto something or simply leading his people to ruin.

Once the reader is hooked, Goines gives the series over to action-packed episodes of violence and flight. Books 1 through 3 conclude with dramatic scenes of death, destruction, and outlaws on the lam, which are then picked up at the start of books 2 through 4. *Crime Partners*, for example, ends with Billy and Jackie's shooting deaths, which are ordered by a drug boss, King Fisher, as retaliation for their hit against one of his dealers. *Death List* (1974) commences with Benson and Ryan arriving at the double-murder scene moments too late. Kingfisher (his name is changed to one word in the second book) is himself assassinated in the course of the novel, and *Death List* closes with Kenyatta and a handful of his followers escaping a police raid on their countryside commune just outside of Detroit. The appropriately titled *Kenyatta's Escape* (1974) follows the group literally in flight as they hijack a plane with the aim of transporting themselves to a country "where a Black man is treated like a man."[56] The plane does not make it to Algiers. Instead, it crash-lands in the Nevada desert, where Kenyatta then makes plans to move his ragtag group to Los Angeles. Benson and Ryan spend the entire novel chasing shadows, trying to help local and federal authorities bring Kenyatta to justice. They always remain one step behind the outlaws. *Kenyatta's Escape* closes with Kenyatta and four surviving followers again narrowly escaping from the law after an explosive gas station shootout. *Kenyatta's Last Hit* (1975) commences about a year after the second escape, but we still find Benson and Ryan smarting after their failed capture. They return to Los Angeles to make one final grab at Kenyatta. Once they arrive, they discover he now commands a two thousand–strong following in Watts.

If Benson and Ryan's pursuit of Kenyatta lends the series its internarrative propulsion, Kenyatta's unshakable belief in his rectitude results in the kind of shock and awe that keeps the reader hooked. Cleaning up Detroit's streets by any means necessary turns out to be a bane for Kenyatta and his associates. Violence begets violence until it spins out of control, taking on a life of its own and, in the process, undermining the moral distinction between guilt and innocence. In *Crime Partners*, Kenyatta's targeted killing of two racist policemen leads to an all-out bloodbath. Nine men are slaughtered, including a gang member whom Kenyatta shoots because he flubbed the getaway. In the same novel, Billy and Jackie's hit on the drug dealer Little David leads directly to their own deaths, as well as those of their lovers, by order of King Fisher. Although Kenyatta is technically responsible for starting the cycle of bloody reprisals, *Death List* begins with the detached observation that it was Billy and Jackie's fate that they should have died so violently: "Blood ran freely down off the sidewalk into the gutter as the lifeless forms of four young black people lay in the filth and hopelessness of the hard-pressed neighborhood." The victims have been acted upon—"Billy was spattered with the blood of his loved one," and Jackie "kept falling until the hard pavement struck him in the face"[57]—but Goines's prose absolves Kenyatta of responsibility for their deaths. As with *Black Gangster*, his passive-voice description of violence gives the impression that a timeless and agentless fate—what I earlier called a narrative death drive—has destroyed his characters.

The bodies keep piling up, with both loyalists and officers suffering massive losses. In *Kenyatta's Escape*, a police raid on Kenyatta's rural commune leaves eight officers and over twenty of Kenyatta's followers dead in a shootout, at the end of which the group's farmhouse is set ablaze. Kenyatta manages to leave the commune in the nick of time, knowing his people will perish. In this way, what starts off as an ostensibly noble cause devolves into Kenyatta's efforts to evade the law. Indeed, as his crimes catch up with him, Kenyatta is shown constantly in flight, leaving his followers to die at the hands of police. Terrence T. Tucker interprets this novel as affirming the leader's "commitment to his organization and its members," saying it is "unyielding" because he feels a measure of "guilt" after leaving them behind to perish.[58] Yet Kenyatta's attempted flight to Algiers is no act of solidarity—it is an act of self-preservation. Jerry H. Bryant offers a soberer take when he says that "Kenyatta's methods doom him to failure."[59] Like Prince in *Black Gangster*, the professed revolutionary's dedication to his community turns out to be a hollow promise.

Goines's stone-cold cynicism about Black Power was in keeping with Pinnacle's revenge plots, but it also may have reflected his own despair at not being able to kick the habit. Indeed, a narrative death drive could have been Goines's way of writing about the hopelessness of his situation. On October 21, 1974, life really did imitate art. Goines was putting the final touches on *Kenyatta's Last Hit* when two white men whom Shirley Sailor supposedly knew came into their apartment. Goines and Sailor were shot to death, he near his typewriter, she in the kitchen. Their young daughters had been spared, but having watched their parents' execution, they then had to spend the night with their bodies. It was not lost on anyone that the horrific scenario could have been taken straight from one of Goines's novels.[60]

At the time word on the street was that Goines had been killed for one of three reasons. The first theory was that he himself had been selling dope in order to break even with his habit. So a dope deal gone wrong. The second theory was simple robbery. He had received $900 in the mail that morning, but the police found only seventy-six cents in the apartment the next day. The third theory was that Goines was preparing to pull off the proverbial last big deal—dealing in what was unspecified—so that he could have enough money to leave the country for good. Highland Park police arrested two suspects, but they were released for lack of evidence.[61]

Goines's murder was a boon for Holloway House; it authenticated the street-level experience that its authors were said to have lived themselves. Goines never sought the limelight in the same way Slim did. But now, in death, Morriss and Weinstock would make sure he became their star. They tapped a local white hack, Carlton Hollander, to pen Goines's life story for speedy publication.[62] Under the pseudonym Eddie Stone, Hollander immortalized Goines in *Donald Writes No More* (1974), at once a sensational biography of the man and an extended advertisement for his novels. In many respects, this single book sealed the company's claim to an urban black readership. Goines had lived and died by the code of the street, *Donald Writes No More* proposed, and his novels were hard-hitting testaments to that fact. For his part, Stone ensured that generations of black readers would be sympathetic to the publisher that had given the author his big break. Musing on the sympathetic treatment of Ryan, the white partner in the detective duo giving chase to Kenyatta, he wrote:

Prior to coming to California, [Goines's] associations with white men had been limited. And very few, if any, had been productive. But in California, that situation had changed. His editors, who were at the time white, his lawyers and the people around the publishing business helped him greatly and gave him much needed encouragement. Donald began to see that not all white men were racist, and that not all white men were trying to compromise him with liberal rhetoric. The men he worked with in California showed him another side. They were genuinely interested in him as a writer, and as a man. They treated him fairly and he respected that.[63]

This specious, lopsided account accorded Holloway House all the credit while claiming Goines's views of race had changed for the better. The author himself could not contest it, and that was the point. Goines was the perfect icon around which black pulp fiction could be built: dead in real life but whose image could be sold in perpetuity.

That came to pass when *Kenyatta's Last Hit* was released posthumously, in early 1975. Though the cover gave byline credit to Clark, the blurb underneath it announced, "This book is the last in the great Kenyatta adventure series written by the late DONALD GOINES under the Al C. Clark pseudonym." The belated recognition found an uncanny echo in the novel itself. With a reconstituted army of followers in Los Angeles, Kenyatta goes after the prime mover of the ghetto's drug economy, a mysterious businessman named Clement Jenkins. Kenyatta has concluded that these corporate types "were the controlling powers, the fat honkies who sat back in their leather office chairs dealing out death and corruption with one flick of their pudgy pink fingers. These were the men whom Kenyatta had always been after, yet men whom he had never really seen."[64] Kenyatta's belated insight suggests that his previous attempts at cleaning up the streets missed the point that the true exploiters of the ghetto are those who orchestrate law-enforcement corruption and drug distribution from a distance. Ironically, then, it was corporate white men's invisibility that, earlier in the series, made beat cops and drug dealers such visible targets of Kenyatta's wrath. His "last hit" promises to take out Jenkins as the real agent of black suffering.

After setting Kenyatta up for a climactic confrontation with Jenkins, and with so much riding on his finally doing justice for his people, Goines concludes the series on a note of despair. Kenyatta tracks Jenkins to Las Vegas, and in a showdown between his followers and

Jenkins's guards, Kenyatta is hit with the realization that he may have "underestimated his man." He is, in essence, overawed by the task of killing the Man himself. When shots do ring out, it is Kenyatta who wounds Jenkins on the shoulder, sending him falling to the floor. Yet in an inexplicable seizure of action, Kenyatta simply waits. He waits "to see the white man crawl, the white millionaire who dealt in death." He waits for what seems like an eternity, and Goines points out that he "would wait all night to see it, to see a man whom he had hated in the abstract for so many years beg him for his life." But in that decisive moment, of waiting for the abstract to become real, Kenyatta is cleanly eliminated with a single bullet to the head fired by one of the guards. In the melee that follows, Jenkins manages to escape via a waiting helicopter while the lone surviving member of Kenyatta's group runs for his life, recognizing that "no matter what he did in his lifetime he could never bring the big man back."[65]

With this ending had Goines foreshadowed his own demise? Could Kenyatta's last hit have been an allegory for his writing life—going through the motions but freezing up when it came time for decisive action? It certainly seemed like the perfect confluence of life and art. But that, again, was by design. Carlton Hollander was not only Goines's biographer—he was his ghost. As the author's heroin addiction severely diminished his writing capacities, Holloway House hired Hollander to "edit and rewrite" his books. He visited Goines in Detroit to work on manuscripts with him in person. In that light, he may have been the one to suggest including a black-white detective duo in the series at all. After Goines's untimely death, Holloway House commissioned *Donald Writes No More* but also asked Hollander to finish his last three books, including the stand-alone novel *Inner City Hoodlum* (1975). According to Hollander, he "shared the royalties" from these books with Goines's mother.[66] Out of a terrible tragedy, Morriss and Weinstock had orchestrated their greatest feat yet: using a white man to turn Goines into the patron saint of street culture.

The front page of the October 10, 1974, edition of Los Angeles's *Herald-Dispatch* featured a kicker that was sure to catch the reader's attention: "SHE STOLE FROM ME," it blared, ventriloquizing Bentley Morriss's accusation against former *Players* editor Wanda Coleman. The front-page story fell under the headline "Sex Mag. Charges Black Woman Editor." In it the author filled in the details of a lawsuit that had been filed with the Los Angeles city attorney. "Morris Bentley" had charged Coleman with "walking off with numerous materials vital to the publication of Players magazine," presumably as she was leaving work for the last time. The court hearing was scheduled for October 29, and the story made it a point to say that Coleman was being represented by a black attorney, Carl Sherman.[67]

But all of these details were a pretext, it seemed, for the author to make a broader point about the suing party. "Players magazine," he wrote, "one of the many white-owned black communications seeping into the black community via blacks 'fronting' for white controllers, is a sex oriented publication depicting young under-paid nude black women." The *Herald-Dispatch* was an African American newspaper—a lesser-known cousin to the *Sentinel*—and it used the occasion of the lawsuit to lambaste "wise ethnic white owners" who were "gulping up the dollars meant for the black-owned press." By exploiting the desire for race-oriented fare, white owners had diminished the ability of "legitimate black communications" to compete in the media landscape and thereby "retain[ed] control of black thoughts, black children and black men and women."[68] The *Herald-Dispatch* made sure Bentley Morriss knew exactly what it thought of him in the court of public opinion.

But Coleman did not get off lightly either. Though critical of Morriss, the author implied Coleman had brought the trouble upon herself. "The blacks 'fronting' for white corporations are numerous," he lamented. "Once the white corporation, with the help of the black front, gets a 'toe hold' in the black community, they are finished with 'the catching n . . .' The commodity becomes salable and dollars go out of the black community never to return again."[69] According to the author's logic, by "fronting" for *Players*, Coleman had lent the magazine a credibility that made it appealing to a black audience. Her identity as the magazine's black woman editor had allowed *Players* to gain entry into the black public sphere. Once it established itself in that sphere, Coleman became expendable—no longer necessary to Morriss's business plan. In this analysis, Coleman was Morriss's "catching n . . ."—the bait for unsuspecting readers.

The *Herald-Dispatch* was onto something. Coleman's papers support the view that she built *Players* from the ground up while Morriss reaped the financial rewards. They also show that she was exploited for her labor, and that her editorial vision was appropriated by Players International Publications. Joseph Nazel could easily pick up where Coleman had left off because *Players* itself constituted the formula for a modern pornographic magazine targeting black men. When he took over the editorship from her, it was reported that the magazine had a "circulation base of 300,000, reaching over 1,500,000 readers."[70]

Yet, for these very reasons, the *Herald-Dispatch*'s "fronting" language was perhaps slightly off the mark. Coleman was not just the "front" of *Players* but its entire structure, top to bottom. Indeed, beginning with her editorship, both Players International Publications and Holloway House welcomed an unprecedented number of black talent into their ranks. That included editors, authors, critics and reviewers, cartoonists and illustrators, photographers, and, of course, models. To be sure, Morriss still owned the means of production, and Ralph Weinstock did his bidding as a middle manager. But it would be a mistake, I think, to reduce their output to an inauthentic representation of black interests. Compared to the era of sleaze that preceded it, the conjunction of white capital and black talent at Melrose Avenue generated print commodities that were written by black authors for black readers. The problem was that, in order to realize this goal, Morriss and Weinstock exploited black talent in ways that made them feel like cogs in a mass-market machine. So while their pulps and pinups felt authentic to experience, unique to black readers' interests and tastes, they produced them in a wholly unoriginal way: working on tight budgets and tight schedules, and using formulas and templates that were proven to succeed. The transformation of Holloway House and *Players* into a black communications circuit was complete.

SEVEN

Reading the Street

Players made one notable appearance in popular culture before it became largely invisible to the white gaze. In April 1975, it was featured on network television, in an episode of the sitcom *The Jeffersons*. Developed by Norman Lear as a spin-off of *All in the Family*, the series had debuted on CBS in January of that year. *The Jeffersons* featured a black middle-class family whose patriarch, George Jefferson (Sherman Hemsley), had risen up out of the ghetto to become a respectable businessman, the owner of a successful dry cleaning business. A staunch advocate of self-made success and personal responsibility, George's middle-class masculinity was loud, confrontational, and unapologetic about its investment in individual advancement. Yet much of the series' comic purchase arrived at George's expense: his wife Louise (Isabel Sanford) never failed to remind him where he came from, and the moral upshot of many episodes was that the Jeffersons' middle-class life could never really be severed from the blighted streets of Harlem that used to be their stomping grounds.

Midway through the episode in question, we find George lounging on the sofa in the family's spacious living room. He is wearing a plush robe over a casual outfit and is flipping through the pages of *Players* magazine. When Louise asks him if he is ready to go to bed, George opens up the centerfold and blithely comments, "In a minute." By way of clarification, George tells Louise he is reading their son's magazine. But he has a little fun at her expense when, referring to the foldout centerfold, he quips, "Ain't she tall?"

Louise expresses disgust at the pornography, saying she "wouldn't pose like that for a million dollars." George retorts, "They'd never pay you a million dollars." Louise leaves the room in a huff but not before she holds this little jibe over George's head, promising to "remember" it when they retire to bed.

After Louise retires, the Jeffersons' son Lionel (Mike Evans) happens upon his father scanning *Players* and jokes, "I bet you didn't have anything like that when you were a kid." George responds, "Of course we did. We just didn't put it in magazines." Lionel and George share a laugh over this cross-generational point of male affiliation. Here father and son recognize each other in their respective skirt-chasing activities, and *Players* is cast as the modern, glossy counterpart to long-standing forms of black male leisure—and bonding. Though brief, the scene featuring the magazine dramatizes a larger point about George and Lionel's relationship, one that is encapsulated in the episode's title: "Like Father, Like Son."

The Jeffersons episode demonstrated how much *Players* had helped Bentley Morriss and Ralph Weinstock reorient their enterprise. The (now) monthly periodical helped connect a readership with which they had been barely familiar to the production processes at 8060 Melrose Avenue. The black literary underground developed out of and alongside this new communications circuit. With black pulp fiction, *Players* magazine, and *Players*'s sister publication, the all-nude *Pictorial*, Morriss and Weinstock had effectively cornered the market niche for black men's leisure reading. What made their operation underground had little to do with obscenity statutes or censorship. It had more to do with attitude: a cross-class, cross-generational entitlement to opinion and pleasure that, in most other contexts, would probably be suppressed, derided, or both. This is how black men came to embrace Holloway House and *Players* as their own. Morriss and Weinstock's print commodities gave them a popular medium through which they could delight in stories, sentiments, and visuals that may have been moderately impolite (at best) and dangerously offensive (at worst)—if, that is, they were consumed in front of whites, women, or people who affected a certain level of taste. Black porn and pulp fiction rejected all of it, essentially saying that what bound black men to each other—George to Lionel, but also George to the neighborhood in which he grew up—was their ethos, or orientation toward life.

That ethos was difficult to define. It could be conservative and progressive, illiberal and broad-minded, sordid and righteous. It hewed to no single ideology. What it did was closely identify with the street—coming up on it, surviving it, earning one's reputation through it, or simply looking like one had. In short, the inner-city thoroughfare was imagined as a proving ground for black men, regardless of their background. On the street, one learned that the entire world was a hustle, and that black men were the key players in it. How one negotiated the hustle was not simply a matter of exercising street smarts—it was also a matter of displaying a certain kind of style. One could still play the part, in other words, without ever having stepped foot on the street.

These points should sound familiar. Robin D. G. Kelley, Shane and Graham White, and Davarian L. Baldwin, among others, have traced how urban black men's style, from fashion and musical tastes to dance and other forms of public movement, have played a crucial, if underappreciated, role in modern African American cultural politics.[1] Morriss and Weinstock's operation was unique, however, in that print was the means of transmitting urban black men's style and itself the bearer of that style. In other words, the simple act of reading black pulp fiction and *Players* was tantamount to living the life of leisure fictional pimps and real-life celebrities seemed to enjoy.

This chapter tracks the way Holloway House's and *Players*'s businesses were intertwined between 1975 and 1977. By now the question was not whether Morriss and Weinstock had enough stock in black pulp or if they had the wherewithal to run a monthly black men's magazine. The question was how to keep black men reading both. *Players* and pulp needed to be understood as imagining two sides of the same coin. In laying out my analysis, I follow the basic contours of one letter-writer's assessment of *Players*'s editorial direction in early 1976:

Count me as one of those who feel that you have a beautiful magazine and you're getting better. I'd like to compliment you on your choice of the young ladies who model in Players. I would also like to compliment your advertising various books by black authors, particularly those of Donald Goines. I have read several of his books. He was such a fine writer to have died such a tragic death. I also would like to compliment you on your open forum. You present all viewpoints in favor of, and against the way Players is going. Go and get down with it.[2]

Women to look at, books to read, and an "open forum" to which readers felt empowered to contribute: these were the constitutive elements of the black literary underground. I examine each of them below, in reverse order.

Reclaiming the Street

"Old Hustler Recalls Silky Life of a Pimp." The headline on the front page of the April 22, 1974, issue of the *Detroit Free Press* might have applied to Iceberg Slim, but the subject of the story was fifty-three-year-old local Andrew Stonewall "Stoney" Jackson. A white reporter visited "the back room of an inner city barber shop," where he found Jackson "talking grandly about the splendor of his career and crowing about the ease of his latest hustle—writing books." Like Donald Goines, Jackson had been inspired to write while reading *Pimp* and *Trick Baby* in Jackson State Prison. And, also like Goines, after Jackson had submitted his manuscript over the transom, Holloway House offered to be his publisher. The result was his 1973 memoir *Gentleman Pimp*, a book that, as the *Free Press* noted, "tells floridly of his ventures past—of the pimp's 'silky life,' as Stoney calls it, of those eight years of glory long ago when he was able to 'change cars twice a year.'" Indebted to the vernacular flair and bildungsroman structure of *Pimp*, *Gentleman Pimp* was, in truth, an inferior copy of the original. Indeed, the news story could not help but point out that the book was "poorly written, ridden with cliches [*sic*] and boring repetitions." But that hardly mattered to Jackson, whose book was intended for readers like the black men who surrounded him in the barbershop. Not content to let the Los Angeles–based All America Distributors Corporation handle his publicity, Jackson would walk around downtown Detroit, "checking the book racks at the Greyhound station, then trekking to the newsstand in Grand Circus Park, and finally trudging down to Broadway Books," making personal appeals to buy his book along the way. He was so successful that, as the owner of Broadway put it, *Gentleman Pimp* "killed off 'The Pimp' by Iceberg Slim" in sales.[3]

This time around, Slim was not to be outdone. He announced his intention to reclaim the street of his literary imagination in the winter 1974 issue of *Black Collegian* magazine. It was fitting that he sat down for the interview with Black Arts poet and social activist Kalamu ya Salaam (formerly Val Ferdinand). In some respects, both men had remade themselves in the mold of the changing politics of the era, with the emphasis falling on how to stay black in integrating institutional contexts (i.e., the white college or university). Though Slim began the interview repeating some of the cautionary advice he had given in the past, he also signaled his taking leave from the redemptive anachronicity line. Addressing the question of what he considered his "purpose in life now," Slim admitted, "With the young people, that's purely a selfish motive. It keeps me young when they're interested in me. You might say I'm a kind of sociological vampire. I feed upon this youth, their enthusiasm. It keeps me young." This was a far cry from *Naked Soul*'s self-effacing valorization of the Black Panthers as the real black men of the day. To Salaam, Slim was building up his image as a revitalized teacher, someone who both fed off young people's admiration and could claim to teach them a thing or two. And that was how it played out in the interview. For instance, where Slim used to envy younger pimps precisely for their youth, he now found much at fault in their pimping style. The problem: they typically did not have a "bottom woman," or main prostitute who could manage the petty affairs of the other women in the stable. Pimps today had to do all the work. To which Slim retorted: "I don't know of any pimps I came up with that would stay up all night and miss their rest! Don't get no rest? That's the name of the pimp game, restin' and dressin'."[4] Young pimps had forgotten the leisurely side of pimping, Slim contended, and he was here to bring it back.

Slim made good on redeeming himself the following year when he released an album of toasts, or long narrative poems rooted in oral tradition. Titled *Reflections*, the record was not a Holloway House production. Instead, it came out with Los Angeles's ALA Enterprises and featured backing music by legendary jazz musician Red Holloway. Holloway was a fellow Chicagoan and also the son of Southern migrants. Having played tenor saxophone since the age of twelve, he honed his craft in the city after a tour with the armed services. In 1967, Holloway moved to Los Angeles, where he would eventually lead the house band at the Persian Room, a jazz venue of some renown.[5] Whether Slim knew Holloway from Chicago or Los Angeles is unclear, but the latter did introduce the author to David Drozen, a record producer specializing in black vernacular culture. Drozen's most celebrated records featured sets by black comedians, including Redd Foxx, Richard Pryor, and LaWanda Page. But he also worked with the Watts Prophets, a trio coming out of the Watts Writers Workshop, to release *Rappin' Black in a White World* (1971), an album of poetry set to a fusion jazz-funk beat. This album, along with spoken word poetry by the Last Poets, was an important forerunner to hip-hop.[6] Between Holloway and Drozen, then, Slim had a team that could bring his pimp persona to life, thereby solidifying his claim to street authenticity.

Slim's languid delivery in *Reflections* is complemented by the Red Holloway Quartet's smooth jazz sounds; together they lend the poetry an aura of street-tested timelessness. In "Broadway Sam," for example, the narrator relates the story of the titular "big mackman," a pimp who slides into drug addiction at the behest of Mabel, his "dope fiend whore." The narrator warns:

She was the best in the East and the West,
Once, a long time ago,
But an arm full of junk will take all the spunk
Out of the very best whore.

Slim lingers over "once," highlighting the pastness of Mabel's fame. That she is already hooked on heroin by the time Sam meets her is an oversight that has tragic consequences for him. As soon as Mable introduces Sam to the drug, it is not so much that the tables have turned as the entire game has been switched around on him. The toast continues:

He was king of them all till he took that fall,
Till he made that fatal slip.
He thought it was boss when he shot that horse;
He thought he was being hip.

Soon Sam is in a desperate race, chasing the next fix and losing everything in the process. His fall from grace is complete when, with Mabel stuck in jail (thus losing his only source of income), he "got so sick he went down on a mick. / Big Sam had turned a trick." Slim's variation on the line "He got so sick he sucked a dick," underscores Sam's sexual and racial debasement ("sick"/"mick"), for "mick" is a derogatory term for an Irishman. So it is not just that Sam "sucked a dick" for money but that he sucked a white man's. Echoing the sexual and racial debasement of Otis Tilson, the abject Sam turns into a "used-to-be man," a sometime cross-dresser who (it is implied) sells his body for drugs until one tryst ends with his death "behind a store," "his asshole tore."[7]

Toasts gave meaning to the phrase "cautionary tale" where sleaze confessionals could only approach it with a wink and a nudge. Working in a medium more conducive to aural performance, Slim, in "Broadway Sam," reappropriated the meaning of *Pimp* and *Mama Black Widow* to black vernacular art. Indeed, that seemed to be the running idea behind the album as a whole: rewrite, as it were, Slim's fiction as toasts. The album only had four tracks—"The Fall," "Durealla," and "Mama Debt," in addition to "Broadway Sam"—but they were enough to effectively draw out the street from the sleaze. It was not just that stereotyped personas on the page were animated in ways that made them easier to identify with and relate to. It was also that the rhyme patterns, the jazz backing, and the performative assurance that this was part and parcel of the poet's craft created the illusion of being in a homosocial milieu where such toasts would be shared. *Reflections* simply did not afford the kind of visually oriented, voyeuristic consumption that Slim's early work had appealed to.[8]

The act of reclaiming the street through *Reflections* was not limited to the album itself. It could not have been a coincidence that versions of the four recorded toasts appeared that same year in an academic book titled *The Life: The Lore and Folk Poetry of the Black Hustler*. Edited by two English professors, Dennis Wepman and Ronald B. Newman, and a sociologist, Murray B. Binderman, the University of Pennsylvania Press collection featured toasts Wepman had collected while serving time in "Sing Sing, Clinton, Attica, and Auburn"—all prisons in New York.[9] Slim's books were among those listed in the bibliography of works consulted, but he was not credited with direct assistance, as had been the case in the Milners' *Black Players*. Regardless, *Reflections* put his previous subjection to the white ethnographic gaze—everything about which he had complained in *Naked Soul*—behind him. In performing the four tracks, it was as though Slim was repatriating what Wepman had taken from black men, transposed to the page, and subjected to academic analysis. Now, through Slim's voice, they lived to tell their tales again. Far from being displeased, Morriss and Weinstock likely encouraged the comparison. For even though Pennsylvania had published the hardcover edition of *The Life*, Holloway House came out with the paperback edition, also in 1976. Unlike his experience with the Milners, this time Slim got to play the expert: "A Stone Authentic Collection of Toasts," read his blurb on the front cover (figure 7.1).

The final act marking Slim's return was naturally his appearance in *Players*. Between 1975 and 1977, the magazine went through three editors: Joseph Nazel, Art Aveilhe, and Michael St. John. Though that high turnover rate might suggest that Wanda Coleman's worst fears came true, in fact the quality of the magazine did not appreciably suffer during these years. *Players* continued to advertise the good life for working-class and middle-class black men, relying on a fantasy of the urban hustler to bridge real socioeconomic differences between the two. Complementing that cross-class lifestyle campaign was an effort to show that black literary taste was more capacious than, perhaps, the mainstream marketplace would allow. So, for example, it was during this period that *Players* managed to reprint short fiction by James

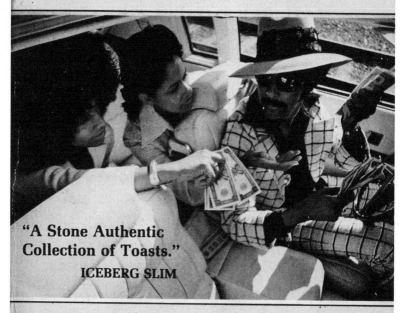

BH613 **$1.95**

The Life

The Lore and Folk Poetry
of the Black Hustler

"A Stone Authentic
Collection of Toasts."
ICEBERG SLIM

Dennis Wepman
Ronald B. Newman
Murray B. Binderman

FIGURE 7.1 Front cover of *The Life: The Lore and Folk Poetry of the Black Hustler* (1976).

Baldwin ("Sonny's Blues," July 1976), Amiri Baraka ("The Screamers," August 1976), Larry Neal ("Abdul's Avatar and the Sun Sister's Song," September 1976), and William Melvin Kelley ("Cry for Me," November 1976) alongside the more familiar pulp stories for which Holloway House was known. The December 1976 issue featured an interview with Maya Angelou (as well as film criticism by Donald Bogle, who presented a condensed version of his argument in the 1973 study *Toms, Coons, Mulattoes, Mammies, and Bucks*), while the February 1977 issue featured the first of several installments excerpting material from Chester Himes's 1972 biography *The Quality of Hurt*. Aveilhe, a former editor at J. B. Lippincott and the man behind James Baldwin and Margaret Mead's *A Rap on Race* (1971),[10] was probably the main reason why these writers came to the magazine. But his editorship nonetheless reflected the general tone of *Players*'s early years.

After a long hiatus, Slim started writing again. His shorts stories would appear in *Players*'s hybrid literary discourse, which, because it included a range of black male writers (not least Slim's old critic Larry Neal), assured the legitimacy of the black literary underground. It could not have been a coincidence that his first short story, "Air-Tight Willie and Me," came out in the same issue promoting ALA's *Reflections*; in fact, the ad for the record appeared on the first full page of the story's text. The interrelationship between story and record went beyond the fact that Slim was the star of both. "Air-Tight Willie" was a slight effort at best, a story that used the Iceberg persona to recount a joint con (concocted by Willie, executed by Willie and Iceberg) that ends up being a con and a double cross (on Iceberg). The details of the con were largely forgettable, and the plotline itself followed that of a classic toast. But therein lay the reason for its publication: it was Slim's first real effort to "write black." By that phrase I do not mean *Pimp*, *Trick Baby*, and *Mama Black Widow* were any less "authentic" than his later work. Rather, I mean to say that, prior to the publication of *Naked Soul*, Slim had gone into Holloway House expecting to write for a white sleaze audience. It took black readers reading past that intention for Morriss and Weinstock, as well as Slim, to change course and respond to what they thought black readers wanted.

"Air-Tight Willie" was the author's first stab at that. As such, it made sense that the plot points should be unmemorable, for the whole purpose of reciting a toast is to lead listeners to believe that they've heard it all before. But if the plotline was already a given, where did Slim invest his creative energy? Style. The very beginning of the story sets the tone:

Back in the days when bad girls humped good bread into my pockets, con man, Air-Tight Willie and pimp . . . me. . . . lay in a double bunk cell on a tier in Chicago's Cook County Jail. I was having one bitch kitty of a time tuning out the interracial sewer mouth shucking and jiving and playing the "dozens" from cell to cell on our tier.

"Lee, your mama is a freakish bitch that hasta crap in a ditch 'cause she humped a railroad switch."

"Hal, your raw ass mammy had bad luck. That drunk bitch got platoon raped in an army truck."

Air-Tight Willie leapt of his bunk screeching and made it a "dozens" roundelay. "Dummy up you square ass punks. Both you mutha fuckah's [*sic*] got mamas so loose and wide they gotta pay the zoo to cop elephant woo."[11]

Though Slim nods to the "interracial" field of inmates playing the dozens, there can be no mistaking that he attributes this form of sparring to blacks' oral tradition. Perhaps this is why Willie, his fellow black inmate, lays down the ultimate cap ("mutha fuckah's") in dispatching the other two (unseen) players. At any rate, the scene's placement at the beginning of the story is all-important. Though it has absolutely no bearing on the plot, it sets the stage for the homosocial milieu in which this toast will play out. Willie and Iceberg do their planning in jail before taking their con to the street. Listening in on the dozens at the beginning puts the reader in that masculine imaginative space.

Yet, in trying to have his prose accord with oral tradition, Slim, paradoxically, may have ended up sounding white. There is a reason the above passage does not quite add up. It has less to do with the dozens and more to do with what surrounds them. The misuse of the phrase "shucking and jiving" (which, though interracial, is about black subversion of white authority), the oddness of the phrase "bitch kitty," and the simply weird inclusion of the word "roundelay"—all of it bespeaks a hyperawareness about what writing black should sound like. Slim's style had always tended toward the baroque, as can be seen in this passage from *Pimp*, where Blood plays hard to get with a woman at the bar: "My turn down of her measly first offer [of a drink] had her jumpy. It was a slick sharp hook twisting in the bitch's mind. Her juicy tongue darted out like a red lizard past her ivory teeth. It slithered over the full lips. She wiggled toward me in an uneven race with the bar keep. He was sliding her green drink between me and the elephant [large male patron]." A decade later, he wrote a similar scene (the narrator leading a woman on so that he can turn her into his prostitute) for *Players*: "My ticker rioted. A delicious stealing lust electrified my genitals. She was dap and down in a black chiffon chemise vine. A white mink stole was draped casually across her shoulders. She smiled frostily as she side stepped through a gantlet of cracking and hitting players to a stool at the bar."[12]

Pimp's style was less "showy" than Slim's late style. Why? It is too pat, I think, to reduce it to the idea that *Pimp* was somehow closer to "authentic" experience. Instead, I think it had to do with the genre conventions in which Slim's style took root at various stages in his career. Whereas the sleaze confessional gave him license to speak with a bravado that was florid but pointed, the "short story toast," so to speak, restricted his voice to a hall of racial masks.

This is why next to no one talks about Slim's late fiction.[13] The collected short stories *Airtight Willie and Me* (1979) and two novels from 1977—*Death Wish*, a Mafia novel, and *Long White Con*, the sequel to *Trick Baby*—seem regrettable, as though they were written by a different author. These works do not receive extended treatment here either. But my reason for ignoring them is simple: their mere publication, I argue, was all that Holloway House and *Players* really wanted out of Slim. Individually considered, these works could have been penned by one of Morriss and Weinstock's hacks. Taken together, however, and attached as they were to the Slim persona, they formed the glue that reclaimed the street for the black literary underground.

The Reality Effect

In some respects, this was Morriss and Weinstock's most challenging masquerade yet. It was not men ghosting as women, or whites pretending to be black—at least as far as readers could tell. It was black men representing the streets they knew so well. By "representing" I mean both the object of narrative and the performance of authorship. The marketing of Goines and then of Slim created a demand whereby readers now expected Holloway House authors to have lived the lives they recounted in fiction. Morriss and Weinstock promoted that belief regardless of when or whether it cohered with authors' actual biographies. The *reality effect*, which they branded with the label "the black experience," became their biggest selling point.

Take, for example, the interview with Iceberg Slim that appeared in the May 1977 issue of *Players*. Subtitled "Pimping the Page," interviewer Nolan Davis welcomed Slim back to the "restin' and dressin'" life, except this time as an author, not a procurer. Four photographs at the beginning of the feature showed Slim at his leisure: bewigged and wearing a frilly black mascot, standing next to a gleaming luxury car (in one picture) and sitting astride a huge dalmatian mix on the sofa (in another). Davis hewed closely to this frame narrative. Indeed, in catching up with the author after his hiatus, the whole point of the interview seemed to be that Slim had gone from turning out women to turning out books of popular fiction. Following up on Slim's anodyne point that he had used some of his underworld skills in the square world, Davis asked, "Are you saying that writing is like pimping?" Taken aback, Slim could only reply that he had told stories both as a pimp and as a writer. Davis realized that Slim was missing his point: that he had modeled how professional writing could be like pimping, for isn't that how he had become such an underground success? Slim did not find the analogy apt. Instead, he talked about how the author, far from being a pimp, must actually write to his audience: "He has a certain publication that he's going to shoot for with his writing. If he's signed by a particular publisher, well then he knows what that publisher's audience is. From precedent."[14] Though many people would not have known it at the time, Slim was talking about the experience of writing *Pimp* not for the black men who were now reading him but for the white sleaze audience that had been the backbone of Morriss and Weinstock's enterprise.

As the interview went on, Slim's description of the writing life became so unsexy, as it were, that Davis finally likened him to a "whore." Slim's response was to say: "Well, in the case of a whore, one has the elegance of the pimp facade." In other words, he could very well be a whore, but his authorial persona would suggest otherwise. The implication, of course, was that those photographs of him living a life of leisure had been staged for *Players*'s benefit. Sensing that his analogy was about to be flipped, Davis quickly backpedaled, likened the reading public to a "whore" ("Must not the public be seduced?"), and spent the rest of the interview driving home that point (thus reasserting the "pimping the page" angle). Slim tried to rearticulate his experience as a professional author, interjecting that writing, for him, was "tortuous labor." But Davis would have none of it. By the end, Slim was repeating the made-up story of how he had earned the "Iceberg" moniker on the street. Once he got that out of him, the analogy slid back into its proper place. Davis's final question was "Have you been pimping this interview?" Slim could only rely on a cliché in response: he had been baring his "naked soul" the whole time.[15]

This was a significant departure from the way Holloway House had marketed its serial fiction only a few years earlier. As I discussed in the previous chapter, adventure serials like Iceman, Rhodes, Radcliff, and, yes, even Kenyatta were derivative of pulp formulas that had been brought back into mass circulation by Pinnacle's paperbacks. Though sensationalist in tone, these serials were obviously not based on first-hand experience. Take, for example, Joseph Nazel's announcement of the next installment of the Iceman series for the *Philadelphia Tribune*: "Hey, action fans! Iceman's back! And this time that bolder-than-Bond Black man is up to his neck in trouble as he tries to save an old friend who's risen to the top of the superstar pile, while trying at the same time to keep one step ahead of the Mafia bullets."[16] The bit of self-promotion fell under the headline "Book Review," and Nazel made no mention of his authorship, his background as a seasoned journalist, or his editorship of *Players*. For a brief window between 1973 and 1975, this formula-driven strategy seemed to work.

That all changed, of course, following the death of Donald Goines. The tragedy showed Morriss and Weinstock how much the confluence of life and art meant for black readers. Sensation could help readers feel like they were experiencing what was written on the page, but the idea that the author himself had experienced it cultivated something more enduring: readers' belief that it was true. "True" not in the sense of verifiable, empirical facts (readers understood they were reading fiction) but in the sense of the profound truth that life continued to be a struggle for black men in America, and that they had to rely on grit, muscle, and street smarts (never anyone else) to get over. When Memphis's *Tri-State Defender* covered Goines's open-casket funeral, it mentioned that "a cultish following had built up around the successful Black author." Worship of Goines was so intense that a copy of one of his books, which the family had wanted to bury with him, was "stolen out of his lifeless hands" during the visitation.[17] Such belief is what saved Morriss and Weinstock's enterprise from becoming a footnote in a larger narrative about race-oriented fads in the age of blaxploitation. By reorienting Holloway House's catalog toward the reality effect, they acknowledged an investment in black pulp fiction that exceeded formulaic copying.

That effect was reinforced as advertisements for black pulp fiction appeared in every issue of *Players*. Though the magazine, as a rule, did not publish excerpts from Holloway House's paperbacks, it created a milieu in which the promoted books were deemed coextensive with the featured writing. So, for example, the visually arresting advertisement for Charlie Avery Harris's 1976 novel *Macking Gangster* (figure 7.2)

Murder, tragic-magic, and a rebellious stable of "hos" plague the flashiest Mack on the Streets! / A Mack's Calling Card is his flash, his dress, his spiel, his hog, and all of these ploys of the game. Junius had it together. Under a smooth coat of grace and charm lay the most dangerous product spawned of the ghetto, as Junius brutally earned the title Godfather of Pimps! ■ And then he meets Demon, a teenage youngblood, who, along with his vicious dog Wolf, is hellbent to make successful hustling a black fact. Junius has his stable of "hos" and Demon has his corps of ghetto hoodlums who will do anything for him. ■ But Demon gets in over his head, and starts dealing in heroin, the tragic-magic that lulls the senses, brings in the bread, and gets him shot. When Junius stalks revenge, he discovers an incredible secret!

MACKING GANGSTER

by Charlie Avery Harris

FIGURE 7.2 Advertisement for *Macking Gangster,* in *Players* (August 1976).

arrived in a 1976 issue whose front cover shouted, "BULLSHIT! BASEBALL IS A WHITE MAN'S GAME—AL DOWNING SPEAKS OUT," and, "AMIRI BARAKA'S MOST EXPLOSIVE SHORT STORY." By way of clarification, managing editor Yazid Asim-Ali (standing in for Aveilhe, who had just joined as editor) explained:

What hath the Bicentennial wrought? The past year has us mystified, mesmerized, propagandized and calcified by the awe and wonder of the Bicentennial. . . . In light of all the revelations that have occured [sic] concerning all sides of our precious sacred cows, it would seem to me that the time is more than right for us to *finally* begin to think for ourselves. . . . We must *all* begin to realize that nobody really gives a shit about us *but* us, and that the blame for what we do or don't do lies with us.[18]

This self-reliant, self-possessed ethos pervaded the magazine, which in turn reflected back on Harris, even though *Macking Gangster* was, strictly speaking, a hack job based on Goines's oeuvre. *Players*'s valorization of urban black masculinity was about big-picture branding, not sweating the details.

Again, as I emphasized in the previous chapter, though it may seem this situation only benefited the owners, it was, in reality, a doubly invested enterprise. Without the support of readers—that is, following Darnton's notion of the communications circuit, readers-cum-authors—the whole enterprise would have collapsed (as blaxploitation had). The opportunities for publication that Morriss and Weinstock made available were real, as one letter-writer acknowledged:

PLAYERS offers a healthy outlet for the creative flow of black free lance [sic] writers. This, in the midst of a marked slump in today's literary market, can only result in creating renewed vigor and vitality as well as an increase in productivity among those of us chasing the creative writer's dream of . . . what else . . . creating. I believe that writing should be a natural outgrowth and extension of one's experiences. PLAYERS has given writers a shot in the arm by providing an appreciative audience.[19]

The metaphor could have referred to medicine, or it could have referred to drugs. Either way, the writer invited readers to wonder what his "experiences" may or may not have been given his invocation of the needle. This was itself a performance of the kind of writing that *Players* and, by relation, Holloway House, had created a market for.

Like Stoney Jackson, Charlie Avery Harris seemed to relish being linked so directly with his fiction. His local newspaper, the *Afro-American*, covered the release of both *Macking Gangster* and his other Goines-inspired potboiler published that year, *Whoredaughter*. "Those readers of Players Magazine and Sepia [the lifestyle magazine I discussed in chapter 4] have already been introduced to him," wrote columnist Ida Peters. Identifying Harris as a "native Baltimorean," Peters revealed details about Harris that only a true local would know: for starters, that he was "the youngest son of Mrs. Geneva Avery of Woodyear Street," and that he was "single, handsome, [and] in his 40's." She went further and disclosed that Harris's real name was Junius Ellis Avery, and that he went by the nickname "Slim Fingers" around "B-More."[20] Peters did not say how she knew these things, but the effect of bringing them up was to make Harris a flesh-and-blood person, a man with a genuine claim to the city about which he wrote.

Indeed, far from diminishing the power of his fiction, Peters's act of exposing the man behind the pen name paradoxically propped it up. In summarizing *Whoredaughter*, she noted the book's focus on "an incredibly evil, utterly deadly young girl" who started turning tricks at the age of twelve. Explaining how she destroys everyone who falls for her, Peters dramatically announced that "only one man could cope with her." That would be Junius, the titular "macking gangster" from the other novel, "who saw her for what she was and forced her to degredation [*sic*]." Making that connection allowed Peters to highlight how knowing Harris's real name, Junius, actually added to both novels' authenticity. That each was largely cribbed from Goines did not matter. What was important was that (so the assumption went) Harris had cast himself in the role of the fearsome antihero. Peters conceded that the novels were more of a "remembrance of the early '30s–'50s with an attempt to make it the '70s," but she still contended that they were "well written," containing details that "[rang] true to this old news hen."[21]

Harris's write-up in the *Afro-American* may have been unusually intimate, but the reality effect took hold even when readers encountered authors from across the country. J. Lance Gilmer, for example, was, like Roosevelt Mallory, from the Bay Area. And, like Mallory, he was a middle-class professional: a reporter for the *San Francisco Examiner*. There was, however, a critical difference between them as far as Holloway House was concerned. Mallory's job as a mid-level executive for Hewlett-Packard kept him safely ensconced in Silicon Valley, in a nearly all-white workplace. Gilmer's job, on the other hand, brought him in close and regular contact with urban black neighborhoods. That, at least, is what the publisher emphasized in his author's biography: "J. Lance Gilmer, San Francisco newsman, caused an immediate sensation with his first novel, HELL HAS NO EXIT. His second, HELL IS FOREVER, is even more powerful. Read it—and learn the truth about the grim underworld of drugs and crime, where death takes many strange forms."[22] Gilmer's fiction was given an extra lift because it had come out of "real-life" experience. Mallory's, by contrast, garnered little to no public interest, perhaps because his biography lent no weight to the idea that he was writing from experience.

With Gilmer's reputation preceding him, readers near and far welcomed his novels for shedding light on San Francisco's drug trade. In the local paper, the *Sun Reporter*, Donald Ray Young tipped his hat to Gilmer's ability to "eloquently report [on] prep sports." Presumably that beat allowed Gilmer to write a searing debut in the form of *Hell Has No Exit* (1976). This "hard-hitting novel," Young asserted, "tells what it's really like in the ghetto and what it's really like to be an addict." That sentiment was echoed all the way in Norfolk, Virginia, where Thomas L. Dabney was even more effusive in his praise. He prefaced his review by saying that, though "the characters [of *Hell Has No Exit*] are not real . . . the likes of them are found in any city where the drug traffic is wide open, and there are such places all over the United States," and that, though "the novel is fictitious . . . the message it has is solid and real." Dabney's gesture of recognizing both the fictionality of the book and the broad (social) applicability of its "message" was, in essence, the key to Holloway House's reality effect. Who could deny, Dabney averred, after reading Gilmer, that "the drug business is hell, and there is no escape from the consequences of using drugs or participating as pushers"?[23] The reporter had brought that whole horrible situation to life for black readers across the country.

If there was anything Goines's death taught Morriss and Weinstock, it was that even a notorious reality effect could be good for sales. Bruce C. Conn's name may have caused some readers to do a double take, as they had done with Robert deCoy the previous decade. But that was his actual given name, and it was his own experience growing up in a Chicago housing project that led him to write *The Horror of Cabrini-Green* (1975). Still in his mid-twenties, Conn was hailed by the *Los Angeles Sentinel* for his "probing honesty," giving readers a "realistic and often caustic look at what it means to grow up in a Chicago project." Having lived in the Cabrini-Green Homes himself, Conn was accorded a certain authority in representing life there as he saw it. True to its title, the novel was jam-packed with scenes of "death, vice, sex, [and] perversion." The "gang activities" in which the protagonist got caught up included "frequent use of nearly every kind of drug imaginable as well as planned and unplanned murders at the drop of a hat." Despite the overt sensationalism of the book, the reviewer concluded, "All in all, the book is too realistic to put down once it has been started. That is, unless the reader is unable to deal with a true look at what the youth of the past decade have had to contend with in order to survive."[24] Once again, the book's takeaway was viewed not as external to but inherent in the most lurid and outlandish details of its telling.

Residents of the Homes apparently did not take kindly to Conn's novel. One retrospective account recalls overhearing that Conn was "kicked out of Cabrini after he wrote the book." He then moved out to California—probably Los Angeles, as Goines had done—and sold the rights to the novel. However, the account concludes, when "the money ran out he had to come back to Cabrini."[25] Even as gossip, or word on the street, this tidbit says a lot about the ground-level reception of Conn's work. Morriss and Weinstock's enterprise enmeshed black pulp fiction in local reading publics to the extent that the stakes of mass-market publishing felt intensely personal and real. Their self-interest might have been guided by niche considerations, but the effect of their business was to create an enduring underground discourse about race, manhood, and inequality in urban America. For that reason, the next time Conn popped up in the newspapers, in 1981, we might speculate that readers felt sorry for him, or that he had received his just desserts. Still only thirty-one years old, he, his wife, and three children were being evicted for not being able to pay rent. Perhaps knowing that some readers would find his fate deliciously ironic, Conn tried to spin things toward his favor: "This may be the best thing. . . . I've been wanting to get out of the place for a while now. But once you're in, it's almost impossible to get out."[26]

There was one author in the catalog, though, who kept a low profile: Eddie Stone. After publishing *Donald Writes No More* in 1974, he came out with his own Goines-inspired fiction: *A Victim of Rape* (1976), *Black Hunter* (1976), *Black Fugitive* (1977), *Street Games* (1977), and *Twenty Miles to Terror* (1978). Stone was more productive than any of the aforementioned authors, and his novels were regularly advertised in the pages of *Players*. Yet the author himself remained an enigma.

We know why, of course: Stone was the pseudonym of Carlton Hollander, Donald Goines's ghostwriter. According to Hollander, Stone received offers to speak at colleges and universities across the country, and once to address an audience in Zimbabwe. As tempting as these offers were, he declined each time, suspecting that "fans would be disappointed he wasn't [the] black writer they [had] envisioned."[27] The reality effect had its limits, then, when it came to acknowledging white authorship of black pulp fiction.

Yet Hollander, perhaps secretly proud of the mask he wore, could not resist penning a dark satire about the exploitative system that went into producing that effect. In September 1977, *Players* published his "Full Moon Rising," a short story that, in a highly reflexive way, told the inside story of the black literary underground. The protagonist, Lincoln Cole, is a struggling black writer living in San Francisco. He writes for Inner City Publishing, headed by one Jules Cochran. For Cochran, Cole's books, filled as they are with "pimps, hustlers, whores, addicts, and hit men," represent "the Black man as he really [is]." Written from a gritty urban perspective, they offer black readers "a little fantasy violence, some bloodshed in the harmless context of a novel." When Cochran gives Cole feedback on his work, the advice is to go for one thing and one thing only: "Descriptive violence, Lincoln. Reality!"[28]

An aspiring writer whose heroes are "Milton, Melville and Hemingway" and "Fitzgerald, Wolfe and Steinbeck," Cole detests Cochran's directives. But rather than leave Inner City, he commits to ramping up the depravity of his novels, thinking that, at some point, he will go too far even for his publisher. He pens six novels in six months, capping off this streak with a scene in which five black children are killed with a sawed-off shotgun, "their tiny heads emanating horrible gurgling sounds as they departed their yet fulfilled bodies." Yet, instead of being appalled, Cochran crows, "Nothing like it anywhere. The Black experience is alive on these pages!" In disbelief, Cole proposes writing an equally obscene scenario in which a shotgun is triggered between a woman's legs. Unfazed, Cochran notes that the woman should be a virgin because "blowing out a used cunt just doesn't have the same impact!"[29] Cole leaves the meeting knowing there is no limit to what Cochran won't publish.

Back in his apartment, Cole mulls over the death and destruction, sorrow and suffering, he cooked up for his six books. What was it all for? "A legacy befitting the Black King of Literature," he notes bitterly. Cole's next act is to give in to the futility of his situation. He goes out into the street and confronts "five men, all Black, wearing trenchcoats and eyeing the passing cars with the furtive glance of the pimp/dealer. All players." Cole takes out his shotgun and blows them away, effectively acting out a scene from one of his novels. Far from being cathartic, however, the killings bring even more dread on him. When the police pick him up, Cole overhears one cop say, "Probably did his fucking race a service." His partner agrees: "Save us a lot of hassle."[30] Cole must now face the fact that his act of defiance played right into racist whites' hands.

A young black man later visits him in jail. He has been sent there by Inner City to write a biography of Cole. "You're a legend," the up-and-coming writer beams. Flash forward to his cell on death row, where

Cole has left "The Biography of Lincoln Cole—The Ghetto Executioner" untouched on his cot. For him, it is enough to know that "he had become legend."[31]

"Full Moon Rising" combined elements of Joseph Nazel's and Donald Goines's actual biographies with Hollander's own experience ghostwriting as Eddie Stone. It is remarkable that it was published in *Players* at all. For one, Bentley Morriss did not come across well in the thinly veiled character of Jules Cochran. Craven and opportunistic: the publisher has no scruples when it comes to exploiting "the black experience." More broadly, though, "Full Moon Rising" aligned a deadening of the spirit with the kind of writing Inner City Publishing, a.k.a. Holloway House, demanded. Cole's soul-crushing work leads him to act out the dark fantasies he has been paid to churn out. That the reading public rewards him for this is, of course, the ultimate irony.[32]

But what if publishing "Full Moon Rising" was not remarkable at all? What if holding up this mirror to Morriss and Ralph Weinstock's infrastructure only burnished their reputation for publishing the most "real" print commodities in the black literary marketplace? From this angle, the story would have been like Cole's pitch to Cochrane: a test to see how far Morriss would go. Evidently the publisher didn't flinch. The story's appearance in *Players* ensured that it would be read as yet another entry in black pulp fiction's catalog of "authentic" narratives of urban life.

Bottom Women

If the blood-and-thunder plotlines of black pulp fiction were outlandish, they were nothing compared to the characterization of women, and specifically black women, at Holloway House and *Players* magazine. I have already described how, even under Wanda Coleman's editorship, the nude models in *Players* were essentially framed as working girls. The problem with this fantasy lay not in any one pictorial but in Morriss and Weinstock's presumption that erotic black womanhood could only be represented as a function of down-market taste. That editorial line became more entrenched between 1975 and 1977. With Sid Smith continuing to mediate between publisher and editor, Nazel, Aveilhe, and St. John all signed off on a pornographic aesthetic that seemed to delight in showing off how much it could subordinate black women to the black male gaze.

Jazz critic and writer Stanley Crouch wrote the informal manifesto for this aesthetic. In the awkwardly titled "Black Women and White Men: An Indication of Something," Crouch situated *Players*'s readers at a crossroads. On one hand, they had lived through an age where black men sleeping with white women had been all the rage. Crouch's loquacious style performed the very critique he intended to level on that passing fancy:

Certain black men, trying to evade the total social context of their sorrow and post-plantational slavery went after white women in urban areas as they were symbols, however illusory, of *freedom*—the talk, the close dancing, the fucking, the strutting with the vanilla ladies in the gaudy daylight, either as merely a lover or as an artist or communist, sometimes even as a husband. In some cases, the flaunting of legendary sexual powers over white women who had white men nutting out all over film screens, was a grotesque protest which only indicated the true depth of the social impotence of the black man.[33]

Though Crouch was taking aim at a general cultural practice, the reference to "nutting out all over film screens" was a fairly specific reference to the sexploitation-blaxploitation conjunction, and thus, by analogy, to the age of black sleaze. His point was that black men's flirtation with the novelty of interracial desire played right into white men's hands. Facing up to their "total social context" would require letting go of the hoary fantasy that sleeping with white women constituted any kind of "freedom."

What made the moment a crossroads, according to Crouch, was that black women were not putting up with such fickleness anymore. He quoted an anonymous source as saying: "I go with a white man because he can buy me the things I want. Take me where I want to go. Help me get over and can tell anybody to kiss his ass and nothing will happen. *Nothing* will happen." Whether or not he made it up, the quotation dovetailed with Crouch's point that white men had long fantasized about seizing this opportunity. Again, relying on the testimony of an anonymous source (whom he only identified as a "white drummer"), Crouch relayed: "He liked black women more than white women [because] they didn't give you a bunch of lip, were sexually freer and were always behind their men, would go out and work to keep their men together—*unlike* white women who were always bitching, spending money, looking to be pampered." No surprise, then, that now, in 1975, the black woman and the White Negro were prepared to conjoin and leave the black man behind. This, Crouch wrote, was yet another example of "the social impotence of the black man."[34]

Thankfully, the solution to this dilemma was literally in readers' hands. Crouch never stated the point explicitly, but he implied that black men should intervene in the aforementioned dynamic and take black women back for themselves. (Who wouldn't want a woman who "would go out and work to keep [her man] together"?) This goal required the cultivation of a self-reliant, self-possessed ethos—such as that propagated by *Players*, conveniently. Black women "want the good life," Crouch said, but they "are tired of hearing, just as white people are tired of hearing, about the problems of black men—regardless of how real those problems may be." The struggle was real, he concluded, but it was solely up to "the black male" to get over it.[35]

Nazel, who was *Players's* editor at the time, evidently received a high volume of correspondence related to Crouch's essay. We can assume so because he devoted an entire column of "Conversin'" to readers' responses to it. There were, to be sure, some critical responses. One man, who claimed to have "recently emigrated to New York" from another country, complained that none of it would make a difference because white racism was an intractable problem in the United States. He was experiencing it firsthand, (presumably) living for the first time in "a white majority country." Another man, who seemed versed in black nationalist thought, articulated the most damning critique, figuring Crouch had given too much credence to white men's social power, which then affected everyone's choice of partner. He punctuated his letter with "Where is the damn method?! Fuck this, I got something to do!" But more letter-writers backed Crouch's call, which one summarized in the motto "Black man, get your stuff together" and another in the saying "Black on Black is right." A college student even drew out the implications of this ethos for the black literary underground. He had had enough of "literature by caucasian [*sic*] anthropologists" that was committed to "probing into the field of the Black pimp and hustler." It was now time to celebrate *Players* as the organ of "the new Black intellectual, aware and concerned."[36]

That pornography was part and parcel of this discourse cannot be denied. Just as *Adam* and *Sir Knight* had reflected the ideology and aesthetic of sleaze, so did *Players* reflect the ideology and aesthetic of Holloway House's urban imaginary. To be clear, that imaginary did not have as clear an ideological correlate as sleaze had had with momism. Black men had never been afforded the domestic security that momism required as a baseline condition for its operation. Iceberg Slim may have written sleaze, but he did not write it for black readers. Still,

I would contend that the textual, visual, and discursive subjection of black womanhood to black male authority played a critical role in the making of the black literary underground. Just because copy for the pictorials rarely, if ever, mentioned black pulp fiction did not mean that the images had nothing to say to readers of Goines, Slim, and the rest.

The reality effect was most elastic when it came to the pictorials. At times *Players* got so real that it seemed to strip away everything that made fantasy possible. In the April 1976 issue, for example, underneath the picture of a model shown with her head tilted backward in an expression of ecstasy, the copy read:

This beautiful creature is Sandy. As you gaze into her eyes let your mind wander back in time. . . . Back to the hot, densely tropical climate of Brazil. Picture a tall, 5'8", dark-haired bronze complexioned, and well proportioned, 36-27-36, Amazon, . . . Excuse me brothers, hate to interrupt but we'd better save that fantasy for later. This Sandy was born in Poplar Bluff, Missouri but for all intents and purposes, she is a native Californian. She is presently enrolled in El Camino college, and her present day ambition is to perfect her modelling style.[37]

By "got so real," I do not mean to imply that any of this copy was factually true. Rather, I mean to argue that one way *Players* framed its models was to deny the conditions for fantasy in the first place. This particular text was egregious not only for going through the motions of conjuring a "tropical" fantasy (a move that, in and of itself, subverted the structuring principles of fantasy) but also for then articulating the falseness of the whole premise. The only real takeaway from this affirms something I have been arguing over the past two chapters: namely, that the woman is exposed for being a professional model, or, to extend the fantasy, a working girl.

The other way *Players* framed its models took the complete opposite approach when it came to tone. Black women were still not so innocent, but they were framed in terms that were bizarrely sappy, as if they could only appear through a soft-focus cloud of turgid prose. Or, in the case of a pictorial from April 1975, poetry:

Adelaide, Adelaide,
My sweet cocoa-brown ghetto goddess
Black pearl of slave ships
And of freedom trains

Come here and rest your head beside me
And touch your man again.

Adelaide, Adelaide,
Sweet Black citylady
Lay back and groove me from your golden chair
(lay back and groove me).

The model pictured next to this paean to beauty was shown posing on a recliner ("golden chair") and wearing a pearl necklace ("Black pearl"). Beyond that, it made no sense to refer to her as a "ghetto goddess" or "citylady," much less someone borne of "slave ships." Yet the entire pictorial was framed as presenting the quintessence of black womanhood to the black male gaze. "I watched you while the slave ship sailed," it continued, "I touched you on the auction block / And kissed you 'til the hot chains cracked."[38] Modern, urbane black womanhood, which is what the pictures conveyed, was undercut by copy that returned Adelaide to the hold and the auction block.

Between de-fantasizing realism and baroque sentimentalism, the reality effect of black womanhood in *Players* can seem puzzling to the contemporary reader. Yet I would argue that it was precisely in the space between being too real and being not real enough that the pictorials propped up *Players*'s appeal to black male fantasy. If, according to Stanley Crouch, black men had been fighting off "social impotence" all their lives, it would stand to reason that the pornographic aesthetic they desired would not be able to see black women for who they were. We might call this the *pornographic exception* to the reality effect. To be sure, black men and *Players* were hardly unique in subjecting women to a distorting gaze. It could very well be argued that, historically speaking, this was, and is, the point of all male heterosexual porn. My point, then, is simply that this general condition, the pornographic exception, took on a specific shape in the field of the black literary underground. In *Players*, black women were framed so as to ensure that the black male gaze remained on top, even if the cost of doing so was to reaffirm racist (because gendered) stereotypes.

This effect was not simply a matter of ill-advised text-image juxtapositions either. On their own, many photographs hewed to the realism-sentimentalism binary I described above. Take, for example, the May 1977 issue featuring "Conchita" as its cover girl. The choice of photograph to grace the cover (figure 7.3) was curious, to say the least. It shows Conchita biting into the gristle of a half-eaten rib. Her look

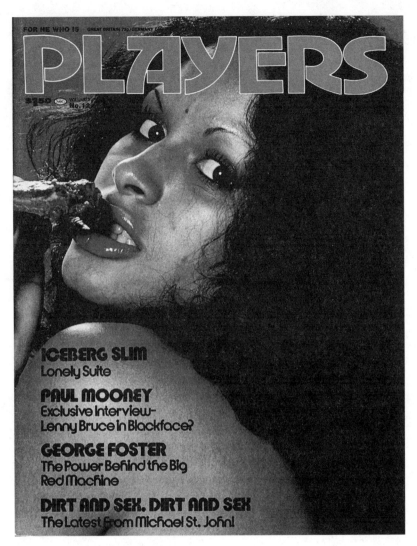

FIGURE 7.3 Front cover of *Players* (May 1977).

means to be seductive (the classic "come-hither" I mentioned in chapter 1), but the viewer's focus inevitably is drawn (back) to that rib. The effect is magnified in the pictorial itself, where in one photograph (figure 7.4) Conchita is shown seated, topless, legs spread apart and bent at the knees, holding a knife and carving fork. Between her legs is the real focus of the camera: a slab of ribs. One can see rib sauce splattered on the knife and carving fork, drawing further attention away from the

From one end of Los Angeles to the other, Conchita's services are in demand: at posh parties in the hills, at blow-outs in the city, everybody is hungry for her ribs. What Famous Amos is to the cookie, Conchita is to the rib. Conchita's FornoCatering Service makes it happen. As she says, "You can lick, but don't munch."

FIGURE 7.4 Pictorial image from "Conchita," in *Players* (May 1977). Courtesy of Players International Publications.

model. A textbook example of *Players*'s diminution of visual fantasy through an all-too-harsh realism, Conchita is largely subordinated to gustatory pleasures, but in the process still rendered "dirty." The copy that went along with the pictorial encouraged readers to try her out: "Conchita's FornoCatering Service makes it happen."[39]

On the flipside was *Players*'s visual fetishization of a gauzy, imagined slave past. Whether using the Confederate flag as the backdrop to a model's wistful pose (figure 7.5) or depicting a cover model breaking free from her chains (figure 7.6), the magazine was drawn to the iconography of slavery as a means of sexualizing the black female body. The alibi for referencing such imagery tended to be that *Players* wished to highlight how far black women had come. The cover model image is self-explanatory, in that regard. As for the other model, she was photographed in different settings, wearing different outfits, in subsequent photographs, leading up to final page, in which she appeared fully clothed, sporting an Afro, and holding a copy of a document titled "Bill of Rights." "Perhaps at last, my pretty girl, you and I, can be about the business of being you and me," read the copy. "We've come a long way, baby."[40] No wonder this pictorial was featured in the same issue that readers' responses to Crouch's essay were published. But that

FIGURE 7.5 Pictorial image from "Gaye," in *Players* (May 1975). Courtesy of Players International Publications.

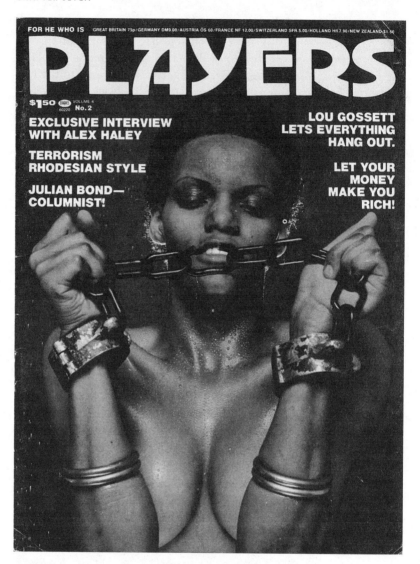

FIGURE 7.6 Front cover of *Players* (July 1977).

placement underscores exactly why both images are deeply problematic. The iconography of slavery ensures that black women start out at the bottom, yes. But its more cunning implication is that the telos of their liberation is not self-actualization or self-development, much less women's empowerment, but simply being with a black man ("being you and me"). This, then, is what true freedom looks like for black women: being subject to a revitalized black male gaze.

All of this may seem beside the point when it comes to black pulp fiction. How could the pornographic aesthetic of a men's magazine, a visually oriented format, reflect the predominantly textual discourse of black pulp fiction? Except Morriss and Weinstock could call on just the man to connect the two. It was not Nazel this time but a familiar name from the old sleaze days: Leo Guild. In the mid-1970s, Guild returned to his trashy worst, penning a number of books for Holloway House that essentially put *Players*'s copy into wider literary circulation. By my tally, between 1974 and 1977, he published the following:

Swingers Three by Cherri Grant (1974)

Black Bait by Leo Guild (1975)

Black Champion by Mary Turner, as told to Leo Guild (1975)

The Black Shrink by Dr. Phyllis James, as told to Leo Guild (1975)

Street of Ho's by Leo Guild (1976)

The Senator's Whore by Cindy Kallmer, as told to Leo Guild (1976)

Josephine Baker by Leo Guild (1976)

Cons and Lovers by Leo Guild (1977)

Black Streets of Oakland by Kelley Eagle, as told to Leo Guild (1977)

Based on this list, it should be noted that, aside from *Swingers Three*, Guild did not conceal his identity by using only a pseudonym. The wink-and-a-nudge masquerade of the 1960s had largely given way to the overt obscenity of the 1970s. When the blurb on the back cover of *The Black Shrink* assured readers, "It's not a casebook,"[41] it meant to stress its confessional (rather than sexological) structure, but it could just as well have gestured to the fact that it no longer needed to be a casebook to pass muster with the censors. Guild was writing in a completely different era, and for a completely different audience, than what he had been used to in the 1960s.

How did Morriss and Weinstock get away with publishing Guild alongside Goines, Slim, and the many black men who now wrote for them? Though recognizing that Holloway House had undergone a shift in business orientation, Guild was not going to change anything about his style. And so it proved. *Black Streets of Oakland* was an unfortunate reworking of *The Girl Who Loved Black*, and *The Senator's Whore* was an equally unfortunate recycling of the central conceit of *Some Like It Dark*. *Black Bait* was a faux confessional written entirely from Guild's perspective, though he ventriloquized his fictionalized subject, Lila, as playing innocent with the line, "I really am just a sweet ol' little nigger."[42] In a different era, these books would have been identified as the quintessence of black sleaze. But now, given their place in Morriss and Weinstock's communications circuit, they had the contextual validation of being associated with, if not being part of, black pulp fiction. Times had changed, but they also hadn't.

This point was driven home when Holloway House reprinted *Some Like It Dark* in 1977. It had been eleven years since the sleaze confessional's debut, sporting the subtitle *The Intimate Autobiography of a Negro Call Girl*. In preparing the book for republication, a few changes had to be made. The subtitle was adapted into a blurb ("The Best-Selling Autobiography of a Black Call Girl"), and all references to "Negro" within the text were replaced by the word "black." Most important, the cover image of a model taken from the pages of *Adam* was replaced by one of a model who clearly belonged in *Players*. Positioned on all fours and facing the camera, the heavily made-up black woman rested her head in her hands while, in the blur of the background, her naked haunches could be seen slightly raised in the air.[43] This is how Holloway House repackaged white-oriented sleaze for a new black readership.

Between 1975 and 1977, the black literary underground became virtually synonymous not only with the print commodities put out by Holloway House and Players International Publications but also with the discourse that shaped how these commodities should be read. For even though Slim put out *Reflections* and a host of other writers appeared in their local black press, all of it went back into supporting black pulp fiction's promotional bottom line. Here the skepticism that had greeted Iceberg Slim and Robert deCoy in 1967 was replaced with the belief that black pulp fiction reflected "the black experience" itself. Though the murder of Donald Goines was the single most important event to help prop up that belief, the rebranding of Slim and the many smaller confirmations of author's street credentials helped make Holloway House's communications circuit run smoothly from publisher to reader to author and back again.

But insofar as *Players* was the key promotional vehicle for all black pulp fiction, "the black experience" itself was subtended was a very particular fantasy of control—that of black masculine self-possession. With the magazine now tightly associated with their books, Morriss and Weinstock were in the business of producing print commodities that specialized in what Beth Coleman has called "pimp theory." Using the black pimp as a figure to reflect on the mass-marketing of urban black masculinity, Coleman writes, "Pimp theory is a formal read-dress of the mechanism of mastery even as it is a form of repetition compulsion. It relies on the double spin, playing the black fetish. . . . Pimp theory says, 'We being an intelligent people, we knew that it was happening any way so we had to benefit from it.'"[44] In this account, pimp theory might be described as an epistemology of the skull book: knowledge of the world and one's surroundings that is premised on the belief that black men turned the tables on white men by leasing "their" women's bodies out to them. To be clear, not every book published by Holloway House was invested in pimp theory, and I am in no way claiming that any author or editor at the press was himself pimping at that moment. The point, rather, is that an exploiters' way of viewing the world predominated in Morriss and Weinstock's total conception of the black literary underground. They cultivated the fantasy that it was inherently a man's world, and that, for black men in particular, "It was better to be a taker than one of those who got took!"[45]

EIGHT

The Difference Within

Odie Hawkins started out at Holloway House in the early 1970s. Like Wanda Coleman, he had been a member of the Watts Writers Workshop, a collective of local artists and writers who, in the wake of the riots, sought to give voice to the ghetto's voiceless.[1] Once he joined Holloway House, Hawkins, like Coleman, learned how that heady idealism could be exploited for profit. He published his first book, *Ghetto Sketches*, in 1972. In both style and substance, it resembled Donald Goines's lurid *Dopefiend*, then only a year old. His next two books, the con man novel *Chicago Hustle* (1977) and the pimp novel *Sweet Peter Deeder* (1979), owed a debt to Iceberg Slim's early fiction. These were followed up with *The Busting Out of an Ordinary Man* (1985), an action-adventure novel that could have been mistaken for one of Nazel's potboilers. Having sampled all the major forms of black pulp's urban imaginary, there was only one thing left for Hawkins to try out: sleaze. His *Chili: Memoirs of a Black Casanova*, also published in 1985, chronicled "the loves of one man's life," a player who "looks upon sex as a recreational sport, a hobby to be enjoyed to its fullest extent!"[2] True to its title, the inspiration here was not a fellow black writer but Paul Gillette's "translations" of Giacomo Casanova's memoirs. Like those two books, *Chili* was structured as an episodic romp, a young man's coming into sexual maturity as retold through bawdy tales.

Hawkins would write many more books for Holloway House, nearly all of them variations on previously published work. Yet the fact that he wrote under his own name, and that Hawkins remained close to the Watts community from which he sprang, lent his titles the kind of street-level credibility that Bentley Morriss and Ralph Weinstock's enterprise had become known for. Nazel may have been Holloway House's most prolific author, but Hawkins was its most versatile, moving across styles and genres to buttress the company's reality effect. With copycats, Slim's and Goines's status as the godfathers of black pulp fiction would be confirmed by the catalog itself. Writers like Hawkins thus provided the necessary backdrop for Slim and Goines to be received as the originators of "the black experience" novel.

If the logic to this seems circular or tautological, that is because it was: Holloway House was going in circles. By which I mean Morriss and Weinstock's communications circuit was operating at peak efficiency in the niche market for black pulp fiction. Publishers, booksellers, readers, and authors were almost perfectly aligned in the way they mirrored each other's interests and fed into each other's perceptions. *Players* was there too, of course, to tie up any loose ends. This was the black literary underground at work.

It could not have been an entirely pleasant system to work within, at least for an author of Hawkins's ambition. We know as much from *Hollow Daze*, his 2013 self-published roman à clef based on his experience working at Holloway House. Hawkins holds nothing back in this thinly veiled skewering of his former employer and colleagues. There is the unscrupulous Benton Marsh (Morriss), owner of Hollow Daze Publishing Company (Holloway House), a fiction factory that exploits black talent for profit. At his side is racist Ron Wildstock (Ralph Weinstock), who comes up with ever more extreme scenarios of black women's degradation for the pornographic magazine *Duh Playa* (*Players*). Then there is Clay Block, based on Holloway House editor Raymond Friday Locke, who curates "Hollow Daze's 'Black Experience' line" through an alcoholic haze. And, finally, there are the writers: Icepick Slim (Slim), the writer and still full-time pimp; Ronald Cummins (Goines), the strung-out hack; and Jack Mozel (Nazel), the Iraq War veteran about whom Marsh wonders, "My God, how many books has this guy written for us?"[3] Black writers working themselves to death. White writers masquerading as black. *Hollow Daze* confirms the expropriation of labor that underlay Holloway House's appropriation of culture in the making of the black literary underground.

But does Hawkins truly escape that underground by telling it like it is? The only figure who avoids skewering in *Hollow Daze* is Harvey Dawkins—Hawkins's alter ego. Dawkins believes his work is of some literary value, and Block concurs that he is "the best of the [lot], the best period." Yet every time he submits a manuscript, Dawkins knows Hollow Daze is "going to slap another one of those horrible-ass covers on the book," cheapening his claim to art.[4] But in distinguishing Dawkins's ambition from Hollow Daze's crass profiteering, Hawkins reveals his to be a twice-told tale. The novel is a direct descendant of Carlton Hollander's short story "Full Moon Rising," from the September 1977 issue of *Players*. Both are extremely critical of the black pulp fiction enterprise, yet both rely on the very techniques that make this enterprise run: masquerade, sensationalism, and a certain valorization of black masculinity. Thus, just as Hollander's story climaxes in the protagonist's violently acting out his darkest fantasies, *Hollow Daze's* narrative pivots on Mozel's choking Wildstock to death, a literalization of the violence he became accustomed to writing.

The black literary underground can sound like a closed circle when only taking into account the print commodities over which Morriss and Weinstock exercised near-total control. Their system required that black readers consume books and magazines in ways they could predict and, indeed, orchestrate. But what happened when readers didn't do that? When they consumed Holloway House's paperbacks yet did not feed back into the communications circuit Morriss and Weinstock oversaw? This was, of course, the story of black pulp fiction itself: how it emerged out of the sleaze industry to become a popular literature written by black authors for black readers. But in the late 1970s, those readers started to define authorship on their own terms, wresting black pulp narrative out of the hands of Morriss and Weinstock's enterprise and moving into their own circuits of communication.

First, there were black women readers. Whether at Holloway House or at Players International Publications, black women had long been deemed the object of white and black men's desire, sexualized property to be exchanged between men. But by the early 1980s, it had become abundantly clear that black women were, in fact, some of black pulp fiction's, and even *Players's*, most devoted readers. In response to an article on the controversy surrounding the Rolling Stones' song "Some Girls," from the 1978 album of the same name, one reader wrote in to *Players*, "As a self-respecting Black Woman I couldn't care less if Mick Jagger sings about Black women wanting to fuck all night. Why get upset over the words to a song? And why not be honest? Some of us do!"[5] Frank opinions such as this one—at once "self-respecting" and sexually self-possessed—challenged the masculinist ideologies on which sleaze, pulp, and pornography had rested. Black women's sexuality was something these formats only ever ventriloquized, and their erotic agency was at best dimly recognized. In the early 1980s, Morriss and Weinstock tried to integrate this demographic into their enterprise, bringing out black women's pulp in a handful of genres. The results were mixed, and most of these titles are long forgotten today. Black women readers eventually left the circuit to write their own popular novels, which proved far more successful.

The second group was young black men like Ice-T (Tracy Marrow), who grew up reading Slim's books in South Central, Los Angeles. These young men took what they wanted from Holloway House and adapted it to new cultural forms—namely, the aural and sonic flows of rap. Morriss and Weinstock proved even less capable of bringing these readers back into the fold. For while rappers became huge fans of Slim and Goines, they did so by repositioning them within the context of street culture and black oral tradition. For these readers, Slim and Goines bridged older cultural forms such as toasts and the dozens with the contemporary desire to address urban poverty, police brutality, and the everyday violence of the black underworld. Thus, by taking Holloway House's books out of the print communications circuit, rappers were able to constitute a vernacular art that was responsive to conditions on the ground, not in the pages of a magazine.

In this final chapter, I juxtapose the circuitous masculinism of the black literary underground with the internally variegated genres and forms that arose out of the same. My argument is that, in the face of a totalizing system of production and distribution, black readers began to make black pulp fiction their own. In so doing, they not only took leave of prescribed modes of reading black pulp fiction but also expanded the black literary underground to include producers and distributors other than the consolidated business under which Holloway House and Players International Publications operated.

Recycling the Street

Joseph Nazel understood quite well that his novels could never be mistaken for reality. In hewing to the Pinnacle formula, he was drawn more to the plot intricacies of conspiracy than to the finer points of setting and characterization. When Nazel's potboiler *Black Uprising* came out in 1976, Cleveland's *Call and Post* reviewer rightly claimed that it was "strictly fantasy with underdeveloped characterizations and loose ends." But, he conceded, if readers were up for "an evening's light reading," then *Black Uprising* would certainly "fit the time-slot."[6] Norfolk's

New Journal and Guide put a more positive spin on this type of reading. *The Black Gestapo* was Nazel's novelization of the blaxploitation movie of the same name, alternately known as *Ghetto Warriors* (both 1975). This was schlock through and through, a fantasia of racial supremacy that sat uneasily alongside the fad of Nazi exploitation films. Yet the *New Journal and Guide*'s critic took it in stride, admitting that the book reminded him of "childhood dreams of some form of conquest or revolution to free blacks from the domination and control of the white man." Set within the context of personal fantasy, he was able to appreciate Nazel's gestures to "the work of Nat Turner and Toussaint L'Overture [sic]" and "what happened to both men and their cause."[7] He recommended it unconditionally.

Overtly formulaic novels stood on their own as slight diversions at worst, pleasing entertainments at best, but they did not speak to readers in the same register as, say, Goines's novels did. Nazel was an experienced newspaperman, and he knew how to produce copy at a clip. So it should come as no surprise that he wanted to try writing for the reality effect. The problem, of course, was that readers already knew him as a Los Angeles newspaperman, editor of *Players*, and author of the Iceman series. Nazel's solution to this dilemma was to do what he knew best: write under different pen names, thereby creating new authorial personas. Based on the available copyright evidence and what we know about Nazel's career as a hack,[8] I have been able to link him to two pseudonyms that have heretofore been taken as real authors. The first, Amos Brooke, was credited with *The Last Toke* (1977), *Doing Time* (1977), and *Black in a White Paradise* (1978). The second, Omar Fletcher, was credited with *Hurricane Man* (1977), *Walking Black and Tall* (1977), *Black against the Mob* (1977), *Black Godfather* (1977), *Miss Annie* (1978), and *Escape from Death Row* (1979). Under these pen names, Nazel could pretend to have personally experienced the gritty urban scenarios about which Brooke and Fletcher wrote. To be sure, he would not be making any public appearances or revealing much about himself in blurbs. Nazel relied mainly on the writing and advertising to bring about the reality effect.

When Omar Fletcher debuted with *Hurricane Man* in 1977, the full-page advertisement in *Players* made sure to highlight the author's street credentials. "The brutally honest story of the agony and savagery of prison life—by a man who's been through it!" read the copy. But just who was Fletcher exactly? The ad would only say that he was "a great new Holloway House discovery in the tradition of Donald Goines."[9] San Francisco's *Sun Reporter* was initially skeptical, pointing out that the novel, whose protagonist is "Rubin (Hurricane) Cartwright," was obviously "based on the life of Ruben [sic] (Hurricane) Carter," the professional boxer serving time for a triple homicide he claimed he had not committed. (Carter's 1974 prison autobiography, *The Sixteenth Round*, inspired Bob Dylan's 1975 protest song "Hurricane.") The review went on to say that the plot was "a bit typical and overused." Still, it found that Fletcher did a good job of "vividly bringing the characters to life," and that these characters helped "make the story seem realistic." Cleveland's *Call and Post*, meanwhile, yawned, "The story is casually written, takes only limited concentration and can be finished in an evening's brief reading time." Its review ended with essentially the same recommendation it had given to *Black Uprising*: read it if you need to "replace any of television's re-runs."[10]

Nazel's chasing the reality effect may have flopped with his pen names, but it succeeded when he took the dynamic literally and began publishing hack biographies of black culture heroes. Under the pen name Rugio Vitale, he published *Joe Louis: Biography of a Champion* in 1979, and under his own name he published *Paul Robeson: Biography of a Proud Man* and *Richard Pryor: The Man behind the Laughter* in 1980 and 1981, respectively. Some of this biographical material either got its start or was excerpted in *Players*, whose lifestyle focus ensured that black celebrities were featured on a regular basis. Because he was taking up widely known figures, there was no need for Nazel himself to prop up his own lived experience. Instead, he wrote about his subjects with a veneration that obviously struck a chord with his readers. Norfolk's *Journal and Guide* was moved by the Robeson biography, for example, in part because it deftly interwove the star-cum-activist's personal achievements with African American social and political movements. "It was unusual that a man of his intellectual and physical ability should remain psychologically and sociologically a member of the masses," the paper noted. To his credit, no matter how famous he became, Robeson "never lost the touch of the masses." The *Journal and Guide*'s title for its review summarized the feeling Nazel conjured in the biography: "His Soul Was Not for Sale."[11]

In its sleaze days, Holloway House had published slapdash biographies of well-known figures who happened to be in the news. Ernest Hemingway (at his death), Robert F. Kennedy (during his run for the Democratic nomination for the US presidency), Dr. Martin Luther King Jr. (after his assassination): if someone made headlines, Morriss and Weinstock would consider doing a biography of him. Once Nazel's biographies took off, the publishers applied the same logic to the black literary underground. This is actually what Carlton Hollander, writing as Eddie Stone, ended up doing after giving up the blood-and-thunder stuff. In 1980, he published well-received biographies of New York Yankee baseball player Reggie Jackson, former US ambassador to the United Nations Andrew Young, and R&B singer-songwriter Teddy Pendergrass. In 1984 Stone came out with a biography of Jesse Jackson during his run for the Democratic nomination for the US presidency. Holloway House made sure to reprint it for Jackson's 1988 run. Also in 1988, to "commemorate the national holiday honoring Dr. King on January 18 and Black History Month" in February, Holloway House brought out a new edition of Louis Lomax's *To Kill a Black Man* as well as a new study by Michael North titled *The King Conspiracy*. In a bizarre fusion of hack journalism and pulp conspiracy, North posited that James Earl Ray had not been the (only) guilty party in King's assassination. Yet that was far from a novel idea, for as the *Columbus Times* in Georgia noted, Lomax himself had argued the same in his book, originally published twenty years earlier.[12]

If Holloway House was stuck recycling storylines, *Players* found itself in a similar rut. In particular, nude layouts were being recycled sometimes just a few years after their first appearance. The "Gaye" pictorial I addressed in the last chapter, for example, reappeared exactly four years later, in May 1979, as the centerfold feature "Gayle Thomas: The Roles and Faces of a Foxy Lady," albeit with some different shots. The cost-cutting could be seen in other areas. Having shed the pretense of being a cutting-edge black men's lifestyle magazine in the late 1970s and early 1980s, *Players* accepted the kind of down-market advertisements—for sex toys, sexual aids, and, inevitably, pornographic videos—the likes of which *Adam* and *Knight* had been taking in for decades. The quality of writing tanked too as Morriss and Weinstock invited white freelancers from *Adam* and *Knight*, including notorious pornographer William Rotsler, to write for *Players*, usually without the cover of pseudonyms. Soon original fiction by black authors went missing entirely, replaced by sex advice columns and "reviews" of (read: advertisements for) Holloway House paperbacks. Last but not least, there were the models *Players* did manage to shoot for upcoming issues. Comedian Chris Rock once explained what he thought was "recycled" in these pictorials. Complaining about the disparities between the "whiteness" of *Playboy* and the "blackness" of *Players*, he observed, "In *Playboy*, the women are posed sensually, like they're happy and getting paid. In *Players*, the women look mad, like they're only getting ten dollars and their pimp is taking eight. In *Playboy*, the women don't have a blemish on their bodies. In *Players*, the model's got stretch marks from the eight kids she's had, plus the bullet wound from that time she got shot in the ass."[13] Though meant in jest, Rock's assessment redoubled the misogyny inherent to *Players*'s shoddy production value.

This relentless, cost-cutting drive to the bottom not only diminished the quality of the magazine—it also yielded ideological effects that made the pornographic exception more extreme. Stereotypes that one might usually attribute to white racists found expression in the magazine in the early 1980s. For example, in response to the January 1982 cover story on the ostensible gulf separating black men from black women, a letter-writer from Jersey City, New Jersey, complained:

I'm tired of this sob story of the poor black women, black men calling them bitches and everything. Well, black men will stop calling them bitches when they stop acting like one [*sic*]. You black men out there know when you treat a black woman good and take care of home and family, a black woman will dog you and you are seen as a square to be used.

But if you spend your money on a big car and sharp wardrobe, don't call and, yes, even smack them around they can't keep away from you. So the dictionary says a bitch is a female dog. I go one step more and say one that bites the hand that beats them (is a dog). Black women will get respect when they stop acting like female dogs.[14]

Part momism, part vernacular insult, the writer's misogyny and racism combined the very worst elements of Morriss and Weinstock's enterprise. Yet, in many respects, this was now a key part of what made the black literary underground tick. Indeed, the writer might have had J. Jason Grant's pulp novel *Bitch* (1979) in mind when he reasoned why black women deserved to be called the epithet.

This steady devolution saw even Sid Smith, the longtime associate publisher of *Players*, forced out of the company. In 1981, he sued Morriss, Weinstock, and Players International Publications for $10 million in damages. The basis of his suit was that he had come up with the idea for the magazine and shared it with Morriss back in 1973. Rather than sign a contract, though, Smith, like Wanda Coleman, had "entered into an oral agreement" with the owner, "whereby [he] would be named vice president and publisher and that the proceeds would be divided into three shares, with Smith and Morris [*sic*] each getting a share and Weinstock . . . receiving the final share." There would be no salary either, as Smith had agreed to be paid in royalties and advertising revenues. After working for the magazine for six years, Smith came to the conclusion that Players International Publications' accounting was suspect, that he had unintentionally signed away his rights to the magazine, and that he was an officer of the company in name only. Having been forced out in July 1979, Smith could now see why Morriss had needed him there. The most damning allegation of the suit was that he was merely a black face, or lure, to "induce advertisers and organizations to advertise with [the] magazine."[15] Though it remains unclear if or how the suit was settled, Smith's rancorous departure from the enterprise goes some way to explaining the magazine's precipitous decline in quality.

Since *Players* and black pulp fiction had a synergistic relationship, it was only a matter of time when the White Negro erotica that Leo Guild had been publishing for years would become a model for black writers to take up in the 1980s. After all, if *Players*'s down-market track was any indication, only the most abject representations of black women's sexuality would be welcomed by Morriss and Weinstock. Things seemed to pan out that way when a spate of novels featuring black women main characters came out in the early 1980s. The crudely rendered illustrations on their covers recalled *Pimp*'s original design from 1967. And each of those covers titillated the reader with a synopsis drawn from between the covers. For example, Jesse Jones's *Midnight's Daughter* (1981) promised "the scorching, shocking story of a woman of the streets and her search for happiness in a hostile, confusing and bruising world of drugs, prostitution, violence."[16] L. K. Wilson's *Celluloid Trick* (1982) tempted the reader with "the story of a beautiful, young, black girl lured into the seamy, sordid world of pornography in order to protect her heroin-addict sister and her innocent young nephew."[17] And, finally, Rae S. Stewart's *Treat Them Like Animals* (1982) hinted above a tableau of an all-women's prison yard: "A brutal, haunting account of what it means to be a black woman in jail in America." As if the visual suggestion were not enough, the back cover clarified: "It is an unsparing portrait of all the savagery, lesbianism and, ironically, tenderness and camaradarie [sic] that exists within the unique society of prison."[18]

These books had all the trappings of the old sexploitation-blaxploitation conjunction, such as the women-in-prison sleazefest *Black Mama White Mama* and the avenging Amazon movie *Coffy* (both 1973), both of which starred Pam Grier. But they also harked back to Goines's less formulaic fiction, *Black Girl Lost*, about a young woman who succumbs to the vices of the fast life, and *White Man's Justice, Black Man's Grief*, a prison novel modeled on Chester Himes's fiction and his own experience doing time (both 1973). And despite their sensationalist packaging, these titles, on the whole, simply did not abide the pornographic exception in the way other books and certainly *Players* did. *Treat Them Like Animals* even had time for a literary flourish that cracked a joke at black men's expense:

> Boredom is . . .
> > when you and your partner
> > start feedin bread crumbs
> > to the mice . . .
> > and watch em fight over
> > the same piece
> > > (like two niggers
> > > > fightin over
> > > > > the same woman)[19]

Stewart had already been recognized as a black lesbian poet who wrote powerfully about her experience serving time. She had even published a short story about the same in the New Jersey prison arts periodical *Inside/Out*.[20] Taking these points into consideration, it becomes easier to appreciate how Stewart's novel, however modestly, gave voice to an antimisogynist politics from within the company's catalog.

All of which may help explain why my personal copies of these paperbacks, which I have bought secondhand over years of conducting research for this book, contain women's names on the inside flaps, indicating their previous ownership. What is more, I have found that these handwritten traces are unique to these books and to one other, Cole Riley's *Rough Trade* (1987), which also recounts the story of a black woman who finds herself in a world of trouble. (Riley is the pseudonym of black erotica author Robert Fleming, whose explicit renderings of black sexual pleasure have never been strictly tailored to the male gaze.) If we can safely conclude that black women read such fare from Holloway House, then we can begin to understand certain developments in the black literary underground later in the decade and into the 1990s.

Hidden Figures

One of the more interesting characters in *Hollow Daze* is a black woman by the name of Alice W. Hiker. She is among the pulp publisher's most popular writers, though her particular genre tends to be overshadowed by the black men at the company. Hawkins has a dig at the kind of writing in which Hiker specializes: black women's erotic fiction. Her books have guffaw-inducing titles like *Lickin 'n' Stickin*, *The Quiet Vagina*, and *Momma's Baby, Daddy's Maybe*. But Hawkins also has Hiker sincerely explain why she, and presumably other women writers, ended up at Hollow Daze. Over dinner with her girlfriends, she confesses, "I actually had an interview with a well-known Black publisher in Chicago who told me, straight up, 'Alice, there's no need for you to be writing this kind of filth. I think you're just trying to shock us, to be naughty for the sake of being naughty.'" That experience played itself out over and over again, with white publishers rejecting her out of hand and black publishers enforcing a "hypocritical puritanism" when it came to her writing.[21] She ended up at Hollow Daze, then, because it was the only publisher willing to "be naughty for the sake of being naughty"—not in spite but because of its sleazy reputation.

Morriss and Weinstock must have recognized fairly early on that black women were a major part of their readership, even though all of their print commodities did not reflect that fact. A slight nod toward that demographic appeared in February 1977, when they debuted a new monthly magazine called *Now*. Published in small digest-sized format, *Now* had the look of Johnson Publishing Company's *Jet*, the long-established celebrity and news magazine for African Americans. In editorial content, however, *Now* tried to approximate the success of *Essence*, the relatively new (its first issue had come out in May 1970) lifestyle magazine targeted specifically to black women. *Now*'s debut reflected this hybrid approach (figure 8.1): the smaller format focused attention on the celebrities appearing in the issue, while Natalie Cole's cover was appealing in a wholesome, respectable way. The only hint that *Now* was, in fact, a product of Players International Publications was the story on "sex symbol" Lola Falana, though even here, her interview stressed the business side of show business, allowing her to fit right in with her fellow black celebrities (among them actor James Earl Jones, television journalist Gail Christian, musical conductor Joyce Brown, and figure skater Linda Allen).

In the end, though, Morriss and Weinstock's initial effort to target black women readers was a flop. *Now* is forgotten in the annals of black periodical history, and it is unclear how many issues even came out. One explanation for its demise is that, in being entirely derivative of successful black-owned periodicals, *Now* was not trailblazing in the way Morriss and Weinstock had been with their other race-oriented properties. Whereas they had identified and cornered the market for black pulp

FIGURE 8.1 Front cover of *Now* (February 1977).

fiction and black pornography, they were entering into a crowded communications circuit when it came to black news and lifestyle periodicals. Another explanation follows from this. The middlebrow aesthetic that defined the general interest magazine was not Morriss and Weinstock's specialty, and it certainly was not what readers came to their print commodities looking for. In this, the fictional Alice Hiker (who Hawkins teases us into thinking is really Alice Walker) would have been exactly right: the Los Angeles operation was the place to get your kicks, not indulge in stereotypically "feminine" (read: bourgeois) discourse.

Holloway House was more successful in appealing to black women readers, but to do so it had to rely on a new group of freelancers to produce books that were distinct from its usual fare. There were the women-in-peril novelists like the ones I mentioned above. But staking out her own terrain was Genia Fogelson, a former instructor of comparative literature at Tougaloo and Millsaps (the latter was her alma mater) in Mississippi.[22] Having recently moved to Los Angeles, Fogelson published her first novel, *Jewel: Undercover Cop*, with Holloway House in 1979. Quite unlike any other character in the catalog, Jewel Smith was the literary equivalent of Pam Grier's 1974 blaxploitation hero Foxy Brown. Smart and self-possessed, Jewel moved between using her brain, brawn, and body to make sense of the various conspiracies at hand ("I was trying to put the pieces of this puzzle together").[23] Like Foxy Brown, she combined the playboy elements of the Iceman with the law-enforcing goodness of Rhodes. But Jewel Smith embodied it all as a black woman.

Another freelancer was Brett Howard, a Jewish woman who had grown up in Memphis, Tennessee, and Santa Fe, New Mexico, the daughter of a department store owner. Howard was a longtime contributor to Morriss and Weinstock's magazines, and, like Leo Guild, she took on ghostwriting assignments for them as well as for other publishers.[24] (Her most infamous of these assignments was 1976's *My Uncle Theodore*, a tell-all biography of Theodore Dreiser by his niece.) But in the early 1980s, Howard started publishing fiction under her own name; her specialty was black women's historical romance. *One Drop of Blood* (1981), *Love's Fire and Glory* (1982), and *Memphis Blues* (1984) all took place in the interwar years, and essentially along the axis connecting Harlem to the South. Though drawn to well-worn tropes of interracial melodrama such as the passing plot, Howard wrote with a fairly sound grasp of history that added yet another dimension to Holloway House's catalog.

These single-author contributions were merely the prelude for Morriss and Weinstock's most ambitious project since they had gambled on *Players* in 1973. As the *Atlanta Daily World* reported in March 1983, Holloway House was starting "the first romance line oriented for a black female readership." Under the editorship of Raymond Friday Locke, Heartline Romances would feature black characters in "contemporary" settings and storylines that reflected their "very specifically ethnic" experiences. The first batch of paperbacks included the following:

Flight to Love by Beverly Joye
Love's Velvet Song by Geraldine Greene
Texas Passion by Leah Guild
Silk and the Lady by Raye Ward
Lover's Holiday by Joyce Lezán
Love Note by Barbara Howard[25]

The emphasis on black romance's contemporaneity was important. While historical romance surely offered many pleasures to black women, it was modern romance that offered clearer, perhaps more aspirational, points of identification with their own lives. Heartline's covers conveyed that very point. Composed by graphic designer Marshall Licht and illustrated by local artist Roxanne Skene, both of whom were white, these covers invited gender- and class-based fantasies of upwardly mobile blackness. Figures 8.2 and 8.3 reveal the distance Heartline's books aimed to put between themselves and the proverbial street.

Upon closer inspection, however, one can see some familiar names hidden between the lines of this story. Barbara Howard was Brett Howard, Leah Guild was Leo Guild, and Joyce Lezán was Joseph Nazel—"Lezán" being "Nazel" spelled backward and Frenchified with an accent mark. Literary historian Valerie Babb also links Nazel to Kimberly Norton,[26] which may have been a veiled reference to his son, Kim Renard Nazel. Finally, Genia Fogelson pitched in with *Tides of Passion* in 1984. In short, most of the Heartline series was penned by a small group of hacks with whom Morriss and Weinstock had been working for years. Yolande Bertrand and Felicia Woods may have joined Fogelson as Heartline's black women authors, but biographical details on both are scant. The most Holloway House revealed could be found in Bertrand's dedications and in the note that Woods was a "student at the University of Mississippi" when her novel *Southern Nights* was published in 1984.[27]

FIGURE 8.2 Front cover of *Lover's Holiday* (1983).

FIGURE 8.3 Front cover of *Love Note* (1983).

As we have seen throughout this book, Holloway House was adept at stage-managing authorship as a kind of racial masquerade. But in taking up Guild's model of cross-gender masquerade for Heartline, the company may have left the series with the most awkward examples of black pulp fiction in the entire catalog. As Joyce Lezán, for example, Nazel once wrote:

As she ate Ebony allowed herself the secret pleasure of fantasizing about a future of breakfasts with Joe across the table from her. What was the harm in a little dreaming, to break the pressures of work. Yes, she imagined, they could wake on wintry mornings, before the first sign of light, ski until the darkness slipped away, taking a leisurely shower *together* on their return, before a hot filling breakfast. Then, by the flickering, dancing light of a whispering fire, make love.[28]

Nazel's prose was workmanlike at best, straining to wring sentiment out of his female characters' interior lives. His use of free indirect discourse did not seem to help, for as this example shows, he never quite allowed his imagination to roam free of the literality of narrative itself. That Ebony's romantic fantasy is tethered to the fact that she happens to be eating a hearty breakfast perhaps reveals where Nazel's mind was wandering to in the actual moment of composition.

Yet, as in most things at Holloway House, Guild's pseudonymic turn as Leah Guild made his fellow hack look like a master of the genre. In the aforementioned *Texas Passion*, Guild narrated a couple's separation like so: "He left her standing there, all her juices flowing," and then, "In the end, he dressed and left, left her with all her needs and desires. She cried. She was torn. She cried herself to sleep." Where Nazel had at least tried to inhabit his female character's consciousness, Guild made no such effort. In fact, he seemed incapable of writing the romance from anything but a vantage point that was tailored to male ego gratification. In the same book, Guild described part of a tryst this way: "He moved her to the couch. He handled her easily. He tossed his jacket on the floor, and the shirt followed, and the trousers followed that. He had on a pair of jockey shorts. They covered nothing."[29] Guild was never the most versatile of hacks, but this was bad even for him. Going through the motions, he wrote about sex as if it were a mechanical process that left absolutely nothing to the imagination. Holloway House's assembly-line model of literary production had evacuated any human feeling from his prose.

Despite the debatable quality of their romances, Morriss and Weinstock pushed Heartline hard on their readers. Mail-order slips for the series could be found in the back of every kind of book they published. Reviews of titles appeared in nonmetropolitan areas, underscoring the idea that these books were for a different kind of reader than what black pulp fiction usually attracted. "Does Jack love Penny or is he only using her to advance his career?" asked Georgia's *Columbus Times*, before noting that Geraldine Greene's *Love's Velvet Song* was suitable for "high school and above level readers."[30] Full-page color advertisements even appeared in *Players*, where the occasional letter-writer did, in fact, criticize the otherwise toxic masculinism of the magazine. In direct response to the Jersey City letter I quoted earlier, for example, a nineteen-year-old from Elmhurst, New York, wrote in to protest how black men talked about black women in the magazine. Urging readers to "be men but not in a sick way," the letter-writer offered:

You sit on your ass with your book and pen, you write she's a bitch, and probably grin.
But if she's a bitch and that's what you say, then who dug the ditch in which she lay?
She's a woman without love, that is what you perceive, but no one can give what they don't receive.[31]

That rap may have articulated a minority opinion, but it displayed the kind of self-awareness that helped carve a small space in the magazine for Heartline. In the same issue, an ad for the series hailed, "Never before such brazen, scintillating, forbidden love written in the black experience!" Six covers illustrated by Skene were featured here, all of which showed black men and women in alternately passionate and warm embraces. "It's exhilarating!" the copy panted.[32]

Ten years later, in 1994, Locke admitted to the *Los Angeles Times* that Heartline Romances had been a failure. As he put it, "there was no market for them at the time." African American romance writer Sandra Kitt offered a more nuanced take in the same story, which covered the diversification of the romance fiction industry. Having made her debut in 1984, Kitt noted that the problem had come down to white publishers, not black readers. "They knew not all of their readers were white," she said, "but they felt . . . if women of color are willing to read romances with white characters, why fool around with it?"[33] It was not until Terry McMillan's blockbuster novel *Waiting to Exhale* (1992) that publishers were finally willing to devote the resources necessary to make black women's voices and experiences central to the production of romance fiction. McMillan's success helped Kitt gain a new lease on the genre, and it led to a general efflorescence of black middle-class romance in the 1990s.

Did that mean Heartline Romances was ahead of its time? Probably not. Taking Kitt's point seriously, the problem with the series was not the lack of a market for black romance—it was Holloway House's utter inability to produce and distribute fiction by black women for black women. There was a clear disconnect between, on the one hand, recognizing that black women were reading pulps and, on the other, targeting that same demographic with newly commissioned fare. Part of the problem may have been that the series had no periodical to complement its circulation. But *Now*'s flopping apparently did not encourage Morriss and Weinstock to rethink their assumptions. They went forward with Heartline, chasing after the black woman reader with middlebrow tastes.

Tellingly, Heartline's demise did not mean women stopped reading black pulp fiction. In fact, Holloway House paperbacks surged in popularity among black women in the 1990s. Crucially, they seemed to be drawn not to the bourgeois scripts of Heartline but to the by now classic pulp fiction of Donald Goines, as well as the women-in-peril novelists who followed in his wake. In their recycled depictions of powerful men who experience a terrible, often tragic, fall, Goines's potboilers gave black women readers an opening to reflect on their own experiences. We know that because of how these readers turned his books into material they could call their own.

Fellow Detroiter Vickie Stringer encountered Goines while serving a stint in federal prison in Bryant, Texas. She was doing time for having been the Columbus, Ohio, connection in a lucrative interstate drug trafficking operation. Police had nabbed her when one of her dealers fingered her to save his own neck. Behind bars, Stringer was inspired by Goines to turn her own life story into the stuff of fiction. She finished her first novel, *Let That Be the Reason*, while incarcerated, and hoped to find a publisher for it upon being released after serving five years. Instead, according to Stringer, she received twenty-six rejection letters from presses big and small. Still believing in her work, she borrowed money from a friend, printed copies of the book herself, and started selling *Let That Be the Reason* at "car washes, corner stores and hair salons"—effectively becoming her own publisher and distributor. (The book was granted copyright in 1999.) The wild grassroots success of that novel led her to write more books and publish other likeminded authors under her own company, Triple Crown Publications, named after her ex-boyfriend's gang in Columbus.[34]

Teri Woods, niece of legendary radio broadcaster Georgie Woods, was working a legal secretary in Philadelphia when she got the writing bug. Inspired by Goines's "style," which she has said "taught me about a new league [of writing]," Woods penned a novel, *True to the Game*, about two friends in 1980s Philadelphia who get caught up in the fast life of the drug trade. Woods based her story not on direct personal experience but on the fact that she had lost loved ones to that life. Like Stringer, Woods had her manuscript rejected by multiple publishers. But also like Stringer, those piled-up rejections did not deter her from reaching her audience. She borrowed some money, taught herself desktop publishing, and printed and bound her own copies of *True to the Game* under the label Meow Meow Productions. (The manuscript was granted copyright as early as 1994 but did not appear in print until 1998.) She sold seventy thousand books from the trunk of her car, hitting beauty shops and sidewalks from Philadelphia to Harlem. Like Stringer, Woods then used the profits to invest in her own company, which she named, fittingly enough, Teri Woods Publishing.[35]

Women like Stringer and Woods were members of a black literary underground that, despite its clear masculinist tilt, found ways of inserting their own women-centered storylines into a contemporary urban imaginary. That they were inspired by Holloway House but could not rely on it—or any other publisher, for that matter—to validate their work revealed the limitations of the company's communications circuit. By having to devise their own means of production, these readers started a new circuit that would diversify the black literary underground from within. Morriss and Weinstock's mistake, perhaps, was to think that what women readers wanted would be distinct from what men wanted. It turned out that the author who had turned their operation away from sleaze and toward black pulp was a favorite among women too.

Beyond the Page

But Iceberg Slim proved he also had staying power. After a decade of flip-flopping on politics and pimping, he emerged at the dawn of the 1980s as the standard-bearer of the black literary underground's masculinist front. Though his late fiction was quickly forgotten, *Pimp* continued to sell remarkably well, going through multiple reprints and becoming the unofficial bible of the underground itself. Further, though he never made another official appearance in *Players*, Slim's pimp persona shadowed the magazine's devolution into just another skin rag. In one mid-1980s issue, the magazine's editor, H. L. Sorrell, was photographed with that month's centerfold model, "Jaylynn," at the X-Rated Critics Organization awards show, which had its own write-up in the issue. In that write-up, Sorrell hailed the "adult movie industry . . . coming into it's [sic] own" and, as a voting member of the organization, considered the "X-rated genre" as "the last motion picture frontier."[36] Approaching his editorship of *Players* as if he were managing a stable, Sorrell blurred the line between model and working girl even more brazenly when, a few years later, in August 1989, he put his own wife, singer Rozlynn Sorrell, on the cover of *Players*.

But if the Slim of Holloway House's communications circuit merely recycled tropes of yore, the same could not be said of his young black fans who brought him back to the street. As rap became one of the most popular musical genres in the early to mid-1980s, Slim's influence on the music became apparent. In particular, the Los Angeles–based subgenre known as "gangsta rap" was understood to have been inspired in part by Holloway House's black pulp fiction.[37] Named after the California gangbanging culture that extended from the prison-industrial complex to the streets (epitomized in the Bloods and Crips conflict), gangsta rap was the West Coast's hard-core alternative to New York's old-school party scene. In Michael Eric Dyson's account, the music coming out of Los Angeles constituted "an indictment of mainstream and bourgeois black institutions by young people who [did] not find conventional methods of addressing personal and social calamity useful."[38] On these terms, black pulp fiction's attention to those marginalized by the rapidly deindustrializing economy shaped the way gangsta rappers at once conceived and performed their art.

That was certainly the case for Ice-T. Born Tracy Marrow in Newark, New Jersey, in 1958, he grew up in "an upscale town" called Summit, enjoying "just a real middle-American life." Marrow moved out to California, however, after his parents died from heart failure four years apart. He lived with an aunt and attended Crenshaw High School, where gangbanging was rampant. But the precocious Marrow adapted to his environment. He became known as "Trey" because Tracy, his birth name, "sounded like a girl's name." It was in this context that he was introduced to black pulp fiction:

All through high school, I was reading Iceberg Slim. I picked up my street name, and later my rap name, from Iceberg Slim. He was the first author I discovered who truly delved into the life of crime and pimpin' and made it *real* to me. I went everywhere with his books, idolizing him. I'd memorized entire sections and could spit them at will. The Crips back in South Central used to constantly say, "Yo, kick some more of that shit by Ice, T."

The more he brought Slim's writing to bear on his practice of reciting "Crip Rhymes," or a South Central–specific version of toasting, the more Ice-T began to embody what would become an iconic rap identity. He listened to Slim's record of classic toasts, *Reflections*, for inspiration. And when he heard the Sugar Hill Gang's "Rapper's Delight" upon its debut in 1979, Ice-T knew he had caught "the rap bug."[39] He would go on to become the standout individual gangsta rapper of his generation.

Ice-T's early albums are testaments to Slim's influence on his art. In his debut, *Rhyme Pays* (1987), the track "6 'N the Mornin'" documents the misadventures of an everyday hustler on the run from the police. While the speaker's gun-toting antics are right out of the pages of a Goines book, Ice-T's infectious rhymes, playful sense of humor, and attention to the finer details of the hoodlum lifestyle are vintage Slim. In the first stanza, for example, Ice-T's rhymes match the propulsive force of each couplet's forward-looking action:

6 in the morning, police at my door
Fresh Adidas squeak across the bathroom floor
Out the back window I make my escape
Didn't even get a chance to grab my old school tape

Recalling an otherwise harrowing getaway, the speaker's attention to the "freshness" of his sneakers (Adidas being a beloved street brand) indicates a certain cool under fire, someone who, despite being on the run, is doing so in style. Not coincidentally, the speaker's self-presentation is maximized for the ladies. After successfully outrunning the cops, for example, he boasts:

Up the next morning, feeling good as hell
Sleeping with a girlie sure beats a cell
Hit the boulevard in my A.M.G.
Hos catching whiplash, trying to glimpse the T[40]

Here the speaker seals his masculine self-possession precisely through the symbolic capital his possession signifies: the "hos" can't help but swing their heads toward the big "T" who drives a slick "A.M.G." (a Mercedes-Benz car model).

In his 2011 memoir, Ice-T remembers how the deceptively simple plot of "6 'N the Mornin'"—"a story about a guy on the run from the cops, waking up one day in Los Angeles, going to the County, hitting the streets, and then getting into a shootout"—took the city, the state, and then the nation by storm. Gangsta-style rap was, in essence, a "crime-story rap," or a hybrid of pulp fiction and urban vernacular traditions. And while it is true that Ice-T observed aspects of gangbanging firsthand, it is important not to assume that his art derived from some unmediated experience of the fast life. Indeed, a large part of it came from reading Slim's books. "I thought he was fly because he was a pimp," Ice-T admits, "but I realized that I really admired him because he was a *writer*." By appreciating Slim's literary qualities, he continues, "I started to develop those same skills in my rhymes, painting these dark portraits of the world of pimps, hustlers, and gangbangers."[41]

Ice-T's three subsequent albums—*Power* (1988), *The Iceberg/Freedom of Speech . . . Just Watch What You Say* (1989), and *O.G. Original Gangster* (1991)—solidified his reputation as gangsta's reigning solo artist. In his vast repertoire of raps about urban life, Ice-T shuttled between misogynist sexual fantasies and deadly serious political insight. *The Iceberg's* titular track, for example, derives from the black pimp's stash of witty repartee:

Out with the posse on a night run
Girls on the corner, so let's have some fun
Donald asked one if she was game
Back Alley Sally was her name
She moved on the car and moved fast
On the window pressed her ass
All at once we heard a crash
Donald's dick had broke the glass[42]

Like the best toasts, Ice-T takes the homosocial code of sexual exchange to extreme, even absurd, lengths.[43] Such crude humor is offset in *O.G.*'s titular track, where Ice-T warns against romanticizing the hood:

Anybody who's been there knows that
Life ain't so lovely on the blood-soaked fast track
That invincible shit don't work
Throw you in the joint, you'll be coming out feet first
. . . .
I rap for brothers just like myself

Dazed by the game in a quest for extreme wealth
But I kick it to you hard and real
One wrong move, and your cap's peeled[44]

These examples demonstrate how, in combining phallic humor with social commentary, activating the silly and the smart, Ice-T transformed Slim's early work into a cultural phenomenon that was as entertaining as it was instructive.

The standout gangsta group was Niggaz With Attitude (N.W.A.). Hailing from Compton and South Central, N.W.A. featured the likes of Eazy-E (Eric Wright), Ice Cube (O'Shea Jackson),[45] and Dr. Dre (Andre Young)—each a groundbreaking artist in his own right. The group's debut studio album *Straight Outta Compton* came out in 1988. Though not explicitly referenced in the lyrics, black pulp fiction formed the narrative backdrop to many of the album's tracks, including "Fuck tha Police," "Gangsta Gangsta," and "Dopeman." In "Fuck tha Police," for example, MC Ren (Lorenzo Patterson) spat,

Smoke any motherfucker that sweats me
Or any asshole that threatens me
I'm a sniper with a hell of a scope
Taking out a cop or two, they can't cope with me[46]

It was a fantasied threat, a Kenyatta-type scenario of righteous vengeance. It did not sit well with the Los Angeles Police Department, however, which accused the group of advocating retaliatory violence against officers. N.W.A. was banned from several concert venues, yet that only seemed to make people even more interested in the music. The group enjoyed incredible commercial success with the album, while its lyrics set "the benchmark for the subgenre's antipolice, antistate rebelliousness."[47] *Straight Outta Compton* helped gangsta go mainstream and gave hip-hop the momentum it needed to take over American popular culture in the 1990s.

After N.W.A. split, two members went on to have enormously successful careers. Ice Cube and Dr. Dre became icons of the West Coast scene, releasing solo albums that elaborated on the vision of potent and militant black manhood *Straight Outta Compton* had deployed. Ice Cube's solo debut *AmeriKKKa's Most Wanted* (1990) "demonstrated how black nationalism as an embodied-social politics [was] dependent not only on performative blackness . . . but also on performative masculinity."[48] Like Ice-T, Ice Cube blended the black pimp's flair with the black revolutionary's politics in a way that Slim himself had failed to realize in the 1970s. Dr. Dre, meanwhile, cofounded what would become the enormously influential label Death Row Records and through it released his solo album *The Chronic* (1992). Musically, the album established the unique G-funk sound of West Coast hip-hop, while performatively, Dr. Dre became the standard-bearer of a smooth, seemingly effortless, flow. Yet these achievements were bound up with virulent misogyny and homophobia, which Dr. Dre expressed in his lyrics as a way to prop up his own hypermasculine persona. That these revanchist expressions were pitched not only to young black men but also to young white men revealed the rap industry's own White Negro dilemma.[49]

Slim was not merely part of the milieu surrounding N.W.A.'s and its members' successes. In a sense, he was intrinsic to that success at an early stage. Though largely forgotten today, one of the group's founding members was Kim Nazel, who went by the stage name Arabian Prince. Joseph's son had been a producer and in-demand club deejay when he collaborated on producing the group's earliest music. He worked on N.W.A.'s first single "Panic Zone" and its independent compilation album *N.W.A. and the Posse* (both 1987) before turning to *Straight Outta Compton*. But financial disagreements led Arabian Prince to walk away from the project before N.W.A. had finished recording it. The only credit he got on it was for the final track, "Something 2 Dance 2."[50] Still, if Arabian Prince's later solo albums are any indication, he must have been a key figure in bringing Slim's florid, almost self-parodying, misogyny to bear on N.W.A.'s rap. "Never Caught Slippin" and "It's Time to Bone," from *Brother Arab* (1989), and "A Poem from a Pimp" and "A Little Jazz 4 Yo Azz," from *Where's My Bytches* (1993), bespoke a deep appreciation for Slim's many permutations over time. Indeed, the tongue-in-cheek nature of some of the music seemed to play on, and with, the very masquerade that Holloway House had attempted to conceal under the label "the black experience." That was to have been expected, perhaps, by someone whose middle name was Renard.

Holloway House was not unaware of the rise of rap. But without a record label to tack onto, Morriss and Weinstock's profit-making options were limited. The best they could do was publish Jeffrey D. Knuckles's *The Rap! Book* in 1988. Containing twenty original raps by Knuckles, the book was published in a seven-by-eleven-inch format, as if to give ample space to both take in and take notes on the lyrics printed on the page. Many of the raps showed Knuckles to be a shrewd social critic and a capable wordsmith. But, in truth, because the words were inevitably divorced from their performative utterance, and in particular Knuckles's sense of timing and flow, they packed little punch and paled in comparison to the rap circulating through airwaves at that very moment. Even more troubling was the fact that the lyrics were prefaced by an introduction by one David B. Lewis. Without any indication of who he was, Lewis attested to the fact that "rap speaks in the vernacular of its listeners, in the hip, easy rhythms of the street, the funky epithets of the schoolyard." Readers were supposed to take his voice at face value and, in some sense, to find value in Knuckles's writing precisely through his testimony. When Lewis concluded his piece by noting that Knuckles had written the raps "while in prison, where he has spent half his childhood and adult life,"[51] he could only recall the White Negro fetish for Slim in the late 1960s and 1970s, which had subjected urban black masculinity to sociological investigation.

By the time this book came out, it was already far too late. Black pulp fiction had taken on a life of its own in the aural and sonic flows of rap. Soon the hip-hop culture that eventuated from rap's mainstream commodification would regard Slim as a forefather of the old-school art and Goines as an inspiration for contemporary narratives of the street. In the 1990s, rappers as varied as Tupac Shakur (born Lesane Crooks), Too Short (Todd Shaw), Jay-Z (Shawn Carter), and Ludacris (Christopher Bridges) name-checked Slim and Goines in lyrics that fans could later repeat off the top of their heads. Thanks to these readers-cum-lyricists, black pulp fiction stayed alive and relevant, with guaranteed sales as new hip-hop fans sought out their favorite acts' influences.[52]

When *Publishers Weekly*, in 2003, described Vickie Stringer's and Teri Woods's books variously as "ghetto fiction, hip-hop novels, 'street life' novels, 'blaxploitation' novels and urban pulp fiction," it brought to light the conjunction between women and young men in the black literary underground.[53] This new, so-called urban fiction (the umbrella term for the descriptors above) was not a recycling of black pulp fiction—it was its own genre and format, inspired by Holloway House, of course, but more in tune with rap's vernacular aesthetics and hip-hop's "ghettocentric" style.[54] Even more important, on an infrastructural level, urban fiction was not the product of the same communications circuit that had long churned out black pulp fiction. Where Morriss and Weinstock had succeeded in recalibrating their enterprise from sleaze to black pulp fiction, they failed to see the potential of what would come after black pulp fiction itself. In other words, wide swaths of their readership became unrecognizable to them. Again, that did not mean people stopped reading or buying their books, or that they no longer had a place in the black literary underground. What it did mean was that their hold on the underground was no longer dominant, and that it was only a matter of time before Holloway House would be superseded by the very readers who had come of age reading its books.

The company made one final lurch for the young readers' demographic in 1989. Responding to ostensible complaints from some corners that Slim and Goines were bad for kids to read, Holloway House's marketing vice president Mitchell Neal announced the launch of a series of edifying biographies of famous African Americans, including Ella Fitzgerald, Paul Robeson, and Jackie Robinson. These short books came "heavily illustrated, and [were] suitable for a teen-age audience."[55] Despite the hype, many of the titles, published under the imprint Melrose Square, were simply reworked versions of biographies Holloway House had put out years earlier for an adult audience. In other words, aging hackwork—Brett Howard's book on Lena Horne, Rugio Vitale's (Nazel's) on Joe Louis—would be recycled yet again for kids' consumption.[56] Holloway House was running on fumes. With a dearth of original content, the company was desperately trying to catch up with its readers. Those readers were now the undisputed engine of the black literary underground.

Iceberg Slim died from complications related to diabetes on April 30, 1992, at the age of seventy-three. While Slim was on his deathbed at Brotman Medical Center in Los Angeles, riots sparked by the acquittal of four police officers in the infamous Rodney King beating were raging outside.[57] Six days of looting, arson, and violence resulted in nearly sixty deaths, more than two thousand injuries, and over $1 billion in property damage. The riots were concentrated in South Central Los Angeles, among whose neighborhoods could be counted Watts. The parallels to the most iconic urban uprising of the civil rights era were hard to miss. What had changed, really, in twenty-five years? the city's black residents might have asked themselves. As Min Hyoung Song has observed, the 1992 riots "laid bare the many contradictions and pathologies quivering beneath America's skin-deep claims to civil society."[58] "Skin-deep" was another way of describing how Morriss and Weinstock had run their enterprise even as they gained a massive following of loyal readers.

Holloway House made an expected appearance in the obituary, but, in a move reminiscent of the way it had treated Goines's death, the company used the occasion of Slim's passing to announce that it had "just introduced all his titles in a commemorative silver edition celebrating the 25th anniversary since publication of his first book."[59] To be sure, Slim's books had gone through cover redesigns since initial publication. But this edition was special, packaging Slim's writing in as close to a collected works format as Holloway House could manage. It was, at one and the same time, a deep sign of respect for the author's fan base and another crass example of banking on his legend.

The occasion of Slim's death also ushered in the moment of his rediscovery by the White Negro. As we already know, Irvine Welsh happened upon a used copy of *Pimp*, which then gave him the idea to write *Trainspotting*. There was also *Esquire*'s coverage of Slim's passing, which surveyed the author's life and legacy in a way that recalled the ethnographic curiosity of Christina and Richard Milner. Highlighting the scale of Slim's underground reception, the piece noted that his books had sold six million copies before his death.[60] Inquiring readers might well have asked, How could that be? Just who was reading Iceberg Slim? They were eager to find out. Before long, both Slim and Goines were reprinted in trade editions in the United States by W. W. Norton, as part of its Old School Books series; in the United Kingdom, in Welsh's hometown Edinburgh, by Payback Press; and in France (in translation) as part of Éditions de l'Olivier's Soul Fiction series (Slim) and of Gallimard's long-running crime and mystery series, the Série Noire (Goines).[61] Suddenly, reading Slim and Goines had become "cool," a form of symbolic capital whose value accrued from the very reality effect that the black literary underground had cultivated around pulp fiction. Literalist interpretations of Slim and Goines, which have predominated among scholars and professional critics, can be traced to this moment—that is, when white readers sought to appropriate the black literary underground itself.

Yet that newly diversified field of cultural production would not be so easily appropriated. As this chapter has shown, urban fiction and hip-hop had already taken the black literary underground to places beyond white readers' ken. That Holloway House and Players International Publications were becoming increasingly irrelevant to that process of reinvention did not matter. Black readers reappropriated cultural narratives and cultural forms from books that, having gone through an almost assembly-line production process, were always thought of, first and foremost, as commodities to be sold, units to be moved. By engaging with these books beyond what Holloway House prescribed for them, black readers recreated black pulp fiction in their own image, using their own formats. Holloway House's monopoly on determining what counted as "the black experience" was coming to an end.

Epilogue: And Back Again

At the end of "What Is This 'Black' in Black Popular Culture?," Stuart Hall leaves us with a description of his object of study as a site of contestation. He writes,

Popular culture, commodified and stereotyped as it often is, is not at all, as we sometimes think of it, the arena where we find who we really are, the truth of our experience. It is an arena that is *profoundly* mythic. It is a theater of popular desires, a theater of popular fantasies. It is where we discover and play with the identifications of ourselves, where we are imagined, where we are represented, not only to the audiences out there who do not get the message, but to ourselves for the first time.[1]

What I find analytically enriching about this description is not only its antiessentialist standpoint but its theorization of cultural production as a site where recognition itself is contested in the "theater" of consumption. Hall acknowledges that popular culture is perfectly capable of appealing to different groups at one and the same time ("audiences out there" and "ourselves"). Yet, in both instances, recognition is hardly, if ever, a given. In fact, for Hall, popular culture is that site where misrecognition ("do not get the message") and a new mode of identification ("for the first time") are made possible. Thus, to apprehend the "black" in black popular culture, we must forget about finding what we recognize as "black" in that field and focus instead on how "black" itself is the sliding signifier that conducts both misrecognition and identification among different audiences and different consumers.

This, in short, has been the project of *Street Players: Black Pulp Fiction and the Making of a Literary Underground*. Where Holloway House's origin story for black pulp fiction has been taken as self-evident for well-nigh half a century, my aim in this book has been to reconstruct the format's genealogy and demonstrate that its claim to "blackness" and even to "pulp fiction" had to be made—appropriated, commodified, consumed, and reinvented. In tracking this process, I have shown how misrecognition and identification were constantly in play at Holloway House and its associated businesses. For example, the *Pimp* of 1967 appealed to white readers in a way that the *Pimp* of 1971 sought to overturn among black readers, only for that second version to be left behind by the *Pimp* of the years since Donald Goines came onto the scene. Approaching the arc of Iceberg Slim's career from this angle, we can more clearly see how the strategies that had enabled white misrecognition—masquerade, ghostwriting, and hackwork—were repurposed by Holloway House to elicit, and sustain, black identification. Far from being unique to Slim, this repurposing facilitated the entire enterprise's transition from sleaze to street. Yet, as part 3 of this book has shown, that transition was hardly seamless or neat. Even with the rise of *Players* magazine in 1973, which gave monthly, self-referential shape to the black literary underground, the field of cultural production to which Morriss and Weinstock laid claim always showed signs of its conflicted conditions of production. The black literary underground thus should be thought of less as an inherently transgressive subculture than as a print-based conjuncture of competing interests and tastes—a site of contradiction.

My method has been crucial in bringing these dynamics to light. By taking up a structuralist account of cultural production in space (Bourdieu) and over a period of time (Darnton), I have limited what any one actor can say or do to effect change in the black literary underground. That includes myself, in the role of the professional critic. I have resisted the critical tendency to read against the grain of black pulp fiction's conditions of production, imputing irreverent or "resistant" interpretations to an ordinary reader who would share my values, aesthetic or otherwise.[2] Instead, I have outlined the broader structural conditions that made change possible in a system of cultural production. To that end, I have described how Bentley Morriss and Ralph Weinstock exercised near-exclusive control over the black literary underground for the better part of two decades. They did so not only through their print commodities but also through the discourse they cultivated around their books. Change was slow in coming because they controlled the means of production and distribution for so long. It was only after readers sidestepped Morriss and Weinstock's communications circuit and started making their own pulp narratives in the form of urban fiction and hip-hop that the black literary underground expanded to include genuinely new voices (as opposed to those stage-managed through masquerade or ghostwriting) drawn from a totally new pool of talent (in contrast to the fairly small group of writers on whom Morriss and Weinstock relied). Thus, by not looping back in Holloway House's communications circuit, these readers effectively reapprorpriated black pulp fiction for their own uses, which is to say, for black cultural production.

Even here, though, we might refrain from concluding that the rise of urban fiction and hip-hop represents the triumph of black agency over white exploitation. Because the available evidence suggests that, in the very way it operated, Holloway House had been on course to becoming obsolete. If there is anything my extended genealogy of black pulp fiction reveals, it is that the format owed its existence to a highly interconnected field of print culture. For decades, Morriss and Weinstock's pulps and pinup magazines blanketed the country in a vast network of paper, originating out of the All America Distributors Corporation warehouse and intersecting through self-referential citations and cross-publication advertising. In the 1990s, however, this business model collapsed on itself. With the rise of digital media, the print public sphere contracted, consigning huge swaths of the paper-based trades to the dustbin of history. It was difficult enough for transnational conglomerates and news corporations to stay afloat, much less one of the last independent publishing houses in the nation.

For its part, *Players* would have encountered stiff competition from home video and DVD players, cable television and pay-per-view, and, of course, the internet. The magazine tried to keep up with the times by repackaging just its pornographic elements (*Pictorial*), putting out more extreme hard-core content (*Nasty*), and interfacing with the powerful video industry (*Black Video Illustrated*). But these were only stopgaps in the relentless drive toward print's obsolescence. Ralph Weinstock did not live to see the worst of it when he passed in August 1997.

The same could be said of black pulp fiction. Slim and Goines may have been fine, but who was going to read the hacks who had populated the majority of Holloway House's catalog with books? Their cultural references were woefully out of date, and their style of writing seemed like it had come from another time (which, more often than not, it had). Not to mention that books were now competing with an overfilled menu of popular media for readers' attention. Hip-hop, it should be noted, became the dominant cultural force in this turn-of-the-century mediascape. No other cultural form proved more amenable to cross-media adaptation, promotion, and distribution, both within the United States and around the world. Holloway House had a stake in hip-hop's dissemination, but, in truth, it was narrowly focused on just *Pimp* and a few of Goines's novels. Everything else fell by the wayside.

In a last-ditch effort to break into the wider mediascape, Morriss made another go at Hollywood in the early 2000s. This time Fox Searchlight Pictures would bring Goines to the big screen. Based on his 1974 novel *Never Die Alone*, the movie of the same name seemed to have all the ingredients for success. Director Ernest R. Dickerson had made well-received gritty urban crime dramas in the early 1990s, the most famous of which was *Juice* (1992), starring Tupac Shakur. Rapper DMX (Earl Simmons) was cast in the lead role of David, a fearless drug lord who starts an underworld turf war, and his music would anchor the movie's original soundtrack. Yet when *Never Die Alone* debuted in March 2004, it was an immediate flop. Its opening weekend garnered only $3 million in receipts, putting it just outside the top ten, at eleventh, for ticket sales. Receipts declined precipitously from there, such that within a month the movie was screening in fewer than sixty theaters.[3] Michael Sragow, of the *Baltimore Sun*, said the movie "simply wallows in gangsta hyperbole—it's all bling bling, bang bang," while the *Washington Post*'s Desson Thomson quipped, "Possibly the worst thug-life flick to be released in the past 72 hours, this movie sags under the weight of the bling-bling cliches [sic] strung around its headless neck."[4] Just as *Trick Baby* the movie had come late on the heels of blaxploitation, so was *Never Die Alone* adjudged to be late to arrive to the gangsta party. By the time it came out, it could only be viewed as a crass attempt to exploit a tired formula.

Morriss shuttered his various publishing operations in 2008. The *Adam* family of pornographic magazines, which, in a twist worthy of a separate study, had undergone its own rebranding so that it now catered to gay men, was discontinued, as was the *Players* family of magazines. Most of Holloway House's back catalog was sold off to New York's Kensington Books, a mass-market paperback house that remains one of the last major independents in the United States. Interestingly, the company, which specializes in romance fiction, is the successor to the 1960s and 1970s sleaze outfit Lancer. Presumably cofounder Walter Zacharius had made the gender-conscious shift to romance to keep his company afloat. For its part, Kensington agreed to continue publishing all sixteen of Donald Goines's novels under the imprint Holloway House Classics.[5] Today you can purchase any of these books in slick trade paperback editions featuring hip-hop-inspired covers.

The only thing Kensington did not acquire was Slim's oeuvre. In March 2011, his daughter Misty Beck revealed to hip-hop fan website *SOHH* that Morriss had settled a lawsuit brought forward by the Beck family, alleging that Holloway House cheated Slim out of royalty payments for years. Although the settlement's terms meant that the family "didn't win a lot of money" for back royalties, they were "able to get the catalogue back" and thus owned the rights to his work. At least that was the case before a literary agent the family had hired sold those rights to Bryan "Birdman" Williams, cofounder and CEO of Cash Money Records.[6] Having gotten his start as a rapper on the New Orleans hip-hop scene, Birdman, along with this brother Ronald Williams (whose nickname, fittingly enough, is "Slim"), rose up the industry ladder to become a major hip-hop producer. The duo's eye for talent led them to sign eventual stars such as Lil Wayne, Nicki Minaj, and Drake. Now, in spring 2011, the Williamses were debuting a publishing imprint, Cash Money Content (CMC), that would complement their successful record business. Unlike Holloway House, which had long relied on an in-house distribution company, CMC was partnering with Atria Books, an imprint of CBS Corporation's Simon & Schuster, to market and distribute its books. One of the first titles in the CMC catalog would be a reprint of *Pimp*.[7] Today all of Slim's work can be found in slick trade paperback editions from CMC.

It is appropriate, I think, that this book ends by coming around full circuit. Goines is now printed by a company that falls under sleaze's long shadow. Slim is now printed by a company that epitomizes the reappropriation of pulp narratives by urban fiction and hip-hop. In a way, the coexistence of these investments spatializes the temporal shift I have sought to track in this book. To the extent that the black literary underground has a future in the twenty-first century, it will be tied to the structural conditions that gave rise to it long ago and that made it available for constant reinvention.

Acknowledgments

I'm grateful to have had dedicated mentors support this project from the beginning. Thomas Ferraro and Janice Radway were the earliest champions of my work. By their example, I learned how to become a better reader—of social life no less than textual objects. Mark Anthony Neal was generous in showing me where, and how, my work fits into black popular culture studies, and Matt Cohen was equally supportive in introducing me to the book history community. Tomiko Yoda helped me build the conceptual lattice to make this project conversant with gender and sexuality studies.

My scholarly life has been enriched at four institutions, all of which I'd like to recognize here. Duke University and the Graduate Program in Literature deserve the biggest thanks for launching my academic career. I also thank Northwestern University and the Department of African American Studies for awarding me a postdoctoral fellowship in 2010–12, the University of Notre Dame and the Department of English for employing me as an assistant professor in 2012–14, and Princeton University and the Department of English and the Department of African American Studies for hiring me in my current position in 2014. It's been an honor to work at these institutions, and to contribute to the academic life of such vibrant, field-leading departments. My chairs Darlene Clark Hine, Celeste Watkins-Hayes, Valerie Sayers, William Gleason, and Eddie Glaude made sure I had the time, space, and resources I needed to get the job done. At Princeton, my department managers Karen Mink and April Peters, as well as staff members Allison Bland, Tara Broderick, Pat Guglielmi, Jana Johnson, John Orluk Lacombe, Nancy Shillingford, and Dionne Worthy, have made the job far easier.

As long as it's taken me to complete this project's journey, I've been given the intellectual fuel and personal encouragement to keep at it by a number of friends and colleagues. Rather than link each person to a specific moment in my life, I wish to acknowledge everyone together, in the happy muddle that is my memory of time well spent: Anna Arabindan-Kesson, David Ball, Herman Beavers, Wendy Belcher, Alfred Bendixen, Ruha Benjamin, Wallace Best, Martha Biondi, Anne Cheng, Sarah Chihaya, Emalu-Hina Cleveland, Rawiri Cleveland, Adrian Colón, Jesús Constantino, Simone Drake, Rita Felski, Leonardo Francalanci, Alisha Gaines, Simon Gikandi, Loren Glass, Jacqueline Goldsby, Johannes Göransson, Yogita Goyal, Ezra Greenspan, Joshua Guild, Carissa Harris, Tera Hunter, Joseph Jeon, Neetu Khanna, Semyon Khokhlov, Joshua Kotin, Z'étoile Imma, Richard Iton, Cheryl Jue, Greg Jue, Russ Leo, Julia LoPresti, Matthew LoPresti, Emily Marker, Kate Marshall, Joyelle McSweeney, Walter Benn Michaels, Koritha Mitchell, Lee Mitchell, Naomi Murakawa, Vin Nardizzi, Ian Newman, Betty Chau Nguyen, Phuong Nguyen, Chika Okeke-Agulu, Liesl Olson, Chinyere Osuji, Imani Perry, Sandra Richards, Britt Rusert, Gayle Salamon, Nitasha Sharma, Stacey Sinclair, Keeanga-Yamahtta Taylor, Rebbeca Tesfai, Kyla Wazana Tompkins, Alfred Valrie, Azareen Van der Vliet Oloomi, Kenneth Warren, Mary Helen Washington, Sarah Wasserman, Robyn Wiegman, Ivy Wilson, Michelle Wright, and John Young.

Research for this project has been supported by every institution at which I've taught, and I want to thank the libraries and library staff of Duke, Northwestern, Notre Dame, and Princeton for meeting, and often exceeding, my everyday book, periodical, and online needs. The archival component of this project could not have been completed without the assistance of staff at the Charles E. Young Research Library at UCLA and at the Eberly Family Special Collections Library at Penn State University. This project's final form owes much to the papers I consulted at these two libraries.

I also want to thank the specific funding sources that supported research for this book: the Bayard Rustin Professional Development Fellowship at the University of Notre Dame, the Career Enhancement Fellowship from the Woodrow Wilson National Fellowship Foundation, and the Dorothy Foehr Huck Research Travel Award from the Eberly Family Special Collections Library at Penn State University. Last but not least, I'm grateful to Princeton's Department of African American Studies for supporting me with a generous publication grant.

The University of Chicago Press proved to be the perfect home for this book. Alan Thomas was kind to take a chance on my work, and I'm grateful to have had his backing since day one. Kyle Adam Wagner facilitated the review and production process with aplomb, giving me just the kind of encouragement I needed to stick to deadlines and be happy with the results. Mark Reschke's copyediting clarified my voice throughout. I'm indebted, finally, to my three reviewers, whose generous comments helped me turn my manuscript into what I hope is a coherent and readable book.

My family usually isn't sure what to make of my work, but their love and support is all the more meaningful because of that. Thanks to Eddie Buksas, Meaghan Buksas, and Jennifer Clark for providing a home away from home for this island-born son. Oliver, you're a baby and a dog, and you've given me so much love around breakfast and dinner time, and many times in between—thank you. And thanks, most of all, to Mom, Patricia Nishikawa, the last of our small circle, the person to whom I owe my name.

This book is dedicated to Katherine Elisabeth Clark, who has made all of it, everything, infinitely more worthwhile.

Notes

INTRODUCTION

1. Irvine Welsh, introduction to *Pimp: The Story of My Life*, by Iceberg Slim (Los Angeles: Holloway House, 1967; Edinburgh: Canongate, 2009), vi.
2. Welsh, xv.
3. Ice-T, introduction to *Pimp: The Story of My Life*, by Iceberg Slim (Los Angeles: Holloway House, 1967; Edinburgh: Payback Press, 1996), v.
4. Ice-T, v, vi.
5. Eric Lott, *Black Mirror: The Cultural Contradictions of American Racism* (Cambridge, MA: Harvard University Press, 2017), 9. See also Toni Morrison, *Playing in the Dark: Whiteness and the Literary Imagination* (Cambridge, MA: Harvard University Press, 1992).
6. Greg Tate, "Introduction: Nigs R Us, or How Blackfolk Became Fetish Objects," in *Everything but the Burden: What White People Are Taking from Black Culture*, ed. Tate (New York: Broadway, 2003), 4.
7. bell hooks, "Eating the Other: Desire and Resistance," in *Black Looks: Race and Representation* (Boston: South End Press, 1992), 22.
8. This point about Slim's mythos is in conversation with Anthony Reed's deconstruction of hip-hop's "roots" in "Authentic/Artificial," in *Time: A Vocabulary of the Present*, ed. Joel Burges and Amy J. Elias (New York: New York University Press, 2016), 294–308.
9. Quoted in Justin Gifford, "'Something Like a Harlem Renaissance West': Black Popular Fiction, Self-Publishing,

and the Origins of Street Literature; Interviews with Dr. Roland Jefferson and Odie Hawkins," *MELUS* 38, no. 4 (2013): 232.

10. A valuable model for my inquiry is Nelson George's essay on the influence of white small business owners on early hip-hop culture, "Black Owned?," in *Hip Hop America* (New York: Penguin, 1998), 56–75. George's take on white ownership of black cultural forms offers a more nuanced view of the issue than the deterministic account found in Ellis Cashmore, *The Black Culture Industry* (London: Routledge, 1997).

11. On Holloway House generally, see Peter Gilstrap, "The House That Blacks Built," *New Times Los Angeles*, October 15, 1998; and Justin Gifford, *Pimping Fictions: African American Crime Literature and the Untold Story of Black Pulp Publishing* (Philadelphia: Temple University Press, 2013). There are two book-length treatments of black pulp fiction's standout authors: Peter A. Muckley, *Iceberg Slim: The Life as Art* (Pittsburgh: Dorrance, 2003); and L. H. Stallings and Greg Thomas, eds., *Word Hustle: Critical Essays and Reflections on the Works of Donald Goines* (Baltimore: Black Classic Press, 2011).

12. Sleaze remains a woefully understudied pulp genre. The most substantive discussions of it can be found in books that blur the line between collecting, fandom, and scholarship: Michael R. Goss, *Young Lusty Sluts! A Pictorial History of Erotic Pulp Fiction* (London: Erotic Print Society, 2004); Brittany A. Daley et al., eds., *Sin-a-Rama: Sleaze Sex Paperbacks of the Sixties* (Los Angeles: Feral House, 2005); and John Harrison, *Hip Pocket Sleaze: The Lurid World of Vintage Adult Paperbacks* (London: Headpress, 2011).

13. Stuart Hall, "What Is This 'Black' in Black Popular Culture?," in *Black Popular Culture*, ed. Gina Dent (Seattle: Bay Press, 1992), 23, 26, 26–27, 28.

14. Hall, 28.

15. Pierre Bourdieu, *The Field of Cultural Production: Essays on Art and Literature*, ed. Randal Johnson (New York: Columbia University Press, 1993), 37.

16. Robert Darnton, "What Is the History of Books?," *Daedalus* 111, no. 3 (1982): 67.

17. Ed Guerrero, "The Rise and Fall of Blaxploitation," in *Framing Blackness: The African American Image in Film* (Philadelphia: Temple University Press, 1993), 69–111.

18. The studies that have made the deepest impression on this project are Herman Gray, *Producing Jazz: The Experience of an Independent Record Company* (Philadelphia: Temple University Press, 1988); Tricia Rose, *Black Noise: Rap Music and Black Culture in Contemporary America* (Hanover, NH: Wesleyan University Press, 1994); S. Craig Watkins, *Representing: Hip Hop Culture and the Production of Black Cinema* (Chicago: University of Chicago Press, 1998); Jeffrey A. Brown, *Black Superheroes, Milestone Comics, and Their Fans* (Jackson: University Press of Mississippi, 2001); and David Grazian, *Blue Chicago: The Search for Authenticity in Urban Blues Clubs* (Chicago: University of Chicago Press, 2003).

19. See, e.g., Jewelle Gomez, "Speculative Fiction and Black Lesbians," *Signs* 18, no. 4 (1993): 948–55; John Howard, "Representations," in *Men Like That: A Southern Queer History* (Chicago: University of Chicago Press, 1999), 174–229; Mireille Miller-Young, *A Taste for Brown Sugar: Black Women in Pornography* (Durham, NC: Duke University Press, 2014); Paula Rabinowitz, *American Pulp: How Paperbacks Brought Modernism to Main Street* (Princeton, NJ: Princeton University Press, 2014); and Darieck Scott, "Big Black Beauty: Drawing and Naming the Black Male Figure in Superhero and Gay Porn Comics," in *Porn Archives*, ed. Tim Dean, Steven Ruszczycky, and David Squires (Durham, NC: Duke University Press, 2014), 183–212.

20. Hall, "What Is This 'Black' in Black Popular Culture?," 27.

CHAPTER ONE

1. Bob Norman, "Miss Gold-Digger of 1953," *Playboy*, December 1953, 6, 7, 8.

2. "An Open Letter from California," *Playboy*, December 1953, 27, 29.

3. "A Word from Adam," *Adam* 1, no. 1 (1956): 2. Early issues of Morriss and Weinstock's magazines did not specify month of publication. I cite them here by volume and issue numbers, as one would for journals.

4. "Greetings from Sir Knight," *Sir Knight* 1, no. 1 (1958): 2.

5. Though film and media scholars have studied sleaze in relation to the contemporary sexploitation craze, no analogous body of scholarship has been devoted to sleaze's circulation in print. On sleaze in film, see Jeffrey Sconce, ed., *Sleaze Artists: Cinema at the Margins of Taste, Style, and Politics* (Durham, NC: Duke University Press, 2007); Eric Schaefer, ed., *Sex Scene: Media and the Sexual Revolution* (Durham, NC: Duke University Press, 2014); and David Church, *Disposable Passions: Vintage Pornography and the Material Legacies of Adult Cinema* (New York: Bloomsbury, 2016).

6. The literature on US separate spheres is broad and deep, but the touchstone study is still Ann Douglas, *The Feminization of American Culture* (New York: Knopf, 1977).

7. "Stars Will Aid Jewish Bazaar," *Los Angeles Times*, October 12, 1947; "Fords to Get Award," *Los Angeles Times*, February 23, 1958.

8. Reference to Morriss's mother, Mrs. Tillie Schwartz, can be found in the announcement of his marriage to Sonia Zeiger: "Weddings," *Los Angeles Times*, June 19, 1949.

9. Quoted in John Harrison, *Hip Pocket Sleaze: The Lurid World of Vintage Adult Paperbacks* (London: Headpress, 2011), 293. The quotation and confirmation of the name's sources are from Kevan Jensen, the son of one of Morriss's former writers.

10. Robert O. Self, "Sex in the City: The Politics of Sexual Liberalism in Los Angeles, 1963–79," *Gender and History* 20, no. 2 (2008): 291.

11. *Adam* had started out with a companion men's magazine, aptly titled *Eve*, in 1956, but the latter folded almost immediately. This according to

"Adam," in *Cult Magazines, A to Z: A Compendium of Culturally Obsessive and Curiously Expressive Publications*, ed. Earl Kemp and Luis Ortiz (New York: Nonstop Press, 2009), 8.

12. Laura Mulvey, "Visual Pleasure and Narrative Cinema," in *Visual and Other Pleasures* (Bloomington: Indiana University Press, 1989), 19, 18.

13. André Bazin, "Entomology of the Pin-Up Girl," in *What Is Cinema?*, vol. 2, trans. Hugh Gray (Berkeley: University of California Press, 1971), 158. Tellingly, Venus is cited in a little ditty that accompanies the pictorial from which figure 1.3 is taken: "Slick thirty-six had Venus, true, / Our Jean's a perfect forty-two! / And yet, sweet Jean's alone, we find. / Can love be so Venetian blind?" "Trick for the Taking," *Adam* 1, no. 8 (1957): 28.

14. "A Word from Adam," *Adam* 1, no. 12 (1957): 2.

15. "Adam's Tales," *Adam* 2, no. 9 (1958): 54.

16. Dennis, "Made in Texas . . ." [gold-digger cartoon], *Adam* 4, no. 3 (1960): 13.

17. John Calhoun, "Poison Is a Woman's Weapon," *Adam* 2, no. 9 (1958): 32.

18. "Adam's Tales," *Adam* 4, no. 5 (1960): 56.

19. Philip Wylie, *Generation of Vipers* (New York: Farrar & Rinehart, 1942), 188.

20. Dian Hanson, ed., *The History of Men's Magazines: From Post-War to 1959*, vol. 2 (Cologne: Taschen, 2004), 295.

21. "Knight's Gambit," *Sir Knight*, April 1962, 49.

22. Charles Dennis, "Break the Sex Habit," *Adam* 5, no. 7 (1961): 24.

23. "Magazine in Trouble," *San Rafael Independent-Journal*, October 26, 1957.

24. "Indicted Firms Fail in Effort to Get Magazines," *Los Angeles Times*, April 28, 1959.

25. "Adam," 8.

26. *Roth v. United States*, 354 U.S. 476 (1957).

27. Self, "Sex in the City," 292–93, 293.

28. Self, 293.

29. Quoted in "Holloway House New Paperback Firm," *Publishers' Weekly*, September 18, 1961. See also Linda Quinlan, "Holloway House Publishing Company," in *American Literary Publishing Houses, 1900–1980: Trade and Paperback*, ed. Peter Dzwonkoski (Detroit: Gale, 1986), 189.

30. Morriss and Weinstock are usually cited as the driving forces behind Holloway House, but it was Morriss who owned the means of production and distribution.

31. Robert S. Bravard, "A Librarian's Guide to Black Literature," *Choice* 5, no. 8 (1968): 916, 917.

32. Foreword to *The Many Loves of Casanova*, vol. 1 (Los Angeles: Holloway House, 1961), vi.

33. Consolidated Advertising Directors, Inc., purchase order for "The Advance of Medicine," February 20, 1963, and purchase order for "Innkeeper's Daughter," August 19, 1963, Paul Gillette Papers, 1956–90, Eberly Family Special Collections Library, Penn State University, Box 10. As of this

writing, the archive has yet to be fully processed. Thus, I note only box numbers, leaving out folder numbers, when citing materials from this collection.

34. Stephen J. Gertz, "Sexed-Up Literary Classics," *Booktryst*, April 21, 2011, http://www.booktryst.com/2011/04/sexed-up-literary-classics.html.

35. Loren Glass, *Counterculture Colophon: Grove Press, the "Evergreen Review," and the Incorporation of the Avant-Garde* (Stanford, CA: Stanford University Press, 2013), 132–38.

36. Paul J. Gillette, letter to Ralph Weinstock, n.d., Paul Gillette Papers, Box 15. Being able to track Gillette's work flow and composition process should make the kind of inquiry Kathleen Lubey models in "Making Pornography, 1749–1968: The History of *The History of the Human Heart*," *ELH* 82, no. 3 (2015): 897–935, replicable by other scholars.

37. Gertz, "Sexed-Up Literary Classics."

38. Paul J. Gillette, *Satyricon: Memoirs of a Lusty Roman* (Los Angeles: Holloway House, 1965), 81. As the preceding discussion implies, I consider Gillette to be not so much a translator as an author inspired by previously published translations. Thus, instead of citing him as the translator of Holloway House's *Satyricon*, I cite him as its author.

39. Consolidated Advertising Directors, Inc., purchase order for "Interview with a Call Girl," December 20, 1963, Paul Gillette Papers, Box 10.

40. Paul J. Gillette, *Psychodynamics of Unconventional Sex Behavior and Unusual Practices* (Los Angeles: Holloway House, 1966), 126, 127.

41. Mike Bruno and David B. Weiss, *Prostitution, U.S.A.* (Los Angeles: Holloway House, 1965), 30, 31.

42. The self-referentiality of this discourse applied to authors other than Gillette. In the March 1963 issue of *Knight*, e.g., George Starbuck Galbraith of Bakersfield, California, wrote in to compliment the editors on a recent issue of the magazine. He particularly liked its "color work" and *Knight*'s choice of "girls." But then Galbraith also said, "And do keep publishing that brilliant and witty humorist, me. I've hatched a new article that I can hardly wait to send you." The editor indulged Galbraith, replying, "We can't wait, Georgie, because we adore brilliant, witty humorists." The self-congratulatory back and forth was buttressed by the fact that another Galbraith piece, "Male, Female and Their Mail," appeared in the very issue in which his letter appeared. Galbraith, letter to the editor, *Knight*, March 1963, 75.

43. There is more scholarship on this format than there is on sleaze; see George Gerbner, "The Social Role of the Confession Magazine," *Social Problems* 6, no. 1 (1958): 29–40; Maureen Honey, "The Confession Formula and Fantasies of Empowerment," *Women's Studies* 10, no. 3 (1984): 303–20; and Regina Kunzel, "Pulp Fictions and Problem Girls: Reading and Rewriting Single Pregnancy in the Postwar United States," *American Historical Review* 100, no. 5 (1995): 1465–87.

44. Leo Guild, "Confessions of a Celebrity Ghost Writer," *Los Angeles Times*, November 5, 1967.

45. Guild.

46. Barbara Payton, *I Am Not Ashamed* (Los Angeles: Holloway House, 1963), 13.

47. Payton, 100.

48. Payton, 139, 140, 155.

49. John O'Dowd, *Kiss Tomorrow Goodbye: The Barbara Payton Story* (Albany, GA: BearManor Media, 2006), 382.

50. Payton, *I Am Not Ashamed*, 19.

51. Payton, 84, 189.

52. Kipp Washington with Leo Guild, *Some Like It Dark: The Intimate Autobiography of a Negro Call Girl* (Los Angeles: Holloway House, 1966), 7.

53. Guild, "Confessions."

54. Alex Jackinson, *The Romance of Publishing: An Agent Recalls Thirty-Three Years with Authors and Editors* (Cranbury, NJ: Cornwall, 1987), 35.

55. Mills's book inspired the teleplay for the critically acclaimed, Emmy Award–winning biopic *Introducing Dorothy Dandridge* (1999), starring Halle Berry in the title role.

56. Quoted in Guild, "Confessions."

57. Washington, *Some Like It Dark*, 117, 131, 184, 188.

58. Washington, 45, 115, 118, 121, 131, 132, 187, 192.

59. Washington, 153.

60. Rodella's racial background is an open question. There is no mention of it in *Adam*, though it would be a mistake to assume that this means Rodella is white. Her surname indicates ethnic Italian heritage, but given that this is probably a stage name, it could also be a cover for Rodella's blackness or racial ambiguity. "Weekend in Paradise," *Adam* 2, no. 2 (1958): 62–65.

61. Washington, *Some Like It Dark*, 182, 175.

62. "Hollywood Office Building Planned," *Los Angeles Times*, March 10, 1963.

CHAPTER TWO

1. Quoted in Peter Gilstrap, "The House That Blacks Built," *New Times Los Angeles*, October 15, 1998.

2. Mark McCord, "The Next Hustle," *Wax Poetics* 38 (2009): 65

3. Justin Gifford, *Street Poison: The Biography of Iceberg Slim* (New York: Doubleday, 2015), 159.

4. Advertisement for Johnnie Walker's Red Label, *Los Angeles Sentinel*, July 15, 1965.

5. An example of how the legend feeds off itself, without independent confirmation of Morriss's claims and by mere repetition, is Will Turner, "'Ill Parallels': Ice-T, Iceberg Slim, and *Portrait of a Pimp*," in *African American Culture and Society after Rodney King: Provocations and Protests, Progression*

and "Post-Racialism," ed. Josephine Metcalf and Carina Spaulding (Farnham: Ashgate, 2015), 19–47.

6. Morriss has adapted the legend to suit the question at hand. For example, in a 1998 interview with the *Los Angeles Times*, he was asked how Holloway House had gone from "Jayne Mansfield to Iceberg Slim," or, as I frame it in this book, from sleaze to street. His response was "We'd already had some success with a couple black-authored books, like 'The Dorothy Dandridge Autobiography,' which the major houses wouldn't have touched. Word got out that we were actively promoting new writers and that's how Bob [Beck] found us." In fact, Holloway House had published no black writers prior to Slim, and Earl Mills's biography of Dandridge appeared in 1970. Tamar Brott, "Iceberg Slam Dunk," *Los Angeles Times*, November 8, 1998.

7. Gifford, *Street Poison*, 7, 25, 143, 140.

8. Iceberg Slim, *Pimp: The Story of My Life* (Los Angeles: Holloway House, 1967), back cover.

9. I refer to the author as Slim and the biographical subject as Beck hereafter. In so doing, I take up a hybrid approach that acknowledges the slippages between these names and how the person designated by both struggled to reconcile his literary celebrity with his "real" identity.

10. Slim, *Pimp*, 20, 21, 23, 25.

11. Slim, 195.

12. Slim, 220–21.

13. Robin D. G. Kelley, "The Fires That Forged Iceberg Slim," *New Yorker*, August 19, 2015, http://www.newyorker.com/books/page-turner/the-fires -that-forged-iceberg-slim. For similar readings, see Victoria A. Elmwood, "'They Can't Take That Away from Me': Gendered Nationalism and Textual Sovereignty in the Autobiographies of Iceberg Slim and Malcolm X," *Soundings* 90, nos. 3–4 (2007): 245–71; and Justin Gifford, *Pimping Fictions: African American Crime Literature and the Untold Story of Black Pulp Publishing* (Philadelphia: Temple University Press, 2013), 40–67.

14. Slim, *Pimp*, 86–87.

15. Kelley, "The Fires That Forged Iceberg Slim." For similar readings, see D. B. Graham, "'Negative Glamour': The Pimp Hero in the Fiction of Iceberg Slim," *Obsidian* 1, no. 2 (1975): 5–17; and Peter A. Muckley, *Iceberg Slim: The Life as Art* (Pittsburgh: Dorrance, 2003), 15–32.

16. Arthur Kempton, *Boogaloo: The Quintessence of American Popular Music* (New York: Pantheon, 2003), 162.

17. John W. Roberts, *From Trickster to Badman: The Black Folk Hero in Slavery and Freedom* (Philadelphia: University of Pennsylvania Press, 1989), 186.

18. Slim, *Pimp*, 17.

19. Gifford, *Pimping Fictions*, 67.

20. Slim, *Pimp*, 81.

21. McCord, "The Next Hustle," 62; Gifford, *Street Poison*, 88, 159; Richard Milner, quoted in *Iceberg Slim: The Lost Interviews*, ed. Ian Whitaker (Lon-

don: Infinite Dreams, 2009), 20. But note that McCord registers Slim's first nickname as Bobby Lancaster, not Slim Lancaster.

22. Candice Love Jackson, "The Literate Pimp: Robert Beck, Iceberg Slim, and Pimping the African American Novel," in *New Essays on the African American Novel: From Hurston and Ellison to Morrison and Whitehead*, ed. Lovalerie King and Linda F. Selzer (New York: Palgrave Macmillan, 2008), 169, 168.

23. Barbara Payton, *I Am Not Ashamed* (Los Angeles: Holloway House, 1963), 129.

24. Advertisement for Holloway House's *Pimp: The Story of My Life*, *Adam*, May 1967, 29.

25. Bob Blackburn, review of *Pimp: The Story of My Life*, by Iceberg Slim, *Adam*, July 1967, 4.

26. Norman Mailer, "The White Negro: Superficial Reflections on the Hipster," *Dissent* 4, no. 3 (1957): 279, 285.

27. Slim, *Pimp*, 315, 314.

28. Quoted in Christina Milner and Richard Milner, *Black Players: The Secret World of Black Pimps* (Boston: Little, Brown, 1972), 317.

29. Blackburn, review of *Pimp*.

30. Advertisement for Holloway House's *Pimp: The Story of My Life*, *Los Angeles Sentinel*, September 28, 1967.

31. Quoted in "Louis Lomax: The Television Prophet," in *Voices from the Sixties: Twenty-Two Views of a Revolutionary Decade*, by Pierre Berton (Garden City, NY: Doubleday, 1967), 18–19, 12, 13.

32. "Robert H(arold) deCoy, Jr.," Contemporary Authors Online, August 1, 2001, go.galegroup.com/ps/i.do?p=CA&sw=w&u=txshracd2531&v=2.1&id =GALE%7CH1000024188&it=r&asid=3c31e6f35fecf7ba47809e9098edec1c.

33. Dick Gregory, preface to *The Nigger Bible*, by Robert H. deCoy (Los Angeles: Holloway House, 1967), 13, 14, 15.

34. Robert H. deCoy, *The Nigger Bible* (Los Angeles: Holloway House, 1967), 93, 94, 25–26.

35. DeCoy, 56, 59, 64.

36. DeCoy, 150, 160, 162, 163.

37. Quoted in "Author Claims Ad Ban," *Los Angeles Sentinel*, January 26, 1967.

38. "Getting Death Threats, Says 'Nigger Bible' Author," *Jet*, April 13, 1967, 27. See also "Singer Mittie Lawrence Seeks to Shed Hubby-Writer," *Jet*, April 6, 1967, 24.

39. Quoted in Joe Bingham, "White Exec Fired for Negro Efforts," *Los Angeles Sentinel*, April 13, 1967.

40. Quoted in Bingham.

41. Robert H. deCoy, *The Nigger Bible* (Los Angeles: Blawhit, 1967), 3.

42. DeCoy, back cover.

43. "DeCoy's Book Entered in Pulitzer Competition," *Los Angeles Sentinel*, November 16, 1967.

44. Ron Welburn, review of *The Nigger Bible*, by Robert H. deCoy, *Liberator* 9, no. 10 (1969): 19.

45. Iceberg Slim, *Trick Baby: The Biography of a Con Man* (Los Angeles: Holloway House, 1967), front cover, 5.

46. Slim, 9, 10.

47. Slim, 72.

48. Slim, 93, 37.

49. Slim, 146, 150.

50. Muckley, *Iceberg Slim*, 42.

51. Slim, *Trick Baby*, 311, 312.

52. Advertisement for Holloway House's *Trick Baby: The Biography of a Con Man*, *Adam*, March 1968, 29.

53. Slim, *Trick Baby*, 193, 194.

54. Slim, 198, 199, 211.

55. Gifford, *Street Poison*, 166.

56. Slim, *Trick Baby*, 260.

57. Slim, 310.

58. Robert J. Erler, "A Guide to Television Talk," in *Television Talk: A History of the TV Talk Show*, by Bernard M. Timberg (Austin: University of Texas Press, 2002), 272.

59. Quoted in Justin D. Gifford, "'Harvard in Hell': Holloway House Publishing Company, *Players Magazine*, and the Invention of Black Mass-Market Erotica," *MELUS* 35, no. 4 (2010): 136.

CHAPTER THREE

1. Mel Watkins, "In the Ghettos," *New York Times Book Review*, February 25, 1968.

2. Watkins.

3. Watkins. Watkins named Lewis H. Michaux's National Memorial Bookstore in Harlem as one of the few outlets that featured a more diverse range of titles.

4. John Harrison, "The 1970s: When Softcore Hardened and the Sleaze Became Sick," in *Hip Pocket Sleaze: The Lurid World of Vintage Adult Paperbacks* (London: Headpress, 2011), 126–209.

5. Mel Watkins, "Black Is Marketable," *New York Times Book Review*, February 16, 1969. The first three chapters of Paul Talbot's *Mondo Mandingo* offer the best account to date of the Falconhurst series' origin with a small Virginia publisher, development between three white male authors, and popular reception across three decades. Paul Talbot, *Mondo Mandingo: The "Falconhurst" Books and Films* (Bloomington, IN: iUniverse, 2009), 3–76.

6. Louis E. Lomax, *To Kill a Black Man* (Los Angeles: Holloway House, 1968), 10.

7. Lomax, 10, 255, 254.

8. Louis E. Lomax, "Portrait of Malcolm X," *Knight*, March 1969, 97.
9. Sara Harris and Lucy Freeman, *The Lords of Hell* (New York: Dell, 1967), 9.
10. Offutt is the subject of Kentucky-born writer Chris Offutt's memoir *My Father, the Pornographer* (2016).
11. Earl F. Bargainnier, "The Falconhurst Series: A New Popular Image of the Old South," *Journal of Popular Culture* 10, no. 2 (1976): 308.
12. Talbot, *Mondo Mandingo*, 43.
13. Norman Gant, *Black Vengeance* (New York: Lancer, 1968), 111, 112.
14. This point is exemplified by the sympathy-inducing blurb on the front cover of *Black Vengeance*: "Tortured men strike out for freedom against master and mistress alike . . . the most shocking portrayal of slavery ever written."
15. Norman Spinrad, "Darktown Strutters' Ball," *Knight*, September 1969, 19.
16. Spinrad, 21.
17. Susan Courtney, *Hollywood Fantasies of Miscegenation: Spectacular Narratives of Gender and Race, 1903–1967* (Princeton, NJ: Princeton University Press, 2005), 312n24. DeCoy's probable source is Johnson's 1927 ghostwritten autobiography *In the Ring and Out*.
18. Robert H. deCoy, *The Big Black Fire* (Los Angeles: Holloway House, 1969), 57, 129.
19. DeCoy, 162.
20. DeCoy, 305.
21. *Report of the Commission on Obscenity and Pornography* (Washington, DC: US Government Printing Office, 1970), 1.
22. *Report of the Commission on Obscenity and Pornography*, 74.
23. *Report of the Commission on Obscenity and Pornography*, 90, 92–93, 94.
24. *Report of the Commission on Obscenity and Pornography*, 95.
25. Advertisement for Holloway House's *The Girl Who Loved Black*, *Knight*, September 1969, 64.
26. Leo Guild, *The Girl Who Loved Black* (Los Angeles: Holloway House, 1969), 8.
27. Guild, 9, 12, 13, 14.
28. Guild, 27, 36.
29. Guild, 122, 147, 188.
30. This reading is closely aligned with Alisha Gaines's introductory discussion of the socio-structural limits of "empathetic racial impersonation" in *Black for a Day: White Fantasies of Race and Empathy* (Chapel Hill: University of North Carolina Press, 2017), 7–12. For similar studies of racial impersonation (not just blackface or minstrelsy) in twentieth-century American popular culture, see Susan Gubar, *Racechanges: White Skin, Black Face in American Culture* (New York: Oxford University Press, 1997); Gayle Wald, *Crossing the Line: Racial Passing in Twentieth-Century U.S. Literature and Popular Culture* (Durham, NC: Duke University Press, 2000); and Eric Lott, *Black Mirror: The Cultural Contradictions of American Racism* (Cambridge, MA: Harvard University Press, 2017).

31. Guild, *The Girl Who Loved Black*, 81, 67, 87, 124.
32. Editorial assignment, [no month] 1964, Paul Gillette Papers, 1956–90, Eberly Family Special Collections Library, Penn State University, Box 10; "Open Letter to Black Muslim Cassius Clay!," *Cloak 'n' Dagger*, August 1964, 17.
33. Guild, *The Girl Who Loved Black*, 223, 224, 225.
34. Guild, 245.
35. Richard B. Milner, "America's No. 1 Pimp Tells It Like It Is!," *Rogue*, June 1969, 7.
36. Quoted in Milner, 8.
37. Quoted in Milner, 7.
38. J. C. Thomas, "The American Woman Is a Waste of Good Flesh," *Rogue*, June 1969, 79, 82.
39. Here I again signal my departure from readings of *Pimp* that suggest it is a cautionary tale about the perils of exploiting women for money. Slim's reactionary masculinism, which reflected the reactionary masculinism of the sleaze trade writ large, cautioned against one thing: the diminution of manhood at the hands of female or feminine authority.
40. Iceberg Slim, *Mama Black Widow* (Los Angeles: Holloway House, 1969), 6.
41. Slim.
42. Advertising copy for the book explicitly advanced this reading. It identified "Mother's prejudices" as "the instrument of the family's destruction," and it advised readers that Slim "directs his disdain not at those who are sick, but to the sickness itself . . . those blights of the American personality which permit such a thing as a ghetto to exist." The retreat from a structural understanding of racial inequality is clearly indicated in the copy's emphasis on regressive "personality" traits. Advertisement for Holloway House's *Mama Black Widow*, *Knight*, October 1969, 55.
43. My reading diverges from Candice Love Jackson's assertion that in *Mama Black Widow* "neither the South nor the North can sufficiently support the African American community." Though the South is not without its hardships, for Slim, the region sustains the black patriarchal household in ways that are clearly longed for in the novel. Candice Love Jackson, "The Literate Pimp: Robert Beck, Iceberg Slim, and Pimping the African American Novel," in *New Essays on the African American Novel: From Hurston and Ellison to Morrison and Whitehead*, ed. Lovalerie King and Linda F. Selzer (New York: Palgrave Macmillan, 2008), 181.
44. Slim, *Mama Black Widow*, 68, 72, 107.
45. Slim, 105, 113, 127.
46. Slim, 142–43.
47. The report was named after sociologist Daniel Patrick Moynihan, who authored the study while he was assistant secretary of labor at the department.
48. US Department of Labor, *The Negro Family: The Case for National Action*, in *The Moynihan Report and the Politics of Controversy*, ed. Lee Rainwater

and William L. Yancey (Cambridge: MIT Press, 1967), 51, 62, 75. Moynihan's perspective was, like Slim's, influenced by armchair psychology. At the beginning of *The Negro Family*, he wrote, "A fundamental insight of psychoanalytic theory . . . is that the child learns a way of looking at life in his early years through which all later experience is viewed and which profoundly shapes his adult conduct" (51).

49. Slim, *Mama Black Widow*, 291, 236.

50. Slim, 23, 29, 32, 39, 42.

51. Justin Gifford, *Street Poison: The Biography of Iceberg Slim* (New York: Doubleday, 2015), 169; Marlon B. Ross, "'What's Love but a Second Hand Emotion?' Man-on-Man Passion in the Contemporary Black Gay Romance Novel," *Callaloo* 36, no. 3 (2013): 684n10.

52. Editorial assignment, August 1964, Paul Gillette Papers, Box 9.

53. Slim, *Mama Black Widow*, 7, 9, 10.

54. Slim, 244, 245, 246.

55. Slim, 310–11, 312.

56. Slim, 313.

57. Delle Brehan, *Kicks Is Kicks* (Los Angeles: Holloway House, 1970), back cover.

58. Leroy Brown, as told to Roger Blake, *Black Sexual Power* (Cleveland, OH: Century, 1970), back cover.

59. Brehan, *Kicks Is Kicks*, 7, 8.

60. This reading contests Regina Blackburn's analysis of the ostensible agency Brehan exercises in the book: "She went beyond the natural environment, where blackness was subordinated, to determine her goals by her own power; and she saw herself as an independent person." Regina Blackburn, "In Search of the Black Female Self: African-American Women's Autobiographies and Ethnicity," in *Women's Autobiography: Essays in Criticism*, ed. Estelle C. Jelinek (Bloomington: Indiana University Press, 1980), 138.

CHAPTER FOUR

1. Larry Neal, "Brother Pimp," in *Black Boogaloo (Notes on Black Liberation)* (San Francisco: Journal of Black Poetry Press, 1969), 45.

2. Neal.

3. Neal, 46, 45. For other readings of the poem, see Stephen E. Henderson, "Take Two—Larry Neal and the Blues God: Aspects of the Poetry," *Callaloo* 23 (1985): 221–22; Charise L. Cheney, *Brothers Gonna Work It Out: Sexual Politics in the Golden Age of Rap Nationalism* (New York: New York University Press, 2005), 104; and Lee Bernstein, "Prison Writers and the Black Arts Movement," in *New Thoughts on the Black Arts Movement*, ed. Lisa Gail Collins and Margo Natalie Crawford (New Brunswick, NJ: Rutgers University Press, 2006), 306.

4. Iceberg Slim, *The Naked Soul of Iceberg Slim* (Los Angeles: Holloway House, 1971), 5.

5. Milton Van Sickle, introduction to *The Naked Soul of Iceberg Slim*, by Iceberg Slim (Los Angeles: Holloway House, 1971), 9, 9–10.

6. Slim, *Naked Soul*, 60, 61.

7. Slim, 70.

8. Slim, 43, 42, 45–46, 46.

9. Slim, 152, 152–53, 153, 154. Compare this reading to the flawed assertion that "Beck was decidedly disheartened by the Black Panthers' rebuff since he regarded pandering as a revolutionary act against an oppressive American society, not as part of an oppressive cultural structure," in Candice Love Jackson, "From Writer to Reader: Black Popular Fiction," in *The Cambridge History of African American Literature*, ed. Maryemma Graham and Jerry W. Ward Jr. (New York: Cambridge University Press, 2011), 659.

10. John A. Williams, review of *The Naked Soul of Iceberg Slim*, by Iceberg Slim, *Sun Reporter* [San Francisco], August 21, 1971.

11. Slim, *Naked Soul*, back cover.

12. *Black Journal* debuted in June 1968 and was hosted by Lou House. Al Perlmutter, who was white, started out as executive producer, but after the production team walked out on him, black filmmaker William Greaves took over the role. On the series' early years, see Tommy Lee Lott, "Documenting Social Issues: *Black Journal*, 1968–1970," in *Struggles for Representation: African American Documentary Film and Video*, ed. Phyllis Klotman and Janet K. Cutler (Bloomington: Indiana University Press, 1999), 71–98; Christine Acham, "Was the Revolution Televised? Network News and *Black Journal*," in *Revolution Televised: Prime Time and the Struggle for Black Power* (Minneapolis: University of Minnesota Press, 2004), 24–53; and Devorah Heitner, "No Thanks for Tokenism: Telling Stories from a Black Nation, *Black Journal*, 1968–1970," in *Black Power TV* (Durham, NC: Duke University Press, 2013), 83–122.

13. Francis Ward and Val Gray Ward, "Chicago—Kuumba Workshop," *Black World*, April 1972, 38, 37.

14. "Chicago Locale for 'Iceberg Slim' Movie," *Chicago Defender*, September 8, 1971.

15. "Chicago Locale" features a photograph taken on set in which Johnston (going by Alade Alabukon) and "Robert Beck, the real Iceberg Slim," stand next to each other during a lull in the shoot. The picture is captioned "The two Iceberg Slims."

16. The episode does not make clear that Slim is lecturing at Malcolm X College, but contemporaneous coverage of the event confirmed the location. See "Chicago Locale" and "Black Journal to Present Show on Pimps," *Bay State Banner* [Boston], October 28, 1971.

17. Quoted in "The Pimping Game," *Time*, January 11, 1971, 54, 55.

18. Slim, *Naked Soul*, 199, 201.

19. Slim, 204, 205, 206, 209.
20. Richard Milner, "Meeting Iceberg Slim: How's Tricks?," in *Iceberg Slim: The Lost Interviews*, ed. Ian Whitaker (London: Infinite Dreams, 2009), 154.
21. Quoted in Helen Koblin, "Portrait of a Pimp," *Los Angeles Free Press*, February 25, 1972.
22. Quoted in Iceberg Slim, foreword to *Pimp: The Story of My Life*, in *Rappin' and Stylin' Out: Communication in Urban Black America*, ed. Thomas Kochman (Urbana: University of Illinois Press, 1972), 386.
23. Robert Beck, letter to editor, *Playboy*, October 1972, 14. He signed the letter as Robert Beck, but in clarifying the symbolic capital wielded in response to McPherson, the editor noted that the writer was, in fact, the notorious Iceberg Slim.
24. Houston A. Baker Jr., "From the Improbable Fields Down South: One View of Ghetto Language and Culture," in *Long Black Song: Essays in Black American Literature and Culture* (Charlottesville: University Press of Virginia, 1972), 115.
25. Preston Wilcox, review of *The Naked Soul of Iceberg Slim*, by Iceberg Slim, *Black World*, May 1972, 79, 80.
26. Milner, "Meeting Iceberg Slim," 149.
27. Christina Milner and Richard Milner, *Black Players: The Secret World of Black Pimps* (Boston: Little, Brown, 1972), 39.
28. Marvin Gelfand, "Black Pimps: 'Players' Talk about the 'Game,'" review of *Black Players: The Secret World of Black Pimps*, by Christina Milner and Richard Milner, *Los Angeles Times*, April 15, 1973.
29. Bob Moore, "The Inside Story of Black Pimps," *Sepia*, February 1972, 53.
30. The upstart company may have had deeper business dealings with Holloway House given that its physical address was also located on Melrose Avenue in Los Angeles. "Cinema Entertainment Films 'Trick Baby,'" *Sun Reporter* [San Francisco], September 16, 1972.
31. Quoted in "'Trick Baby' Opens at Loop Theatre," *Chicago Defender*, December 16, 1972.
32. Advertisement for Universal Pictures' *Trick Baby*, *Chicago Defender*, December 23, 1972.
33. Quoted in "'Trick Baby' Opens."
34. In the novel, the con is mentioned in passing when the black detective Dot Murray confronts Folks and Blue. Murray threatens to go to Frascati's nephew, the Mafia boss Nino Parelli, fingering them for the scam, unless they give him a cut of their earnings.
35. Kevin Thomas, "Movie Reviews," *Los Angeles Times*, January 24, 1973.
36. Rhonda J. Foston, "'Trick Baby,'" *Sun Reporter* [San Francisco], March 31, 1973.
37. Quoted in Tony Griggs, "Clerics Call Film Racist," *Chicago Defender*, February 5, 1973.
38. "Iceberg Slim's Novel 'Trick Baby' Brought to the Screen," *Los Angeles Sentinel*, January 25, 1973; Kay Bourne, "A Pimp's Eye View of Life," *Bay State*

Banner [Boston], February 1, 1973; Les Matthews, "Pimps Are Charming Con Men Who Hate Women: Iceberg Slim," *New York Amsterdam News*, February 3, 1973.

39. Quoted in "Iceberg Slim's Novel."

40. Quoted in Bourne, "A Pimp's Eye View of Life."

41. Quoted in Joe Ellis, "Iceberg Slim Is Warming Up to Life," *Chicago Defender*, December 16, 1972.

42. Quoted in Matthews, "Pimps Are Charming Con Men Who Hate Women."

43. Hollie I. West, "Sweet Talk, Hustle and Muscle," *Washington Post*, March 20, 1973.

44. Milner and Milner, *Black Players*, 225.

CHAPTER FIVE

1. Hollie I. West, "A Tinseled Pimp-Hero," review of *The Mack*, directed by Michael Campus, *Washington Post*, April 21, 1973.

2. West.

3. Richard Hoggart, *The Uses of Literacy: Aspects of Working-Class Life with Special Reference to Publications and Entertainments* (New York: Oxford University Press, 1970), 221.

4. Eddie B. Allen Jr., *Low Road: The Life and Legacy of Donald Goines* (New York: St. Martin's, 2004), 12–13, 24, 33–34.

5. Allen, 36–38, 51, 82.

6. Allen, 99.

7. Donald Goines, *Dopefiend: The Story of a Black Junkie* (Los Angeles: Holloway House, 1971), 7, 8, 9, 10, 12.

8. Goines, 62, 32, 174.

9. Goines, 81.

10. Goines, 237, 251.

11. Hoggart, *The Uses of Literacy*, 221.

12. Goines, *Dopefiend*, 7.

13. Goines, 253, 254.

14. Michael Covino, "Motor City Breakdown," *Village Voice*, August 4, 1987; Greg Goode, "From *Dopefiend* to *Kenyatta's Last Hit*: The Angry Black Crime Novels of Donald Goines," *MELUS* 11, no. 3 (1984): 42–43; quoted in Kermit E. Campbell, *"Gettin' Our Groove On": Rhetoric, Language, and Literacy for the Hip Hop Generation* (Detroit: Wayne State University Press, 2005), 93.

15. Campbell, *"Gettin' Our Groove On,"* 93.

16. Donald Goines, *Whoreson: The Story of a Ghetto Pimp* (Los Angeles: Holloway House, 1972), 9, 10, 11.

17. L. H. Stallings posits a different reading of this episode, following from her assertion that "Goines's work thematically deals with the process of decolonization following enslavement." In the act of naming her son,

"Jessie, a poor single Black mother whom society oppresses, comments on her neo-slave status." For her, the "name is the visual sign of an unadulterated oppression of blackness, his state of colonization signified in the horror of his name." I do not think the episode is imbued with such political meaning. If anything, Whoreson's name signifies Jessie's effort to fix, that is, entrench, his identity in the underworld. L. H. Stallings, "'I'm Goin Pimp Whores!' The Goines Factor and the Theory of a Hip-Hop Neo-Slave Narrative," *CR: The New Centennial Review* 3, no. 3 (2003): 200, 194, 195.

18. Goines, *Whoreson*, 40, 13, 23, 38.
19. Goines, 199, 24, 25.
20. TreaAndrea M. Russworm writes of the psychoanalytic valences of this scene: "The intertwined hangers visually render mother and son together, making tangible what the son later reconfigures as a phallic tool that remains ever connected to all that the baaaddd mother codifies." TreaAndrea M. Russworm, "Pimping (Really) Ain't Easy: Black Pulp Masculinities and the Flight from Recognition," in *Blackness Is Burning: Civil Rights, Popular Culture, and the Problem of Recognition* (Detroit: Wayne State University Press, 2016), 158.
21. Donald Goines, *Black Gangster* (Los Angeles: Holloway House, 1972), 7, 35, 25, 24, 31.
22. Goines, 64, 65.
23. Goines, 92, 93–94, 94, 95, 118, 119.
24. Donald Goines, *Street Players* (Los Angeles: Holloway House, 1973), 28, 32.
25. Goines, 107, 74, 187.
26. Goines, 189, 190.
27. "A New Magazine for Men," *Sun Reporter* [San Francisco], July 7, 1973.
28. *Miller v. California*, 413 U.S. 15 (1973).
29. Philip H. Dougherty, "Advertising: Changes at Playboy," *New York Times*, July 9, 1973.
30. Quoted in Dougherty.
31. The next chapter explains that Coleman's papers suggest she edited up to the eighth issue of the magazine, though was uncredited for doing so.
32. Quoted in Justin D. Gifford, "'Harvard in Hell': Holloway House Publishing Company, *Players Magazine*, and the Invention of Black Mass-Market Erotica," *MELUS* 35, no. 4 (2010): 116.
33. Gifford, 115.
34. Coleman was behind the "For He Who Is" tagline. It was inspired by her father always saying, "What it is." This seemingly nonce formulation "used to drive [her] crazy," but Coleman intuited that a deeper meaning lay behind its utterance. Quoted in Gifford, "'Harvard in Hell,'" 117.
35. On the centrality of the good life to Hefner's marketing of *Playboy*, see especially Elizabeth Fraterrigo, *"Playboy" and the Making of the Good Life in Modern America* (New York: Oxford University Press, 2009).

36. "Robert M. Cunningham," *Society of Illustrators*, n.d., https://www
.societyillustrators.org/robert-m-cunningham; Yanick Rice Lamb, "Senti-
mental Returns," *Black Enterprise*, December 1989, 79–85.

37. Justin Gifford, *Pimping Fictions: African American Crime Literature and the
Untold Story of Black Pulp Publishing* (Philadelphia: Temple University Press,
2013), 136; Mireille Miller-Young, *A Taste for Brown Sugar: Black Women in
Pornography* (Durham, NC: Duke University Press, 2014), 82.

38. "What's a Girl Like Wanda Doing Editing *Players*, a Black Men's Magazine?," press release, n.d., Wanda Coleman Papers, 1960–2003, Charles E.
Young Research Library, UCLA, Box 150, Folder 4.

39. "Yeah . . ." [two pimps cartoon], *Players*, November 1973, 74.

40. "Hustlers' Cars," *Players*, November 1973, 67, 69, 70.

41. This reading qualifies what Eithne Quinn has called the "lifestylization"
aesthetic of the 1970s "pimp pose." For Quinn, this aesthetic is character-
ized by the apparently incongruous juxtaposition of "flashy, sometimes
overblown spectacle" and "powerful street identification." "Through
outrageous style politics and occupational pursuits," she writes, "the pimp
type is seen to repudiate the 'square world' where workers do 'chump jobs'
for 'chump change.'" But *Players*, I argue, did not completely denigrate the
idea of work, or even of a nine-to-five job. It allowed the working stiff to
see himself as a player too, given the right frame of mind. Eithne Quinn,
"'Pimpin' Ain't Easy': Work, Play, and 'Lifestylization' of the Black Pimp
Figure in Early 1970s America," in *Media, Culture, and the Modern African
American Freedom Struggle*, ed. Brian Ward (Gainesville: University Press of
Florida, 2001), 218.

42. "Good Gracious! Bodacious Ms. Robinson," *Players*, November 1973, 91.

43. "Good Gracious! Bodacious Ms. Robinson," 91, 93.

44. Miller-Young, *A Taste for Brown Sugar*, 84.

45. Gifford, *Pimping Fictions*, 136, 141.

46. Charles Johnson, "Lois" [Panthers funeral cartoon], *Players*, November
1973, 65.

47. The message seemed to stick with Johnson. Though he gave up cartoon-
ing to become a fiction writer, his second novel, *Oxherding Tale* (1982),
includes a reference to *Players*'s debut cover girl. When the enslaved
protagonist loses himself in a reverie, he imagines his female lover as
an exotic beauty: "Her name, now that I think on it, might have been
Zeudi—Ethiopian, ancient, as remote and strange . . . as Inca ruins or
shards of pottery from the long-buried cities of Mu." Charles Johnson,
Oxherding Tale (Bloomington: Indiana University Press, 1982), 16.

48. Huey P. Newton, "Scoring," *Players*, November 1973, 42.

49. Quoted in Gifford, "'Harvard in Hell,'" 117.

50. Quoted in Walter Burrell, "Richard Roundtree: A Players Interview," *Players*, November 1973, 96.

51. Robert E. Weems Jr., with Lewis A. Randolph, "The National Response to Richard M. Nixon's Black Capitalism Initiative," in *Business in Black and White: American Presidents and Black Entrepreneurs in the Twentieth Century,* by Weems (New York: New York University Press, 2009), 127–56.

52. Stephen J. Gertz, "West Coast Blue," in *Sin-a-Rama: Sleaze Sex Paperbacks of the Sixties,* ed. Brittany A. Daley et al. (Los Angeles: Feral House, 2005), 35.

53. Editors of *Swingers World, All about Swinging: A Swinger's Handbook* (Los Angeles: Melrose Square, 1973), 214, 223, 215.

54. The only study of the white-targeted side of Morriss and Weinstock's enterprise after 1970 is David Church, "Between Fantasy and Reality: Sexploitation, Fan Magazines, and William Rotsler's 'Adults-Only' Career," *Film History* 26, no. 3 (2014): 106–43.

CHAPTER SIX

1. Thruman [Thurman] Bunts, letter to editor, *Players,* March 1974, 26; Wambi Kenyatta, letter to editor, *Players,* March 1974, 26.

2. Charles D. Lewis, letter to editor, *Players,* March 24, 26; P. C. B. Williams, letter to editor, *Players,* March 1974, 26.

3. Bunts, letter to editor.

4. Bunts.

5. P.J., letter to editor, *Players,* March 1974, 26.

6. J. E. Robinson, letter to editor, *Players,* May 1974, 25.

7. Richard C. Clenna, letter to editor, *Players,* May 1974, 25.

8. A. J. Perriera Jr., letter to editor, *Players,* May 1974, 25.

9. See my "Race, Respectability, and the Short Life of *Duke* Magazine," *Book History* 15 (2012): 152–82.

10. Wanda Coleman, memo to Bentley Morriss, May 17, 1973, Wanda Coleman Papers, 1960–2003, Charles E. Young Research Library, UCLA, Box 150, Folder 5.

11. Ralph Weinstock, memo to Wanda Coleman, n.d., Wanda Coleman Papers, Box 150, Folder 5.

12. Coleman, memo to Morriss, May 17, 1973.

13. Wanda Coleman, memo to Ralph Weinstock, July 5, 1973, Wanda Coleman Papers, Box 150, Folder 6.

14. Wanda Coleman, memo to Ralph Weinstock, August 8, 1973, Wanda Coleman Papers, Box 150, Folder 6.

15. Wanda Coleman, memo to Ralph Weinstock and Sid Smith, May 1, 1974, Wanda Coleman Papers, Box 150, Folder 6.

16. On *Ebony*'s profiles of success model, see Tom Pendergast, *Creating the Modern Man: American Magazines and Consumer Culture, 1900–1950* (Columbia: University of Missouri Press, 2000), 245–46.

17. "The Gwendolyn Brooks Literary Awards," *Black World,* January 1975, 77.

18. Wanda Coleman, memo to Ralph Weinstock, July 23, 1974, Wanda Coleman Papers, Box 150, Folder 6.
19. Wanda Coleman, memo to Ralph Weinstock, January 22, 1973, Wanda Coleman Papers, Box 150, Folder 6.
20. Andrew L. Tate, review of *White Man's Justice, Black Man's Grief,* by Donald Goines, *Players,* January 1974, 14.
21. Wanda Coleman, memo to Daphne Bolden, February 15, 1974, Wanda Coleman Papers, Box 150, Folder 4.
22. Though Cindy Cook could have been a stage name, in Coleman's papers it is attached to a real person who would later do public relations for *Players.* She is also named as the model posing with actor James Cousar in the "Far Out Fuzzy Wuzzies" fashion feature from January 1974. If the model and public relations agent were, in fact, the same person, it would further buttress my thesis that Coleman had to put the magazine together on her own—even relying on in-house talent.
23. "Cookin' Cindy Cook," *Players,* March 1974, 48, 52.
24. "Karry Onn," *Players,* May 1974, 48, 52.
25. Daphne Bolden, memo to Ralph Weinstock, Wanda Coleman, Bentley Morriss, and Sid Smith, n.d., Wanda Coleman Papers, Box 150, Folder 4.
26. Michelle Kidd, memo, n.d., Wanda Coleman Papers, Box 150, Folder 4.
27. Wanda Coleman, memo to Bentley Morriss, June 26, 1974, Wanda Coleman Papers, Box 150, Folder 4.
28. Wanda Coleman, memo to Ralph Weinstock, July 9, 1974, Wanda Coleman Papers, Box 150, Folder 4.
29. Wanda Coleman, memo to Ralph Weinstock, July 26, 1974, Wanda Coleman Papers, Box 150, Folder 5.
30. Wanda Coleman, memo to Ralph Weinstock, August 1, 1974, Wanda Coleman Papers, Box 150, Folder 6.
31. "Joe Nazel, 62; L.A. Journalist, Biographer of Black Luminaries," *Los Angeles Times,* September 2, 2006.
32. Emory Holmes II, "An Appreciation: Joseph Gober Nazel Jr. (1944–2006)," *Los Angeles Times,* October 8, 2006.
33. West's name is a nod to Henry Highland Garnet (1815–82), the radical abolitionist who was an early advocate of black nationalism and of black emigration to other parts of the world. The reference to Garnet is thin, but his dream of a black American settlement in Africa (i.e., a colony in the desert) might be reflected in West's Oasis.
34. Joseph Nazel, *Billion Dollar Death* (Los Angeles: Holloway House, 1974), 11, 9, 10 13.
35. Dom Gober, *Black Cop* (Los Angeles: Holloway House, 1974), 7.
36. Nazel, *Billion Dollar Death,* 18; Gober, *Black Cop,* 8.
37. Nazel, *Billion Dollar Death,* 25–26.
38. Gober, *Black Cop,* 17, 22.
39. Gober, 21.

40. Nazel, *Billion Dollar Death*, 13, 8, 23.

41. Nazel's short-lived Pinnacle series consists of *My Name Is Black* (1973) and *Black Is Back* (1974).

42. Jerry Palmer, *Thrillers: Genesis and Structure of a Popular Genre* (London: Edward Arnold, 1978), 58. For complementary analyses of the 1970s conspiracy thriller, see also Fredric Jameson, *The Geopolitical Aesthetic: Cinema and Space in the World System* (Bloomington: Indiana University Press, 1992); Paul Cobley, *The American Thriller: Generic Innovation and Social Change in the 1970s* (Basingstoke: Palgrave, 2000); and Patrick Anderson, *The Triumph of the Thriller: How Cops, Crooks, and Cannibals Captured Popular Fiction* (New York: Random House, 2007).

43. Nazel, *Billion Dollar Death*, 33.

44. Gober, *Black Cop*, 38, 40.

45. Nazel, *Billion Dollar Death*, 126, 132, 133.

46. "Powerful resemblance to the bestselling Executioner novels," blared *Publishers Weekly* on the front cover of Joseph Nazel, *Black Is Back* (New York: Pinnacle, 1974).

47. "Get Mallory!," *Measure*, March 1974, 6.

48. "Prisoner-Author Finishes 3rd Novel," *Indianapolis Recorder*, November 22, 1975.

49. Quoted in "Prisoner-Author Finishes 3rd Novel." Readus would publish one final novel: *Black Renegades*, from 1976.

50. Eddie B. Allen Jr., *Low Road: The Life and Legacy of Donald Goines* (New York: St. Martin's, 2004), 149–50.

51. Advertisement for Holloway House's *Crime Partners*, *Players*, March 1974, 78.

52. Quoted in Allen, *Low Road*, 160.

53. Candice Love Jackson, "The Paradox of Empowerment: Colonialism, Community, and Criminality in Donald Goines's Kenyatta Series," in *Word Hustle: Critical Essays and Reflections on the Works of Donald Goines*, ed. L. H. Stallings and Greg Thomas (Baltimore: Black Classic Press, 2011), 39; Justin Gifford, *Pimping Fictions: African American Crime Literature and the Untold Story of Black Pulp Publishing* (Philadelphia: Temple University Press, 2013), 85.

54. Al C. Clark, *Crime Partners* (Los Angeles: Holloway House, 1974), 53, 55, 56, 57.

55. Clark, 57.

56. Al C. Clark, *Kenyatta's Escape* (Los Angeles: Holloway House, 1974), 14.

57. Al C. Clark, *Death List* (Los Angeles: Holloway House, 1974), 15, 14.

58. Terrence T. Tucker, "Revolutionary Hustler: Liberatory Violence in Donald Goines's Kenyatta Series," in Stallings and Thomas, *Word Hustle*, 62.

59. Jerry H. Bryant, *Victims and Heroes: Racial Violence in the African American Novel* (Amherst: University of Massachusetts Press, 1997), 268.

60. Tom Ricke, "The Fast Life and Violent Death of Donald Goines, Writer and Victim," *Detroit Free Press*, March 16, 1975. Ricke's article is the

unacknowledged source for key insights from Allen's biography. I cite it here as the fullest contemporary account of Goines's murder.

61. Ricke. The notorious double murders remain unsolved to this day.
62. Gifford, *Pimping Fictions*, 77.
63. Eddie Stone, *Donald Writes No More* (Los Angeles: Holloway House, 1974), 201–2.
64. Al C. Clark, *Kenyatta's Last Hit* (Los Angeles: Holloway House, 1975), front cover, 160.
65. Clark, 210, 214, 218.
66. Kate Martinez, "The Face behind Donald Goines and Eddie Stone," *Poly Optimist*, April 2015.
67. Robert Reedburg, "Sex Mag. Charges Black Woman Editor," *Herald-Dispatch* [Los Angeles], October 10, 1974.
68. Reedburg.
69. Reedburg.
70. "Players Magazine Names Joseph Nazel Editor," *Atlanta Daily World*, September 1, 1974.

CHAPTER SEVEN

1. Robin D. G. Kelley, *Race Rebels: Culture, Politics, and the Black Working Class* (New York: Free Press, 1994); Shane White and Graham White, *Stylin': African American Expressive Culture from Its Beginnings to the Zoot Suit* (Ithaca, NY: Cornell University Press, 1998); Davarian L. Baldwin, *Chicago's New Negroes: Modernity, the Great Migration, and Black Urban Life* (Chapel Hill: University of North Carolina Press, 2007).
2. Robert Kelley, letter to editor, *Players*, April 1976, 26.
3. Paul M. Branzburg, "Old Hustler Recalls Silky Life of a Pimp," *Detroit Free Press*, April 22, 1974. Importantly, *Gentleman Pimp* did not include the sleaze conventions of a moralizing preface or introduction and a slang glossary.
4. Quoted in Kalamu ya Salaam, "The Psychology of the Pimp: Iceberg Slim Reveals the Reality," *Black Collegian* 5, no. 3 (1974): 34, 35.
5. Don Heckman, "Red Holloway, 1927–2012," *Los Angeles Times*, February 27, 2012.
6. Brett Hamil, "David Drozen, Comedy Archivist," *City Arts*, April 30, 2013, http://www.cityartsonline.com/qa-david-drozen-comedy-album-producer.
7. Dennis Wepman, Ronald B. Newman, and Murray B. Binderman, "Broadway Sam," in *The Life: The Lore and Folk Poetry of the Black Hustler* (Philadelphia: University of Pennsylvania Press, 1976), 96, 97, 98.
8. Here I depart from Jerry H. Bryant's argument that black pulp fiction may be described as "long prose toasts," which "fuse the middle-class literate tradition and the oral folk tradition, mixing the two sets of values, simultaneously romanticizing and criticizing the man of violence." Though

suggestive, Bryant's "toast novel" fails to account for toasts' medium spec-ificity, reducing them to textual discourse that can then be adapted into literary form. Jerry H. Bryant, "A 'Toast' Novel: Pimps, Hoodlums, and Hit Men," in *"Born in a Mighty Bad Land": The Violent Man in African American Folklore and Fiction* (Bloomington: Indiana University Press, 2003), 119.

9. Wepman et al., introduction to *The Life*, 6. I have been able to conclude with a fair degree of certainty that Wepman was serving time for his involvement in the 1953 double murder (by cyanide poisoning) of his roommate's parents. "Indict Son, Pal in Poisoning of Doctor, Wife," *Chicago Tribune*, December 19, 1953.

10. "Author and Editor" [photograph], *Black World*, February 1972, 72; Margaret Mead, "A Rap on Race: How James Baldwin and I 'Talked' a Book," *Redbook*, September 1971, 70.

11. Iceberg Slim, "Air-Tight Willie and Me," *Players*, November 1976, 21.

12. Iceberg Slim, *Pimp: The Story of My Life* (Los Angeles: Holloway House, 1967), 80; Iceberg Slim, "To Steal a Superfox," *Players*, February 1977, 37.

13. The lone extended consideration of these works can be found in Peter A. Muckley, *Iceberg Slim: The Life as Art* (Pittsburgh: Dorrance, 2003), 98–176.

14. Quoted in Nolan Davis, "Iceberg Slim: Pimping the Page," *Players*, May 1977, 10, 29.

15. Quoted in Davis, 30, 31, 83.

16. Joseph Nazel, "Book Review," *Philadelphia Tribune*, December 7, 1974.

17. "Book Author Dies," *Tri-State Defender* [Memphis], January 11, 1975.

18. *Players*, August 1976, front cover; Yazid Asim-Ali, "Say Brothers . . . ," *Players*, August 1976, 6.

19. Isiah Smith Jr., letter to editor, *Players*, February 1976, 26.

20. Ida Peters, "What's Happening: B'more's 'Whoredaughter,'" *Afro-American* [Baltimore], August 14, 1976.

21. Peters.

22. J. Lance Gilmer, *Hell Is Forever* (Los Angeles: Holloway House, 1977), back cover.

23. Donald Ray Young, "For Your Pleasure," *Sun Reporter* [San Francisco], January 6, 1977; Thomas Dabney, "There Is No Escape: Dangers of Drugs Depicted in Novel," *New Journal and Guide* [Norfolk, VA], January 15, 1977.

24. Jim Cleaver, "Horror of Cabrini-Green," *Los Angeles Sentinel*, December 2, 1976.

25. Doreen Ambrose-Van Lee, *Life after Cooley High and Good Times (I Ain't Gonna Rhyme)* (Bloomington, IN: iUniverse, 2009), 12.

26. Quoted in David J. Blum, "Urban Blight: Cabrini-Green Project, Big Ghetto in Chicago, Fights a Losing Battle," *Wall Street Journal*, May 5, 1981.

27. Kate Martinez, "The Face behind Donald Goines and Eddie Stone," *Poly Optimist*, April 2015. According to this story, Hollander later wrote a screenplay based on his experience penning black pulp fiction as Eddie

Stone. He titled it *Blue Eyed Soul*. After shopping the script around, Hollander was alternately accused of "being a racist" and threatened with "never working in Hollywood again."

28. C. H. Hollander, "Full Moon Rising," *Players*, September 1977, 61.
29. Hollander, 61, 62.
30. Hollander, 62.
31. Hollander.
32. As a satire of the politics of American letters, "Full Moon Rising" could be thought of as a predecessor to Percival Everett's *Erasure* (2001). That novel's protagonist is a struggling black writer who achieves commercial and critical success with a novel (*My Pafology*) that plays directly to racist and gendered stereotypes.
33. Stanley Crouch, "Black Women and White Men: An Indication of Something," *Players*, February 1975, 41.
34. Crouch, 96.
35. Crouch.
36. R. Rudder, letter to editor, *Players*, May 1975, 36; Jean De Savieu, letter to editor, *Players*, May 1975, 36–37; William Bland, letter to editor, *Players*, May 1975, 36; Johnny Lee Hewing, letter to editor, *Players*, May 1975, 36; A.B., letter to editor, *Players*, May 1975, 37.
37. "Sandy," *Players*, April 1976, 68.
38. "Adelaide," *Players*, April 1975, 30, 32.
39. "Conchita," *Players*, May 1977, 34.
40. "Gaye," *Players*, May 1975, 35.
41. Dr. Phyllis James, as told to Leo Guild, *The Black Shrink* (Los Angeles: Holloway House, 1975), back cover.
42. Leo Guild, *Black Bait* (Los Angeles: Holloway House, 1975), 16.
43. Kipp Washington, as told to Leo Guild, *Some Like It Dark* (1966; Los Angeles: Holloway House, 1977), front cover.
44. Beth Coleman, "Pimp Notes on Autonomy," in *Everything but the Burden: What White People Are Taking from Black Culture*, ed. Greg Tate (New York: Broadway, 2003), 79.
45. Donald Goines, *Black Gangster* (Los Angeles: Holloway House, 1972), 119.

CHAPTER EIGHT

1. For a contemporary account of Hawkins's participation in the group, see "Watts Workshop Writers Read at Moratorium Rally," *Los Angeles Sentinel*, November 20, 1969.
2. Odie Hawkins, *Chili: Memoirs of a Black Casanova* (Los Angeles: Holloway House, 1985), back cover.
3. Odie Hawkins, *Hollow Daze* (Bloomington, IN: iUniverse, 2013), 22, 21.
4. Hawkins, 55, 35.
5. J.C., letter to editor, *Players*, May 1979, 18.

6.   Jay Vanleer, "Book Reviews," *Call and Post* [Cleveland, OH], December 18, 1976.

7.   Thomas L. Dabney, "Struggle Still On: Childhood Dreams and Black Gestapo," *New Journal and Guide* [Norfolk, VA], November 12, 1977.

8.   My evidence is as follows: one Rugio Vitali or Rugio Vitale is credited as the author behind both pseudonyms. But Vitali or Vitale was very likely a pseudonym itself; there is no evidence of him being a real-life author or person. The only book he published under his name was *Joe Louis: Biography of a Champion* (1979), also with Holloway House. Joseph Nazel used material on Louis in his 1984 novel *Delta Crossing*, and Brooke, Fletcher, and Vitale all write in basically the same style: plot-driven reportage. We know Nazel used other pseudonyms both before and after this period, so I am comfortable concluding that he was, in fact, Rugio Vitale, Amos Brooke, and Omar Fletcher. For the relevant copyright data, see Library of Congress, Copyright Office, *Catalog of Copyright Entries, Third Series, Volume 31, Part I, Number 1, Section 2, Books and Pamphlets* (Washington, DC: Library of Congress, 1977), 2883; Library of Congress, Copyright Office, *Catalog of Copyright Entries, Third Series, Volume 31, Part I, Number 2, Section 2, Books and Pamphlets* (Washington, DC: Library of Congress, 1976), 2135.

9.   Advertisement for Holloway House's *Hurricane Man*, *Players*, May 1977, 12.

10. John Christopher Kim Fisher, "Hurricane Man," *Sun Reporter* [San Francisco], March 31, 1977; Jay Vanleer, "Book Reviews," *Call and Post* [Cleveland, OH], September 10, 1977.

11. Thomas L. Dabney, "His Soul Was Not for Sale: Book Reveals Sacrifices and Life of Paul Robeson," *Journal and Guide* [Norfolk, VA], April 9, 1980.

12. "Black History Month Commemorated by Publication of Two Important Works on Slain Civil Rights Leaders," *Columbus Times* [GA], January 3, 1988.

13. Chris Rock, *Rock This!* (New York: Hyperion, 1997), 22.

14. Floyd T., letter to editor, *Players*, September 1982, 33.

15. James H. Cleaver, "Players Magazine Hit with Lawsuit: Millions Sought by Smith," *Los Angeles Sentinel*, March 19, 1981.

16. Jesse Jones, *Midnight's Daughter* (Los Angeles: Holloway House, 1981), front cover.

17. L. K. Wilson, *Celluloid Trick* (Los Angeles: Holloway House, 1982), front cover.

18. Rae S. Stewart, *Treat Them Like Animals* (Los Angeles: Holloway House, 1982), front and back covers.

19. Stewart, 76.

20. "Poetry Update II," *Lesbian Herstory Archives Newsletter* 6 (1980): 18; Rae S. Stewart, "Beauty and the Beast," *Inside/Out: Special Women's Supplement* 3, no. 1 (1982): 1, 6–7.

21. Hawkins, *Hollow Daze*, 49, 48.

22. Genia Fogelson, *Belafonte* (Los Angeles: Holloway House, 1980), 4.

23. Genia Fogelson, *Jewel: Undercover Cop* (Los Angeles: Holloway House, 1979), 97.
24. Bobbi Olson, "Forgotten Treasure," *Los Angeles Times*, March 21, 1997.
25. "New Books Reflect Black Is Beautiful," *Atlanta Daily World*, March 31, 1983. Some titles and names have been corrected for accuracy.
26. Valerie Babb, *A History of the African American Novel* (New York: Cambridge University Press, 2017), 396.
27. Felicia Woods, *Southern Nights* (Los Angeles: Holloway House, 1984), back cover.
28. Joyce Lezán, *Hearbeat* (Los Angeles: Holloway House, 1983), 56.
29. Leah Guild, *Texas Passion* (Los Angeles: Holloway House, 1983), 21, 45.
30. Greta A. Dawson, "Book Corner," *Columbus Times* [GA], May 30, 1984.
31. Clayton J., letter to editor, *Players*, June 1984, 23.
32. Advertisement for Holloway House's Heartline Romances, *Players*, June 1984, 50.
33. Quoted in Ellen Alperstein, "Romance Novels Embrace Diversity Books," *Los Angeles Times*, September 29, 1994.
34. Jonathan Cunningham, "Romancing the Hood," *Detroit Metro Times*, June 22, 2005. On Stringer, see also Victoria Christopher Murray, "Triple Crown Winner," *Black Issues Book Review*, May–June 2004, 28; Calvin Reid, "Street Publisher Started Small, Thinks Big," *Publishers Weekly*, July 19, 2004; and Dinitia Smith, "Unorthodox Publisher Animates Hip-Hop Lit," *New York Times*, September 8, 2004.
35. Erica Buddington, "A Peek Inside Her Agenda: Teri Woods," *Her Agenda*, October 7, 2013, http://heragenda.com/power-agenda/teri-woods/; "Teri Woods: Author of True to the Game," *New York Beacon*, July 17, 2002. On Woods, see also Al Hunter Jr., "Not Waiting to Exhale," *Philadelphia Daily News*, October 12, 2000; Diane Patrick, "Urban Fiction," *Publishers Weekly*, May 19, 2003; and Nadira A. Hira, "Curling Up with . . . Teri Woods," *Savoy*, August 2003, 42.
36. Quoted in Robin Carter, "The XRCO Awards," *Players*, June 1986, 25.
37. See, contemporaneously, David Mills, "Los Angeles' Gangsters of Rap, Escalating the Attitude," *Washington Post*, May 20, 1990; and Amy Gamerman, "The Icemen Cometh: 'Gangster Rappers' on Set," *Wall Street Journal*, December 17, 1991. From a critical distance, see Robin D. G. Kelley, "Kickin' Reality, Kickin' Ballistics: 'Gangsta Rap' and Postindustrial Los Angeles," in *Race Rebels: Culture, Politics, and the Black Working Class* (New York: Free Press, 1994), 183–227; and Eithne Quinn, "'Who's the Mack?': The Performativity and Politics of the Pimp Figure in Gangsta Rap," *Journal of American Studies* 34, no. 1 (2000): 115–36.
38. Michael Eric Dyson, *Between God and Gangsta Rap: Bearing Witness to Black Culture* (New York: Oxford University Press, 1996), 185.
39. Ice-T and Douglas Century, *Ice: A Memoir of Gangster Life and Redemption—from South Central to Hollywood* (New York: One World, 2011), 5,

12, 27, 40–41, 51, 52. For contemporaneous sources, see Dennis Hunt, "Rhyme Pays for Ice T," *Los Angeles Times*, August 2, 1987; "Straight Outta South-Central," *Newsweek*, June 30, 1991, http://www.newsweek.com/straight-outta-south-central-204078; and Brian Cross, "Ice T," in *It's Not about a Salary . . . : Rap, Race and Resistance in Los Angeles* (London: Verso, 1993), 180–89.

40. Ice-T, "6 'N the Mornin,'" *Genius*, https://genius.com/Ice-t-6-n-the-mornin -lyrics. The lyrics here and below have been slightly modified from the way they appear on the website. They reflect minor corrections based on my own listening to these songs.

41. Ice-T and Century, *Ice: A Memoir*, 91, 92, 113, 92.

42. Ice-T, "The Iceberg," *Genius*, https://genius.com/Ice-t-the-iceberg-lyrics.

43. Naming this character Donald may also be Ice-T's way of referencing Goines.

44. Ice-T, "O.G. Original Gangster," *Genius*, https://genius.com/Ice-t-og -original-gangster-lyrics.

45. Though it is often claimed that Ice Cube took his stage name from Iceberg Slim, he has stated on more than one occasion that his older brother bestowed it upon him after catching him putting the moves on female friends. "How Ice Cube Got His Name," YouTube, March 11, 2012, https://www.youtube.com/watch?v=otQUAqmLOjY; "Ice Cube Answers the Web's Most Searched Questions," YouTube, April 11, 2016, https://www.youtube.com/watch?v=FvPsBd14OG0.

46. N.W.A., "Fuck tha Police," *Genius*, https://genius.com/Nwa-fuck-tha-police -lyrics.

47. Eithne Quinn, *Nuthin' but a "G" Thang: The Culture and Commerce of Gangsta Rap* (New York: Columbia University Press, 2005), 108.

48. Charise L. Cheney, *Brothers Gonna Work It Out: Sexual Politics in the Golden Age of Rap Nationalism* (New York: New York University Press, 2005), 100.

49. Though the literature on white fandom of hip-hop is copious, the best entry point into that discussion is Bakari Kitwana, *Why White Kids Love Hip-Hop: Wankstas, Wiggers, Wannabes, and the New Reality of Race in America* (New York: Basic Civitas, 2005).

50. Martin Cizmar, "Whatever Happened to N.W.A.'s Posse?," *LA Weekly*, May 6, 2010, http://www.laweekly.com/music/whatever-happened-to-nwas -posse-2164896; Mike Sager, "Arabian Prince Left N.W.A. and He's Doing Just Fine," *MEL Magazine*, January 16, 2016, https://melmagazine.com/arabian-prince-left-n-w-a-and-he-s-doing-just-fine-b776410bec32.

51. David B. Lewis, "Introduction," in *The Rap! Book: Lyric Collection*, vol. 1, by Jeffrey D. Knuckles (Los Angeles: Holloway House, 1988), 7.

52. On black pulp fiction's influence on post-gangsta hip-hop culture, see Tracy Grant, "Why Hip-Hop Heads Love Donald Goines," *Black Issues Book Review* 3, no. 5 (2001): 53; Kermit E. Campbell, "The Player's (Book) Club: Ghetto Realistic Fiction from 'His Last Day' to 'Pimpology,'" in *"Gettin'*

Our Groove On": Rhetoric, Language, and Literacy for the Hip Hop Generation (Detroit: Wayne State University Press, 2005), 87–120; and Jonathan Munby, "Keeping It Reel: From Goines to Gangsta," in *Under a Bad Sign: Criminal Self-Representation in African American Popular Culture* (Chicago: University of Chicago Press, 2011), 149–74.

53. Patrick, "Urban Fiction," See also Linton Weeks, "New Books in the Hood," *Washington Post*, July 31, 2004; Judith Rosen, "Street Lit: Readers Gotta Have It," *Publishers Weekly*, December 13, 2004; and Ta-Nehisi Coates, "Hustle and Grow," *Time*, October 16, 2006, 75–76.

54. The term "ghettocentric" comes from Nelson George, "Ghettocentricity," in *Buppies, B-Boys, Baps, and Bohos: Notes on Post-Soul Black Culture* (New York: HarperCollins, 1994), 95–97.

55. David Streitfeld, "Book Report," *Washington Post*, September 24, 1989.

56. Which is not to say the imprint was a failure. In 1994, Locke hailed the young adult biographies—about forty-five in number—as Holloway House's most recent success stories. Ellen Alperstein, "Multiculture, Ink," *Los Angeles Times*, December 18, 1994.

57. Justin Gifford, *Street Poison: The Biography of Iceberg Slim* (New York: Doubleday, 2015), 222.

58. Min Hyoung Song, *Strange Future: Pessimism and the 1992 Los Angeles Riots* (Durham, NC: Duke University Press, 2005), 12.

59. "'Iceberg Slim' Robert Beck, Author, Dies in L.A. at 74," *Los Angeles Sentinel*, May 28, 1992.

60. Phil Patton, "Sold on Ice," *Esquire*, October 1992, 76.

61. These series were interconnected through the transnational work of French cultural critic Samuel Blumenfeld and American editor Marc Gerald, both of whom are white. For personal accounts of how these series came about, see Marc Gerald, "Old School Noir," *Salon*, March 7, 1997, https://www.salon.com/1997/03/07/noir/; and Samuel Blumenfeld, "Epilogue—an Experience in Literary Archaeology: Publishing a Black Lost Generation," in *Race, Ethnicity and Publishing in America*, ed. Cécile Cottenet (Basingstoke: Palgrave Macmillan, 2014), 231–42.

EPILOGUE

1. Stuart Hall, "What Is This 'Black' in Black Popular Culture?," in *Black Popular Culture*, ed. Gina Dent (Seattle: Bay Press, 1992), 32.

2. There are more than enough studies of black pulp fiction that do this, and I have engaged with them throughout this book in the text and in my notes.

3. *"Never Die Alone,"* Box Office Mojo, http://www.boxofficemojo.com/movies/?id=neverdiealone.htm.

4. Michael Sragow, "'Never Die' Never Rises above the Bling, Bang," *Baltimore*

Sun, March 26, 2004; Desson Thomson, "'Never Die Alone': Hackneyed II Death," *Washington Post*, March 26, 2004.

5. "Kensington Buys Holloway Backlist," *Publishers Weekly*, February 25, 2008.

6. Misty Beck, "I Think Cash Money Really Respects My Dad's Work," *SOHH*, May 16, 2011, https://web.archive.org/web/20120123153048/http://www .sohh.com:80/2011/05/i_think_cash_money_really_respects_my_da.html.

7. Jeffrey A. Trachtenberg, "Rap, Parlayed into Books," *Wall Street Journal*, November 3, 2010.

Index

Pages numbers in italics refer to figures.